ARE THERE REALLY TANNAITIC PARALLELS
TO THE GOSPELS?

SOUTH FLORIDA STUDIES IN THE HISTORY OF JUDAISM

Edited by
Jacob Neusner
William Scott Green, James Strange
Darrell J. Fasching, Sara Mandell

Number 80
ARE THERE REALLY TANNAITIC PARALLELS
TO THE GOSPELS?
A Refutation of Morton Smith

by
Jacob Neusner

ARE THERE REALLY TANNAITIC PARALLELS TO THE GOSPELS?
A Refutation of Morton Smith

by

Jacob Neusner

Scholars Press
Atlanta, Georgia

ARE THERE REALLY TANNAITIC PARALLELS TO THE GOSPELS?

©1993
University of South Florida

Publication of this book was made possible by a grant from the Tisch Family Foundation, New York City. The University of South Florida acknowledges with thanks this important support for its scholarly projects.

Library of Congress Cataloging in Publication Data
Neusner, Jacob, 1932–
    Are there really Tannaitic parallels to the Gospels?: a
refutation of Morton Smith/ by Jacob Neusner.
        p. cm. — (South Florida studies in the history of Judaism; no. 80)
    Includes index.
    ISBN 1-55540-867-2 (alk. paper)
    1. Smith, Morton, 1915–   Makbilot ben ha-Besorot le-sifrut ha
-Tana'im. 2. Bible. N.T. Gospels—Language, style. 3. Rabbinical
literature—Relation to the New Testament. 4. Bible. N.T. Gospels—
Extra-canonical parallels. 5. Tannaim. 6. Tosefta—Criticism,
interpretation, etc. 7. Mishnah—Criticism, interpretation, etc.
I. Title. II. Series: South Florida studies in the history of Judaism; 80.
BS2555.S543N48   1993
296.1'23066—dc20   93-7554
                                                    CIP

Printed in the United States of America
on acid-free paper

Table of Contents

Preface ix

Introduction 1

1. Smith's Alleged Parallels: Much Ado about Not Much.............. 15

    I.   Why Reread a Forty-Year-Old Dissertation.................... 15

    II. Know-Nothings, Fundamentalists, and Morton Smith...... 25

    III. Time to Reexamine Smith's Altogether-Too-Secret
         "Secret Gospel"?.. 27

    IV. The Lesser Theses of Smith's *Tannaitic Parallels*.............. 31

         1. *Verbal Parallels* 32
         2. *Parallels of Idiom*.. 32
         3. *Parallels of Meaning*... 33
         4. *Parallels of Literary Form* 34
         5. *Parallels in Types of Association*........................... 35
         6. *Complete Parallels*.. 35
         7. *Parallels of Parallelism* 36
         8. *Parallels with a Fixed Difference*.......................... 36

    V.   Much Ado about Not Much.................................... 36

    VI. For This, a Ph.D.?.. 38

2. Parallels of Parallelism: Smith's Statement of His Thesis........ 41

3. The Character of the Tosefta 65

4. The Facts of Mishnah-Tosefta Relationships [1]: The
   Tosefta as a Commentary to the Mishnah 87

5. The Facts of Mishnah-Tosefta Relationships [2]: The
   Tosefta as a Complement to the Mishnah................................103

6. The Facts of Mishnah-Tosefta Relationships [3]: The
   Tosefta as a Supplement to the Mishnah.................................123

7. Are There Really Tannaitic Parallels to the Gospels?..............131

    I.   Did Morton Smith Understand the Relationship
        between the Mishnah and the Tosefta?.........................131

    II. Smith's Conceptual Bungling...135

III. The Relationship between the Tosefta and the
Mishnah and the Synoptic Problem...............................140

IV. Do Any Documents in Rabbinic Literature Draw on
the Equivalent of a Q?...142

V. Do Any Documents in Rabbinic Literature Give
Evidence of a Shared Protocol of Exegesis or Common
Convention Governing the Selection and Arrangement
of Data?..149

VI. What, Today, Is to Be Learned from the Career of
Morton Smith? 155

Appendix One: Smith's Legacy of Conceptual Bungling: The
Case of Lee I. Levine 161

Appendix Two: Smith's Legacy of Selective Fundamentalism in
the Writing of S.J.D. Cohen: Believing Whatever You Like.....167

Index 179

Preface

When a scholar has completed his work and gone to his eternal rest, scholarly responsibility requires that the legacy be carefully sifted to sort out what remains useful from what can be buried with the bones and books of the deceased. What I here inter is the deceased's claim to have identified "Tannaitic parallels," of the particular set of eight classifications that he defined, to the New Testament Gospels. Specifically, the late Professor Morton Smith, 1915-1991, Professor of Ancient History at Columbia University for most of his career, set forth the notion that Tannaitic literature yields numerous and important parallels to the Gospels. That claim will here be shown factually erroneous, resting on a profound misunderstanding of matters. I shall show that what endures is only the main idea, which hardly was original to Smith – the perfectly commonplace fact that rabbinic literature proves relevant to Gospel exegesis and history. My interest derives from the contrary fact: Gospel research for me has provided an important model of critical study. I learned that fact from Smith's book. But that is all to be learned there.

To the study of Judaism Smith's one weighty contribution is his doctoral dissertation submitted in 1948 at the Hebrew University of Jerusalem. There he alleged that Tannaitic literature exhibits eight important parallels to the Gospels, a proposition announced in the title, *Tannaitic Parallels to the Gospels*, Society of Biblical Literature Monograph Series VI (Philadelphia, 1951). In these pages I briefly examine seven of his eight parallels, and I devote the shank of the book to a test of the other one. Of these eight alleged parallels, two by his own reckoning fail – there are no parallels in the stated categories; five, our survey at the end of Chapter One indicates, prove trivial or simply confused; and one is worth a close reading. That one proves false as to its facts. The upshot is simple. Smith left behind, as his one and only book on Judaism, a trivial and, where interesting, quite wrong, ignorant, and misleading legacy.

ix

This result yields an assessment of the man's scholarly career that he could not have appreciated. While claiming to be a universal expert on the study of Judaism and the Jews' history, in fact the only book Smith wrote on the subject shows the claim spurious. His work was superficial; his knowledge flawed; his confidence in his own judgment, so far as Judaism is concerned, ill-placed. Smith wrote too much, too soon, and too hastily, therefore being guilty of the atrocious slovenliness that he quickly, and with no evidence commensurate to the seriousness of the charge, gleefully imputed to nearly everybody else whenever he could get away with it. While here he alleged that he had made a great discovery, he had in fact not done his homework. Smith's allegations about Tannaitic literature and about the Gospels are, while interesting, undependable and must be checked point by point by any cautious reader.

The demonstration of these facts follows a simple plan. The introduction spells out the indictment, the shank of the book then lays out the case. Then the readers, having read this brief, will write the verdict on this part of Smith's legacy. For they alone serve as judge and jury.

A personal note is in place. Smith meant a great deal to me and, in his way, gave me a great deal, too. He therefore deserves more than a book review or an article. I pay him this tribute of closure: a careful reading and examination of the one idea of his that was important to me, and that I think has still retained some interest for learning in general. Smith not only was the sole really important teacher I ever had, but he also devoted his best energies for many years to a campaign to destroy me as a scholar, to discredit me as a person, and to assassinate my character.

For that, were matters merely personal and political, I should hardly owe Smith a reply. But I do owe him the respect of a rereading of his oeuvre, so far as that work played an important role in my life. Smith aimed at character assassination, but at stake were serious questions of scholarly concern, and that is the field where I shall greet him in paying this last farewell. It takes the form appropriate to objective issues of fact and interpretation: let me take seriously, and at face value, the things he taught me, dismissing out of mind, after a final reprise, the lessons to be learned from Smith about how not to conduct a scholarly life and career.

Smith is not alone in teaching these other, disreputable lessons. In his long campaign, he was only a general staff member. But he served in an army that had more generals than privates. I have already dealt with the others of consequence, each one in terms of not personality but scholarship. Turning sixty this year, I realized that, like Moses in

Midian, I have outlived all my consequential enemies; the men who sought to murder me all have died.

Over the years I have dealt with the scholarship of each one. So far as substantive scholarly and academic issues were ever at stake, I have dealt in other places with Solomon Zeitlin, Ephraim E. Urbach, Saul Lieberman, Louis Finkelstein, and Salo W. Baron. These entirely academic *Auseinandersetzungen* took the forms of a sustained critique of Zeitlin's and Finkelstein's findings about the Pharisees, a major book review of Urbach's magnum opus, an article in *History and Theory* on Lieberman's intellectual pathos, and a reexamination in my *Economics of the Mishnah* of Baron's findings relevant to the topic, on which he claimed to have something to say but about which he said nothing coherent – these sufficed for the five, respectively.

None of them, in retrospect, looms nearly so tall as they all did in life. All of them rapidly fade with time, proving – for those who remember them at all – to have been overrated lightweights. Their scholarly legacy is today valued only by the believers; it proves out of all proportion to the political and institutional power they exercised while among the living. Of the five, Finkelstein's critical editions still deserve attention, and Lieberman is still rightly consulted for the meanings of words and phrases, where he excelled and remains helpful.

No work of mine can omit reference to the exceptionally favorable circumstances in which I conduct my research. But there is a special reason to do so here. I wrote this book at the University of South Florida, which has afforded me an ideal situation in which to conduct a scholarly life. I express my thanks for not only the advantage of a Distinguished Research Professorship, which must be the best job in the world for a scholar, but also of a substantial research expense fund, ample research time, and some stimulating and cordial colleagues. In the prior chapters of my career, I never knew a university that prized professors' scholarship and publication and treated with respect the professors who actively pursue research.

The University of South Florida, and nine universities that comprise the Florida State University System as a whole, exemplify the high standards of professionalism that prevail in publicly sponsored higher education in the USA and provide the model that privately sponsored universities would do well to emulate. Here there are rules, achievement counts, and presidents, provosts, and deans honor and respect the university's principal mission: scholarship, scholarship alone – both in the classroom and in publication.

It is particularly appropriate to say so in this context in particular. For Smith got his American degrees at Harvard, taught at Brown, spent his career at Columbia, and yearned to go back to Harvard or at least to Brown, in the 1970s, while at Columbia seeking positions at Brown (where I tried without success to open the way for him) and at Harvard. He was a true son of the Ivy League (as, alas, was I in my time). Had Smith spent his career in a different kind of academy from the only one he valued, he might have attained that professionalism that would have helped him exercise such authentic power of intellect as he possessed. To him, only the Ivy League counted. But Smith also evaluated opinions and scholarly results by the position held by those who proposed them. That explains why, for his part, he required the prestige that, in his mind, teaching here, rather than there, bestowed upon him; to him, that meant more than solid achievement, and it may account for the rather thin resume that lists all of his writings.

Smith thought his position brought him honor, made his voice heard, and marked his opinion as important. But, in the field of the study of religion, excellence is where it is; there is no correlation whatsoever in that field between the ranking or objective distinction of a university and the ranking and objective distinction of the academic study of religion in said university. To the contrary, the best departments, as measured by all objective measures, are located by happenstance, wherever they happen to be; and the best books come from wherever they come from. Smith lacked the wisdom to realize that it is not the position that honors the person, but the person that honors the position.

He told me very early in my career not to consider, or to retain, a professorship at any publicly supported institution of higher education. These he called "the slums." In scholarship, Smith bought the sizzle, not the steak. For my part so did I. That is why I was able to find and join a genuinely academic community, one with high and rigorous standards of solid achievement for itself, only after I had left the Ivy League.

But I hasten to add, that judgment is unfair to many of the universities that comprise that league, which, after all, have in common only that their football teams compete every autumn. Otherwise, each competes in its own academic league, Harvard with MIT and Cal Tech, Chicago and California, for instance. Brown – as to faculty standing and accomplishment, the things that count – competes not with the far more accomplished faculties of Dartmouth or Yale or Princeton but rather – and only with difficulty – with the intellectual backwaters and their tweedy college teachers at Wesleyan, Trinity, Williams, Swarthmore, Haverford, Amherst, Bucknell, Reed, Pomona, and Oberlin.

For this happy, and intellectually climactic, chapter of my career, I find myself in a university that competes only with itself. The University of South Florida (not to mention the other eight universities of the Florida system, and, I know, the vast university of other state universities and colleges and junior colleges and all the rest) measures itself by how well it fulfills the responsibilities of public service to a vast constituency. For us, success is our, and our students', achievements. And, as a matter of fact, we define the norm. Since approximately 80 percent of all university students attend public universities, and since approximately 90 percent attend universities in their own states, I contemplate with confidence the future of American higher education – therefore of America itself.

When I look back on Morton Smith's sad and arid career, I take special pleasure in finding myself in the mainstream and not a backwater.

JACOB NEUSNER

Distinguished Research Professor of Religious Studies
UNIVERSITY OF SOUTH FLORIDA
Tampa, FL 33620-5550 USA

Introduction

Parallels with a fixed difference and one typical of the relationship of the literatures encompass these cases: [1] Jesus = God; [2] Jesus = the Law.... I think these passages suffice to show that Jesus appears in the Gospels in a number of places where the parallel passages of TL have God or the Law.... A likely inference would be that Jesus occupied in the minds of the authors of the Gospels much the same place as God and the Law occupied in the minds of the authors of TL. *But to make such an inference would involve an act of historical faith, for to pass from the observable similarity of words to the hypothetical similarity of ideas which the words may have been meant to express is to pass from the knowable to the unknown* [italics supplied].

Morton Smith, *Tannaitic Parallels to the Gospels*

The italicized words, the verbal equivalent of nose-in-the-mud groveling, come from a doctoral dissertation that is vintage Jerusalem: sycophantic, learned, and pointless. This is how Morton Smith set forth his *Tannaitic Parallels to the Gospels.* A work full of the bombast of overripe historicism and vacuous positivism but altogether lacking in a critical spirit, Smith's first book replicates with precision that pretentious banality that the doctors of Judaic Studies in Jerusalem value. In fact, despite his humble genuflection before the altar of positive facts, and demonstrative rejection of the sin of "an act of historical faith," Smith's *Tannaitic Parallels to the Gospels'* few facts turn out upon inspection to form large fictions. And for the remainder of his career, Smith repudiated his initial position and adopting the historical faith he piously eschews here.

In fact, when we wade past the dissertation's suffocating banalities and verbose celebrations of the self-evident and reach its startling theses, we shall find out that Smith simply did not know what he was talking about. An enthusiast, he failed to do his homework. A true believer, he never challenged his own results. Publishing too quickly and – by reason of having failed to do his homework – much too much, Smith began his career by displaying faults that continued, for forty years, to discredit his work. Without deep learning, without consequential ideas, he went on for four decades afterward to accuse others of his own faults.

Do not think these harsh judgments exaggerated or abusive. They are well merited and well founded. They draw upon the facts of written evidence, and I assure the reader, for the case at hand (I leave his contributions to the study of Christianity, Old Testament, New Testament, ancient history, and the like to experts in those areas), they will be substantiated, point by point, in what follows.

To show the character of what we are going to examine, I point to the words given above. At the end of his presentation of the stupefying banality that, where in Tannaitic literature we find God, in the Gospels we find Jesus; where we find the Torah ("the Law"), we find Jesus; the doctorand gives his "likely inference." But this is in fact no "inference" at all, but a mere paraphrase of his data. Then, ostentatiously horrified by his own wit, he apologizes for such a daring surmise, in confusion drawing back. But all he has said, and all he apologizes for, are ho-hum observations that scholarship on the Gospels, following a centuries-old tradition of theology on the Gospels, had long since perceived and surpassed. Finishing his dissertation in early middle age, Morton Smith assures the world that he should never commit "an act of historical faith." He should never pass from "the observable similarity of words" to "the hypothetical similarity of ideas which the words may have been meant to express."

He manifests himself at the outset, acolyte of the true faith of positivistic historicism: "Ah, noble, lordly and pure facts – I apologize to you for the remotest hint that you may bear meaning of any kind." That would be the last apology of Smith's scholarly career – and the final humiliation he would suffer in silence. It is also the one and only time that Smith feared to speculate about anything. The rest of his career consisted in his speculations, with special reference to the plausible conspiracies he saw here, there, and everywhere – private paranoia raised to a scholarly hermeneutics.

We do not know why the dissertation's humble author retreats from the one mildly interesting, if unexceptional, idea, in what is otherwise an incoherent mass of discrete facts. It would carry us far afield to speculate on the psychological and intellectual pressures to which the doctorand succumbed in giving up his hard-earned if unremarkable insight. Nor can we productively speculate on the costs that this act of self-humiliation exacted, or on the retribution Smith would, over the next forty years, exact from others in compensation for whatever disappointments and humiliations he suffered in his youth and early middle age.

But this hitherto unnoted statement of his does help us to understand a career devoted to the totally speculative reconstruction of everything and its opposite and to realize that that career began in an act of intellectual subjugation. The same man who, on the basis of a gullible and credulous reading of selected passages of the Gospels (and capricious rejection of other passages of the same writings), would declare Jesus a charlatan, a magician, and a homosexual, here denies an intent to draw from a vast, arid labor of philology, most of it intellectually inert, any conclusions whatsoever. From such beginnings, not tragic but merely grotesque endings are made. His acts of historical faith, especially perfect faith in his own opinion, would multiply.

That violated doctorand said these words at an age at which more than a few young scholars have already molted the constricting skin of their dissertations and begun to grow a mature and well-fitting one of their own. Rising quickly in that halcyon time, Smith went on within the next decade to become Professor of Ancient History at Columbia University and self-advertised expert on Greek and Roman history, Old and New Testaments, Judaism and Christianity, religion, magic, superstition, theology, and myth – and pretty much everything from the Sumerians through to the advent of Islam. He of course was by reason of such a claim to omniscience a great one for advising people to check very carefully everything said in a book he was reviewing. He would forever state as his often repeated act of condescension and contempt that he had found the author unreliable in some way or another. So, he would say, there may be a good idea, "but you have to check the facts point by point." So the book would (in Smith's lordly fantasy) wither under Smith's penetrating inspection, and anyone who reads it be warned.

Here we shall pay him the compliment of taking his advice and determining whether his allegations as to facts are reliable or, as a matter of fact, merely impressionistic and even ignorant. The one genuinely important statement in his *Parallels* – his one and only important book on the study of Judaism – will be shown simply a misconception of the facts of the documentary relationships Smith claims to portray.

I

In this reexamination of his main contribution to the study of Judaism, his allegation of having found Tannaitic parallels to the Gospels, specifically, I show that his specific, factual allegations at the critical point in his argument, the ones concerning the supposed parallel between the relationship between the Mishnah and the Tosefta and that between Matthew and Luke, simply are false. In the very work in which he insisted on the draconian criterion of the pure facticity of all valid knowledge, Smith did not get his facts straight. The other allegations, briefly reviewed in Chapter One, prove trivial and commonplace. No one familiar with Gospel research even then could have found them more than marginal improvements of existing knowledge and method. But the one on "parallels of parallelism" was genuinely original. It struck me, when I first read it, as amazing; I spent forty-three volumes of my *History of Mishnaic Law* checking it, point by point, in my complete analysis of Mishnah-Tosefta relationships. That is why I know Smith was wrong; I also know that, as we shall see in Chapter Two, when he gave a snippet and declared it representative, he was simply making things up as he went along. There was no one to check him.

This careful checking of Smith's facts, this patient reading of his definitions and category formation – these of course, follow in Smith's own tradition. It is what he meant most of the time to contribute, in the quite correct theory that scholarship progresses through trial and error. As we see in the cited passage, he shrunk back from trying very much, but he would be the one to correct error. He published only a few constructive works, but much criticism of the work of others. A review of his publications shows that most of the items on his bibliography are book reviews, in a ratio of something like six to one over published articles; and in his long life he produced only a few books. Of these, fewer still actually enjoy any standing at all as contributions to scholarship and are so designated. The others are summaries, distillations, reflections, and the like – time fillers. So Smith spent his career mostly passing his opinion on other people's books, book reviews forming by far the largest part of his writings.

True, in Smith's own time, scholarly greats, heavyweights of the order of Arthur Darby Nock, made most of their contributions in the context of book reviews. A rereading of Nock's reviews, collected by Zeph Stewart, provides a better education in Nock's field than time spent reading most of the books he reviews. Nock's great debate with Erwin R. Goodenough took the form, on Nock's side, of book reviews. So book reviewing in the hands of a first-class mind forms a powerful instrument of scholarship.

But Nock's reviews were themselves scholarly essays, the book under review providing an occasion for Nock to think through the subject or problem of the book. Nock never tossed off a few supercilious lines to destroy another scholar's life's work. He never passed an opinion in the spirit of "we all know." He patiently assembled evidence, argument, analysis, to make his points; his book reviews were themselves scholarly disquisitions. By contrast, Smith's reviews tended to be lightweight, offhand, breezy, and, of course, nasty, personal, trivial, mordant, and acid; little research lay behind them; they rested on the foundation of his gargantuan confidence in the validity of whatever he said that minute; and no constructive scholarly agenda motivated his book reviewing.

Smith was no Nock. Smith argued no general thesis on the particular occasion of a book, criticized with no larger program in mind (other than demonstrating, once more, his superiority over everyone else), and made no important scholarly contribution through book reviewing. The same man who antiseptically held back from committing "an act of historical faith" unrestrainedly carried out countless bloody acts of indulgence of private opinion and whim. Everybody else's "I think" for Smith was the same as "it is the fact that...."

What is left of his legacy are some articles of enduring interest, which interested readers will identify for themselves, and his books, and, of these, only his dissertation represented authentic and original scholarship. For the rest, what was original – his Clement fragment – was not authentic, and what was authentic – his potboilers on heroes and holy men, on ancient history, and the like – was not original. A review of his bibliography, in the four-volume festschrift I edited in his honor, *Christianity, Judaism, and Other Greco-Roman Cults. Studies for Morton Smith at Sixty* (Leiden, 1975: E.J. Brill), substantiates that judgment. There we see that Smith was not a very productive book writer and also not much of a book reviewer. His books were few, his reviews opinionated but random, covering anything that came to hand, and not specialized, not systematic, and (when reread decades afterward) also not compelling.

That is why it is only just that any look backward over the man's scholarship also should accord a close and careful reading to a major thesis of his. And that is precisely what I do in this examination of the key chapter of the key book, the one and only book Smith wrote on Judaism, and the dissertation on the basis of which Smith represented himself as knowledgeable about Judaism and its sources. Through his career, Smith passed his opinion on scholarship in every aspect of ancient Judaism. He furthermore distinguished himself as one of the few non-Jewish scholars to read the living Hebrew language, of which we Jews are so proud. He even claimed to know rabbinic literature, though, we shall know see, what he knew about rabbinic literature he learned in a dictionary, and it would have been only with much stumbling and considerable effort that he should have tried to read four consecutive lines of the Talmuds. So we do well, now with the end of his career, to examine the bases for his self-portrait as someone who, concerning Judaism, possessed expert knowledge and important ideas. For reasons to be set forth now, I have chosen now to do so, an act of scholarly

responsibility toward the field in which I work and personal
responsibility as well.

II

To explain my engagement with *Tannaitic Parallels to the Gospels*, let
me turn back to record happier times, for were Smith only the nasty old
fool that he came to be, no one would have reason to want to remember
him or to contend with such scholarly legacy as he may have left. Smith
showed another face altogether, especially to young men. And when I
was his student, he was generous in criticism and intelligent in giving
praise (not much, but at the right time and for the right reason). He was,
as I said, the only teacher I ever had, and, having the advantage of study
with him, I required no other. From studies with him, I went on to make
my own way, and I never believed, and today do not believe, that I could
have accomplished what I have without the education that he provided.
His lessons formed my defining moment; afterward, I took over.

Smith entered my education at the dissertation-writing stage. When,
in early autumn, 1959, after a year of study (1958-1959) I had completed
Columbia University's and Union Theological Seminary's doctoral
course requirements and the two sets of general examinations and
embarked on my dissertation, which was a life of Yohanan ben Zakkai, I
first heard his name. A member of the History Department at Columbia,
he was co-opted by the Department of Religion to serve as a member of
my dissertation committee, along with Professors W.D. Davies, Isaac
Barzilai, and Jakob Taubes, under the chairmanship of Salo W. Baron. As
a courtesy I called on each of the members of the committee, and among
them, found Smith the only one who might have anything to teach me.
Beginning to end, Baron contributed nothing, and the others, while men
of goodwill, were marginal to the work and knew nothing about it. They
merely cheered me on and patronized me. But Smith was something
else.

Though merely a member of the committee, and bearing no special
responsibility whatsoever for the result, he took a keen interest in my
work. I brought him each chapter as I wrote it; he turned it back,
annotated from beginning to end. I brought him a second draft, and he
read and corrected that, so a third, and on through the nine drafts of the
project. From the fourth onward, his comments were mainly
substantive; he saw that I had learned the lessons of form. Then the
comments became interesting and illuminating; I had never met anyone
who thought the way he did. I was captivated by his power of argument
and clear thought. He had just a couple of years earlier finished his
Harvard Th.D. dissertation, which became his intellectually most

successful book, *Palestinian Parties and Politics That Shaped the Old Testament* (New York, 1971: Columbia University Press). I took the train up to Boston and in the Harvard Archives read the book. Then, only when I read it, did I fully understand his strengths of penetrating argument.

Precisely what Smith meant to me can be conveyed by a simple fact: he was the first, the only, and the last authentic teacher I ever had: the only one who critically read what I wrote and gave not only specific criticism but also a detailed model of how to improve my work. My prior education consisted of straight A's and no sustained instruction, except as to facts. From kindergarten until the time I met Smith, I had found every teacher and every class both easy and boring, except for one subject, mathematics, which was never boring, and one teacher, Professor Thomas Kuhn, who was never merely informative but always engaging. From Kuhn I learned ideas that shaped my mind from then on, which today people know in his remarkable *Structure of Scientific Revolutions.*

But, from the time that grades counted, through high school and college, I had gotten all A's and lots of prizes and plenty of praise, but little education. I won every sort of fellowship, to Harvard all paid for, to Oxford on a Henry, to Jerusalem on a Fulbright, to the Jewish Theological Seminary of America on their Special Program in Talmud, and enjoyed everything but what I sought and found only in Smith: authentic teaching by demanding teachers. People seemed happy to tell students this and that, but no one offered criticism, and none paid attention to showing, through precept and example alike, the processes of careful, critical thought.

Smith did. In his devotion to line-by-line examination of sentences, paragraphs, and chapters, and sustained, detailed criticism, he provided whatever education from others I have ever gotten – education, as distinct from the mordant self-criticism that has otherwise driven me always. I take pride in the fact that I learned what he had to teach, and, among the many things he wanted to teach, I chose the right things. My entire theory of teaching, both undergraduate and graduate students, derives from Smith: give the most rigorous criticism you can, always demand the students' best, and forever err by asking too much, not too little.

Not only so, but along with his compelling destruction of what I wrote, Smith made little models for me to use in my revisions. That is, he himself wrote sentences and paragraphs as models of what I should have written. The first drafts of the first few chapters came back to me much larger than they had been, so richly annotated were they. For the roughly dozen years, from 1959 to 1971, when he read and criticized my work, he gave unstintingly, and what he gave was his best. For me, at that time, it was very, very good.

In the dissertation year, the experience of actually learning from a sound model proved so stimulating for me that I never conceived I should not succeed in the task. But it was only when he had read the second draft of the third chapter of the book that Smith said – not to me, but to someone else sitting in his office – "This young man is now well on the way to writing a fine doctorate." The work of course did not end there; ultimately, I wrote the book, as I said, a full nine times over, cover to cover, between autumn, 1959, and late summer, 1960. The others on the dissertation committee saw only the final draft and had nothing to contribute. The book went on to publication and received the Abraham Berliner Prize in Jewish History from the Jewish Theological Seminary.

Then Smith read and annotated the published versions of the five volumes of my *History of the Jews in Babylonia; Development of a Legend. Studies on the Traditions concerning Yohanan ben Zakkai;* and my *Rabbinic Traditions about the Pharisees before 70.* The second edition of the *History.* I. *The Parthian Period* contains numerous corrections and additions deriving from Smith. His contributions to the remaining books proved minimal. We parted company after *Development of a Legend.* Reviewing the book in *Conservative Judaism* 1972, 26:76-77, he called it "an example of the long overdue application to Rabbinic material of the techniques of 'synoptic criticism' and 'form criticism.' These techniques seem to me the ones most likely to make possible a systematic distinction, in the masses of Rabbinic material, between early and late, reliable and unreliable reports. Only by such distinction can some solid, historical firmament ever be separated from the seas of the Talmuds."

In these words, of course, Smith announced that he believed "solid, historical firmament" – the "solid" meant, by his criterion, for his purposes – was there to be found. He supposed that there really is an "early" – and therefore historically factual – to be distinguished from a "late" and fictitious, in the rabbinic literature. But my findings never sustained that surmise; I never could find the path that led from the tale to the event, if any, that the tale purported to record; from the saying to the actual sage who, on some one day, to reliable witnesses, made in his very own words the statement the documents much later attributed to him. *Development of a Legend* in its own primitive way inaugurated the critical, historical study of rabbinic literature. What Smith found to praise would soon strike him in a different way altogether. For I took for granted, in the Anglo-American tradition of pragmatism in which I had grown up, what we cannot show, we do not know. I also grasped that what we cannot falsify, we also cannot verify. Smith's lifelong incapacity at philosophy, which he announced at the start and repeated in chapter after chapter of the book before us, left him deaf to these matters.

And this brings us to the sad tale of Smith's bizarre conduct toward me, which I shall narrate in Chapter One. That praise concealed the profound difference between us. But not for long. The explicit results of work along the lines just now set forth emerged in the next two works, *Pharisees* and *Eliezer ben Hyrcanus. The Tradition and the Man.* I realized that fact only later on, when Smith told me that my *Pharisees* was the last book of mine he ever actually read, and, specifically, he had not read *Eliezer* at all. What changed was that in both those works, I produced comments on the state of the written tradition, but no historical facts that seemed to me to form that "solid, historical firmament" that Smith wished me to locate.

Indeed, I said in so many words that a description of the shape and structure of what I called "the tradition," meaning merely, the sayings assigned to Eliezer, the stories told about him, formed the only solid facts we have in hand. So, I maintained, biography and history would now consist of pious (or malicious) paraphrase of (selected) sayings and stories, which struck me as null, or a different kind of analytical work would have to supersede what until then I, along with everyone else, had been doing. I determined to do it, and I did do it. And he responded in a manner most characteristic of the man, showing a face I had not earlier seen.

III

Despite his sorry behavior, I continue to insist the issues were intellectual and concerned scholarship. Smith was a fundamentalist, with a difference: he believed selectively, but with fury and tub-thumping fervor withal. He thought he could determine fact from fiction in literary evidence, and his historical work rested on a firm belief in the facticity of the facts he selected or fabricated. That conviction of his, coming forth for all to see in his biography of Jesus in particular, classified Smith with those he most despised, Christians who believed in the truth (not the facticity, the truth) of the Bible. So Smith took his place in my life as mentor and master; that relationship lasted until I produced results of which he did not approve. Then he parted company from me long before I realized that my loyalty had been misplaced. He conducted a campaign of personal and scholarly vilification, which grew in intensity and achieved public notoriety. But this did not, and should not be permitted to, obscure the substantive, academic issues.

Smith, of course, violated the norms of the academic, and, by the end, showed himself no scholar at all. Along with others whose infirm grasp of the rules of civility in the Western academy did them in, Saul Lieberman, Ephraim E. Urbach, and Gershom G. Scholem, Smith was one of the four horsemen of my personal apocalypse. That is no mere fantasy on my part. In 1981, two years after the first of Smith's public actions against me, the World Union for Jewish Studies asked me to appear on a panel in Jerusalem, along with Urbach, Lieberman, and Smith, to discuss historical method in Talmudic studies. Scholem was supposed to be the honored guest. But I choose my occasions, and that did not present itself as a likely one.

It was by Smith himself that the differences between Smith and me were personalized and therefore trivialized. He proceeded to spend the last decades of his life in a campaign of demonizing me. But in substance they concerned intellectual and scholarly matters, and therefore they are matters for public inspection. Solid and important points of difference between our respective conceptions of history, history of religion, and history of ideas in Smith's mind turned into evidence of disloyalty on my part. He thought he could write a life of Jesus with his Clement fragment.

I thought and told him to his face that his results were nothing more than anti-Christian propaganda and, in a simple, but uncompromising, footnote, as I said, in the published version of my 1979 SBL address, dismissed Smith's account of Jesus, calling it not history but ideology. In our time a great many Christian scholars have done, and would do, no less for Judaism than I meant to do for Christianity: label prejudice and bigotry for what they are, so remove from scholarly discourse what does not belong among decent people. I did not regret then, and do not regret now, enduring Smith's vengeance for doing what I knew, and now know, was right and also required of me.

I said so both in a letter and in print. Smith felt – the only right word is – jilted. But that hardly explains why he undertook a long-term campaign to discredit me as a scholar and to assassinate my character. Long before I wrote him off, he wrote me off. The substantive issues on which we differed cannot be obscured by despicable conduct. Scholarship does survive scholars' unscholarly behavior.

To conclude this personal narrative: Power conceals its own pathos. Where we are strong, there is our weakness. The power of criticism, which Smith in his great years lavished on his students to their benefit, spilled over into insistence on subservience. When I wrote my *Life of Yohanan ben Zakkai*, he rewrote for me vast stretches of the book; these revised passages served as models for me, and I learned a great deal from Smith by imitating them. But when Smith wished not to offer a model but to impose a mold, and when, further, he took enormous umbrage at anyone who broke the mold he had made, he asked more than what that, or any, relationship was worth. Then his capacity for vengeance knew no limits. In hot pursuit of a disciple deemed a renegade, he was even prepared to disgrace himself, as he did, making himself an outcast, losing all standing in the academy. So power corrupted, and politics proved ephemeral. The reason in my case was that, by the early 1970s, I had produced results leading to conclusions that called into question Smith's entire oeuvre and program. And those results, having been announced at the point at which Smith parted company from me, are now to be addressed.

IV

This brings us to the project at hand. The plan of the book is simple. I set forth the basic thesis of the indictment in the introduction. Then, after surveying the seven theses that have not stood the test of time, in Chapter One, I present Smith's statement of his thesis in Chapter Two. This is in his own words, inclusive of his Appendix C, which presents his specific reading of specific texts. No one can accuse me of inaccurately imputing to him things he did not think, or of misrepresenting his words.

But then we turn to a sustained inquiry into the facts that Smith alleges. Since these concern Mishnah-Tosefta relationships, I offer the reader a very considerable repertoire of texts that define the two documents' relationships. Specifically, in Chapters Three through Six, readers are given an ample occasion to check the facts as shown by dozens of actual texts – Mishnah-Tosefta comparisons in detail and in situ – and can form for themselves a judgment on Smith's characterization of matters.

The facts presented in those chapters were beginning to emerge in the middle 1970s, the point at which, as I shall explain in Chapter One, Smith began his sustained, decades-long campaign to discredit me. It would be self-serving to claim that Smith found his motivation in my demonstration that his first and only book on Judaism was really just wrong on its one interesting idea. But such a claim would give Smith too much credit.

Indeed, I am confident Smith paid no attention to the formation of data pertinent to earlier theses of his. He jumped from topic to topic, forgetting one as he came to the next. Not only so, but he rarely learned from other people, and then, when he did, he learned only some new fact. It is easy to demonstrate the opposite of the proposed explanation for his obsession with me. Though the main lines of the discoveries laid out in these chapters had been set forth during Smith's lifetime, he never again published a word on the topic, either calling attention to the conflict with his notions on the parallel of parallelism, or revising his original scheme. Indeed, it is difficult to point, in Smith's oeuvre, to a single time at which he declared a major thesis of his – even a plausible guess – to have been wrong; he never corrected a mistake; he never changed his mind.

That remarkable capacity to ignore what he did not wish to know marked Smith throughout his scholarly life. As we shall see in Chapter One, Smith really was a dilettante, and once he had passed his opinion on a subject, he did not return to it. A review of his bibliography reveals a devastating fact. None – not one! – of his books relates in problem or even topic to any other. He just flitted from this to that, depositing his opinion where he would. He ended up having passed his opinion on many things, but he made a lasting contribution on none. Only through a detailed survey of the data Smith did not consider but chose to ignore – the data set forth in Chapters Three through Six – shall we see the enormity of his ignorance about a matter concerning which he claimed (as usual) authority and certainty. Chapter Seven then points to the grounds for rejecting Smith's thesis as contrary to the facts of the matter.

This examination of Smith's legacy thus identifies two devastating failures of intellect characteristic of Smith's work, beginning to end. First, Smith will be shown a bungler at problems of a philosophical character, defining matters, forming a clear statement of his categories and criteria. My presentation of the other seven theses of his dissertation, in Chapter One, will show time and again how Smith tried with diminishing success and growing frustration to cope with problems of abstract definition; he ends up "defining" by invoking "examples," typical of junior high school students – or tenth-rate minds. Second, Smith's entire oeuvre leaves the picture of a credulous and gullible believer, but with a difference: Smith's fundamentalism was selective. On this I shall have much more to say; and I am by no means the first to make that observation in Smith's oeuvre.

This twin legacy is, alas, not yet lost. Two other students of Smith's – the ones he liked – show even now what is unsound in Smith's legacy. The first is his conceptual bungling, as exemplified just now by a book by Professor Lee I. Levine, Jewish Theological Seminary (Jerusalem). I reproduce my review, showing specifically how the master's legacy yet lives. Asking questions that rest on the premise of the facticity of the sources, therefore expressing Smith's historical fundamentalism, is exemplified by yet another, Professor S.J.D. Cohen, Brown University (Providence). I repeat here observations concerning a major article of Cohen's, which could have been conceived and executed only in the premise that Cohen knew as fact whatever allegations in the sources he chose to affirm and knew as fiction whatever he chose to reject. Why place on display yet again evidence of intellectual incompetence in books and articles of Smith's outstanding heirs? It seems only right that, so long as we address Smith's legacy, we may as well examine those who carry on their teacher's traditions.

Morton Smith, a domineering personality who talked much better than he listened, took great pleasure in telling young men what to say and do. The need to dominate produced constructive results: he devoted himself to the close and careful reading of doctoral dissertations that came his way, even though he was not the dissertation director but only a member of the committee, as was the case with me. I found his instruction sharp and illuminating; he was a great dissertation director. He read every line and criticized every word and every formulation; I valued his criticism and learned much from him. His was a powerful intellect, and he turned it to the advantage of those whom he instructed. He was the only authentic teacher I have ever known, the only teacher in my experience who really engaged with the education of his students. That is why he was important in my life. Now to examine his own contribution and its context.

1

Smith's Alleged Parallels: Much Ado about Not Much

I. Why Reread a Forty-Year-Old Dissertation

Smith's *Tannaitic Parallels to the Gospels* made a deep impression on me when I read it thirty years ago. And in one aspect, it still teaches the same lesson it did then. At that time, it made me realize that, in order to pursue my studies of rabbinic literature, I had to find out what was happening in Gospel research.

When I was a student at the Jewish Theological Seminary of America, I never heard from a professor the notion that other documents of the same place and era as the rabbinic ones were being studied in ways productive for the examination of rabbinic literature, and I doubt that the professors of that period knew or thought important the methods of New Testament exegesis and critical history. Even though Union Theological Seminary was across the street, no JTSA student in my time ever was advised to audit a course there, and I never heard at JTSA the name of a single scholar of biblical studies working at Union Seminary: not Old Testament, not New Testament, not even Apocrypha and Pseudepigrapha. When I enrolled in doctoral courses in the Columbia University-Union Theological Seminary Program in Religion and attended classes at Union – the great James Muilenberg's in Pseudepigrapha, for example – I was publicly condemned in a JTSA class room for doing so. In my time at JTSA, 1954-1960, the school was what the Catholics call "pre-conciliar."

Smith's *Tannaitic Parallels* introduced me to New Testament studies by showing me why those studies would prove instructive in my work, and, because of it, I found my way to the great figures of that field. It was specifically because of reading this book that I turned to the one work that shaped my earliest thinking on the critical study of rabbinic

15

literature, which is Rudolph Bultmann's *History of the Synoptic Tradition*. It was there, in Bultmann's admirable work, that I began to think about the analysis of the formal traits of rabbinic writings. It was with Dibelius that I began to take an interest in traditions-history. It was with Albert Schweitzer that I learned something about critical history and biography. And these were only the highest peaks of a scholarly field of Himalayan heights. True, I never found useful, or even very relevant, the notion of form-history or form-criticism, none of the premises of which could be sustained in the analysis of rabbinic literature. But Bultmann and the lesser figures of New Testament scholarship of this century and the last remained my models, because they taught me how to read a text beyond its philology, which is all that anyone at JTSA was capable of studying. Since it was through Smith's *Parallels* that I first began to ask myself how to learn what was to be gained from New Testament scholarship, it defined a turning point in my education. And now it does again. So what is to be learned from Smith is that important methods found in one field have to reshape studies of contiguous ones.

This item of his, furthermore, remains the one work of Smith's that, thus far, has appeared to stand the test of time. At any rate, it is the only book he wrote that still can be read for its actual scholarship, not merely for the history of scholarship. All of his other books, and most of his articles, survive as mere curiosities. He is today remembered for his despicable characterization of Jesus as a homosexual magician, a theory of the matter that has found acceptance in not a single account of the life and teachings of Jesus written since Smith made that bizarre allegation. His potboilers have been superseded by other people's.[1]

His one really well-crafted argument, his Th.D. dissertation, which became *Palestinian Parties and Politics That Shaped the Old Testament*,[2] exercises no perceptible influence in biblical scholarship. His prevailing attitudes toward the subjects on which he worked, marked by malice and distorted by his prevailing, paranoid premise that everyone conducts conspiracies against everyone else, do not enjoy esteem among most of those exposed to Smith's writing. This then is his last candidate for enduring worth.

I choose to take up a dissertation published more than four decades ago and devote a whole book to demonstrating that its single important ideas is wrong for three reasons. First, *Tannaitic Parallels to the Gospels* persuaded many Gospel scholars that salvation is of the Jews, so that important exegetical and therefore also historical problems reach final

---

[1]E.g., *The Ancient Greeks* (Ithaca, 1960: Cornell University Press), and *Heroes and Gods: Spiritual Biographies in Antiquity* (New York, 1965: Harper and Row).
[2](New York, 1971: Columbia University Press).

solution in rabbinic literature. It was one of the earliest works, after World War II, to call attention to the resources of that literature for New Testament studies. It further established its author as a major player in the study of Judaism and Christianity alike. So Smith's dissertation in its day proved influential and for that reason warrants careful inspection in light of later findings.

The second reason is that, as I explained in the introduction, reading the dissertation and studying with Smith personally made a profound impact on me in my formative years. For an important chapter in my scholarly career, from 1959 to 1973, I was Smith's student and disciple, and, then to now, I regarded his *Tannaitic Parallels* as the defining work. The entire course of my career was shaped by this one book of his, which had brought me to him to begin with, and that is the book examined here. *Tannaitic Parallels to the Gospels* began as Smith's Ph.D. dissertation in classical philology in the Hebrew University with the 1948 thesis, *Maqbilot ben haBesorot leSifrut Hatannaim.*

But why just now, not ten years ago, or ten years hence? This brings me to the third consideration, which dictates that this is the right time for me to do the work. The reason is that I have only just now reached the stage of asking those more narrowly historical questions that Smith insisted on raising when he did: before he had done the homework required for any further inquiry along the lines of interest to him. This interest of mine on the documentary analysis of literature and society, beginning in my *History of the Mishnaic Law of Purities* and the other divisions, which I started at just the point Smith told me he had stopped reading me, would extend through all the other documents of Rabbinic Judaism. It would lead, as a matter of fact, to the work that just now is getting under way. That is why, at the start of a new chapter, I turn back to the examination of the now-completed one, the one the direction and implications of which Smith grasped much before I did.

Specifically, in the earliest of my theoretical probes, before the systematic documentary work got under way, I found that the sayings and stories in rabbinic literature conveyed historical facts, but not history in any conventional sense. Six volumes of experimentation had left me no doubt that an entirely different kind of history was required.[3] Smith,

---

[3]These are *Development of a Legend. Studies on the Traditions Concerning Yohanan ben Zakkai* (Leiden, 1970: E.J. Brill); *The Rabbinic Traditions about the Pharisees before 70* (Leiden, 1971: E.J. Brill). I-III. I. *The Rabbinic Traditions about the Pharisees before 70. The Masters.* II. *The Rabbinic Traditions about the Pharisees before 70. The Houses.* III. *The Rabbinic Traditions about the Pharisees before 70. Conclusions,* and *Eliezer ben Hyrcanus. The Tradition and the Man* (Leiden, 1973: E.J. Brill). I. *Eliezer ben Hyrcanus. The Tradition and the Man. The Tradition.* II. *Eliezer ben Hyrcanus. The Tradition and the Man. The Man.*

as I said, really understood that fact. For my part, by contrast, I acted on it, without much ado at the time.

So my own long-term scholarly work has come to a point of closure and renewal, and, as part of an effort to review the path I have taken and gain perspective on the path I see before, I have in mind a few works of reconsideration. I have now completed my complete, documentary study of rabbinic literature, beginning to end, covering all of the main writings. I have published translations of every document, and introductions to every document. I have systematically examined the relationship between the Mishnah and the Tosefta, beginning to end, in my translations and commentaries to both documents. So I know a great deal more than Smith did about these matters. I was curious to turn back to see what Smith had observed in his superficial and impressionistic glance at documents that I knew start to finish and in every detail. I remembered him as very confident of what I knew to be mere guesses; no one I have known in forty years of scholarship ever announced with greater certitude this morning's bright idea. So, with my own knowledge of the same matters, resting on sustained and painstaking and careful work of translation and commentary, I determined to see what, really, lay behind Smith's confident pronouncements in his *Tannaitic Parallels*.

Accordingly, at a major turning in my intellectual career, I had to return to Smith's dissertation in connection with thinking about the next question I wish to take up, which is narrowly historical: precisely what kind of history can we, after all, derive from rabbinic literature? I refer in particular to the project of identifying the historical questions that rabbinic literature permits us to answer. This will be in a series of six monographs, yielding a volume of systematic conclusions, under the general title, for the monographs, of *From Text to Historical Context. An Historical Reading of the Canon of Judaism,* and, for the conclusions, of *Rabbinic Writings as a Source of Historical Facts: What the Canon of Judaism Tells Us about the History of the Jews in Late Antiquity.* In preparing for that project, which is my next major venture, I had to reconsider Smith's blunders, so as to give thought to the right way to proceed. That is what called my attention to Smith's dissertation after so many years.

We do not waste our time in examining errors – those of others as well as our own. Scholarship progresses at much because of, as despite, the mistakes scholars make. Smith erred in virtually every factual statement in the one important chapter of his book. But in advising scholars of rabbinic literature to learn what New Testament research had accomplished, he opened the way to others to do right what he did wrong. And that is how matters turned out. In 1975, when I edited his festschrift, in the preface I called Smith "one of the great scholarly masters of this generation," and the reason was the work we shall inspect in these pages.

The former date – 1959 – marks the point at which, working on my Ph.D. dissertation, I brought Smith, who was not chairman but only a member of my dissertation committee in the Columbia University-Union Theological Seminary Doctoral Program in Religion, the chapters as I wrote them. Though he was not the principal of the committee[4] I wanted to enjoy the benefit of his criticism. I did the same with the other four members. Only Smith, among the five, had anything to contribute; only Smith worked with me as I went along. Only Smith had anything important to tell me. His contribution was so generous, so illuminating, so stimulating, that the incapacity of the others hardly diminished the opportunity for learning Columbia and Union set before me. As I explained in the introduction, he was not only the best teacher of my life, he was the only good one. But I have also to spell out the other half of the tale. Rereading Smith's one important book on Judaism takes place in a context that should be spelled out. Specifying the personal differences between us allows me also to identify the intellectual points of contention.

That brings us to the latter date, 1973, which records the point at which he informed me he did not plan to read another book of mine, beyond my *Rabbinic Traditions about the Pharisees before 70*. Specifically, he told me when he thanked me for the gift of my *Eliezer b. Hyrcanus. The Tradition and the Man*, he had not even opened the book and did not plan to do so. Since in the interval he had given me detailed, page-by-page comments on my scholarly books and articles as they appeared, his statement marked a turning. In fact, he never again gave me a substantive comment on anything I sent him, from then to 1979, when I perceived the true meaning of his announcement in 1973.

But, in the interim, I did not take amiss what he had told me. I had appreciated his generosity in taking time out to read my work over ten years and had enormously benefited from his criticism. The second, revised edition of my *History of the Jews in Babylonia. I. The Parthian Period* includes many of his comments. Smith concealed his true meaning. Rather, he explained in a way he knew would appeal to me: he cited the Jacob of the Torah. He had his own work to do, he told me, in line with Jacob's statement to Laban: "When shall I take care of my own household?" I did not think of myself as Laban in encounter with his Jacob. I was wrong. Smith was a clever man – not brilliant, in conceptual matters a complete bungler, but clever.

---

[4]The chairman was Salo W. Baron and the other members were Jakob Taubes, W.D. Davies, and Isaac Barzilai.

What he understood, and what I did not grasp for some time to come, is that I had taken a path he could not approve. It was a path that in fact cut across – and cut off – his entire scholarly progress. In three works, I had reached the conclusion that no conventional, narrative history could emerge from the rabbinic literature; that is to say, the writing of history by the paraphrase and commentary upon stories and sayings in that literature in no way conformed to the critical standards of biblical studies and indeed required an act of faith that scholarship could not sustain. That was a position inimical, even threatening, to the same man who had pathetically announced at the beginning of his scholarship, *"But to make such an inference would involve an act of historical faith, for to pass from the observable similarity of words to the hypothetical similarity of ideas which the words may have been meant to express is to pass from the knowable to the unknown."* For that was precisely what he had been doing in the years after 1948 and, by the mid-1970s, proposed to bring to a climax in his biography of none other than Jesus.

So it came about that at the very moment he was writing his life of Jesus, an account that rested in significant part on Smith's knowledge of rabbinic literature and his certainty of the facticity of whatever he declared a fact, I was calling into question the very basis on which he was reading that, and all other ancient, literature. Even my earliest results and methods denied the possibility of using the rabbinic literature in the way in which Smith wished to use it to make the point he wanted to register in his biography of Jesus. While Smith was telling the world about the authentic, historical Jesus, I was demonstrating that the Judaic component of his evidence could not serve for the purpose for which he was using it.

Smith really believed in the philological fundamentalist position: once you have established the correct, original text and accurately defined all of its words, you have a fact of history. History then formed the consequence of philology, narrowly construed. Not only so, but Smith had made his name in part by his knowledge of rabbinic literature, which he used to establish the facts of Judaism that would illuminate the faith of Christianity in the Gospels. Sayings and stories of rabbinic literature in his hands provided facts – unexamined, uncriticized facts – that would permit him to tell the world who and what Jesus really was. But by 1973 I had already demonstrated that the rabbinic literature's facts in no way served as Smith insisted they did.

That explains why nothing in my work beyond my pre-critical period,[5] specifically, nothing after *Development of a Legend. Studies on the*

---

[5]This is the period in which I wrote *A Life of Yohanan ben Zakkai* and *A History of the Jews in Babylonia.*

Traditions Concerning Yohanan ben Zakkai, brought comfort to Smith's selectively fundamentalist conviction and position. His career of perfect historical faith, his power to transform his bright ideas ("hypothetical similarity") into facts bearing only the force of Smith's own dogmatically argued conviction – these were finding their match in my insistence that we cannot show the historical validity of attributions of sayings to named authorities or of narratives of stories to specific occasions. Therefore so far as rabbinic literature was concerned, the sayings and stories, the raw materials of historical narrative, could no longer serve to support the kind of writing Smith did, even then, in his biography of Jesus, to which we shall allude presently. Smith had in mind a life of Jesus in the grand tradition of nineteenth-century narrative, only a Jesus in the image of Smith's own fantasy of conspiracy and fraud: an anti-Christian Jesus indeed: charlatan, magician, homosexual.

To his theory of the use of the stories and sayings of the received writings of Christianity and Judaism, my results therefore posed a mortal threat. I took (and now take) the view that what we cannot both falsify and validate, we cannot demonstrate: what we cannot show, we do not know. Just now I have published a book with that title, and it summarizes part of a whole position. The other part requires specification as well. For as opposed to the pseudo-critical history Smith thought to write, I conceived of writing a history that took seriously precisely what Smith loathed, which was, religion. The sources that yielded Smith's history would produce my account of the formation of the religion, Judaism.

The reason is obvious. Sources not suitable for one purpose serve very admirably for another – the one they were written to accomplish. And, it was becoming clear to me, through a very patient translation of, and commentary upon, each of the documents of Rabbinic Judaism, I wished to find out not what we want to know but cannot, but rather, what the sources as we can describe, analyze, and interpret them, tell us on their own account. That explains the radical turning I was making at just that time, a turning from reading the sources to answer my questions toward reading the sources to discover their questions.

As I said, Smith was clever, if, alas, not endowed with sufficient intelligence to achieve his goals. He understood far more perspicaciously than I did precisely what was at stake. But, then, I was doing the work, and he was only passing his opinion about it. To be sure, he did not grasp the promise of the project, lacking any sort of conceptual insight or power from the beginning to the end of his career, as I shall show in our brief survey of his *Tannaitic Parallels.* But then he was interested in only what interested him, and he had his own agendum.

To me, the correct purpose of the study of Rabbinic Judaism was to describe, analyze, and interpret that religious system. To the history of Jews in the time of the formation of that Judaism the religious writings of that Judaism attested only casually, and not very often. In my view, the correct address of study of Rabbinic Judaism was, and would remain for twenty-five years, documentary: we examine the traits of documents in a process of description, analysis, and interpretation. These documents of religion claimed to set forth religious truth, not historical fact. In due course, I maintained, this literature would yield a further, more narrowly historical study of text, context, and matrix: history not as the tale of things that happened (with lots of asides by the historian, passing his or her opinion) but as a problem, in times past, of the analysis of culture and conviction: the historical study of religion and the social order.

Now to continue the narrative: After Smith told me he had stopped reading my work, I continued to treat him with deference and to appreciate his learning. I did not take offense at his declaration, though he meant it as a writ of divorce. To the contrary, I valued his work and admired it. I did not wish to take away his time from his own projects. Evidence of my continued goodwill is readily adduced: I initiated, organized, edited, and personally financed Smith's festschrift, in four volumes, no less.[6] Smith called it the finest festschrift anyone had ever received. Reviewers concurred. I brought the homage of the world of learning to his feet. To his credit, he acknowledged each article personally to the author and wrote an exceptionally gracious note of thanks to me as well.

But that gratitude, privately conveyed, did not prevent him from soon afterward carrying out public acts of contempt. Only four years after his fulsome thanks for his festschrift, at the Society of Biblical Literature meeting in 1979 in New York City, Smith ostentatiously walked out – smack down the middle aisle of a huge auditorium, slowly making his way from near the front and center, right in front of me, all the way to the back, for all to see and many to find astonishing. This he did in the middle of my plenary address, the first I had been invited to deliver there. Something in my lecture, which he had read in advance and with which he had helped me in some minor details, enormously outraged him. He did not tell me so in advance privately, rather he showed the world publicly.

---

[6]*Christianity, Judaism, and Other Greco-Roman Cults. Studies for Morton Smith at Sixty* (Leiden, 1975: E.J. Brill). I. *New Testament*. II. *Early Christianity*. III. *Judaism before 70*. IV. *Judaism after 70. Other Greco-Roman Cults.*

Now I have printed that address.[7] At footnote 18 – the Hebrew letters for eighteen stand for life – readers will find the fuse to that bomb that exploded in Smith's mind. There I stated, with reference to his *Jesus the Magician*, the implications of the findings that I had in fact uncovered a decade earlier. Smith would now go public; merely walking out of my lecture hardly satisfied his wrath. Indeed, Smith's next demonstration made the newspapers, at least, the ones that celebrate scholarly scandal. Even now, nearly a decade later, people still find it of interest to discuss the incident with me. Here is the story; several hundred people can attest to what actually happened.

At the same society's meeting in Chicago, in 1984, I was given the honor of delivering the annual lecture, "How My Mind Has Changed." The chairman of the evening, Professor W.D. Davies, called for questions from the floor, after I delivered the plenary address in the honorary series. He did not demur when Smith ignored the instructions – questions from the floor – and ascended the podium, took over the microphone from Davies, and proceeded to remove from his pocket a prepared address that had no bearing on anything I had said in my lecture. Uninvited by the SBL, unimpeded by Davies, Smith now gave his own lecture on "how my mind has changed – about Jacob Neusner." In it, for some twenty or twenty-five minutes, he proceeded violently to denounce me as a charlatan. When he came to the end of his prepared speech, he was not done with my case.

Smith proceeded to his next scene. Having prepared long in advance for his demonstration, Smith took in hand shopping bags full of papers, carried by plane from New York City. His speech done, he calmly folded up his manuscript, put it in his pocket again, and then descended from the podium in order to distribute a handout to the scandalized audience. The leaflet was Saul Lieberman's violently critical review of what amounted to a few mistakes in my preliminary translation of a few paragraphs of a chapter of a tractate of the Talmud of the Land of Israel. Found in Lieberman's desk and submitted by an unknown hand only after Lieberman's death, this "review" – the only book review in English

---

[7]It is in my *The Academic Study of Judaism. Essays and Reflections. Third Series* (New York, 1980: Ktav Publishing House), pp. 82-105. A reduced version is in my *What We Cannot Show, We Do Not Know: The New Testament and Rabbinic Literature* (Philadelphia, 1993: Trinity Press International). I also cite some of the paragraphs in the introduction to my *The Doubleday Anchor Reference Library Introduction to Rabbinic Literature* (New York, 1994: Doubleday). I regard that lecture as my favorite among my public addresses of that kind.

Lieberman ever published – had been printed six months earlier by the
Journal of the American Oriental Society.[8]

Smith played the witch of Endor – for an unnamed Saul to be sure –
to Samuel's wraith. This voice from beyond the grave Smith now
invoked to speak up and show me to be – as he said I was – a fraud and a
charlatan. Now – not trusting necromancy, rather passing out his leaflets
from his shopping bag, going from row to row, gesticulating and
murmuring to himself – Smith had gone too far. People in the audience
began to laugh at the spectacle. Only now, with gales of laughter
breaking over him, Davies finally called for order. But no one listened.
With people standing in the aisles and with the floor now littered with
garbage – for that was the fate of the reprint of Lieberman's last words –
Davies called me to the microphone. The audience subsided, Smith
persisted, and people were laughing still. I asked people to stop
ridiculing Smith, who was, I said, my teacher, to whom I bore a debt of
thanks and honor. They did, and the meeting ended in confusion.

While in good company indeed, I found little comfort in the thought
that the charge, fraud and charlatan, is part of what Smith had already
called Jesus, too. Anyhow, Smith was not finished with me. He
proceeded, in the following months, to organize a nationwide
distribution of the same review, enlisting in the cause the then-dean of
Hebrew Union College-Jewish Institute of Religion, who sent it to every
member of the faculty of that institution. The HUC-JIR dean evidently
knew his professors could not be relied upon to go to the library and
read the journals. A local rabbi in Providence, Rhode Island, and long-
time ally of Smith, William G. Braude, did the same for the Reform
rabbis, not to mention the entire administration of Brown University (to
which, as a matter of course, I had already sent the item, without
comment). When, a couple of years later, Northwestern University
asked me to apply for a chair in Judaic Studies, Reform and Conservative
rabbis of its neighborhood pressured the university provost and the
donor of the chair into reversing the university's plan.

All of these actions belie a simple fact. Masquerading as a lynch
mob, Smith and his allies in fact were engaged in a quarrel about
scholarly and intellectual issues; but they could not frame the issues to
their advantage, finding their final solution to the Neusner problem only
in a campaign academically to exterminate the person, the position being
beyond assault. For at stake in this crusade of Smith and his army of
Jewish seminary professors and Conservative and Reformed rabbis were
intellectual and scholarly issues. Smith and I parted company for

---

[8]That is, by the way, a journal that had not for twenty years reviewed a book of
mine, and would never review another.

substantive, scholarly reasons. Publicly to disrupt a major plenary address and to try to embarrass and humiliate a colleague at an occasion called to pay honor to that colleague hardly characterize any authentically academic debate.

People drew that conclusion. I received more invitations to give plenary lectures at national scholarly meetings in the study of religion. Smith did not. He never got another chance at a major academic audience. Smith paid a heavy price in the debacle that followed. I had received half a dozen honorary degrees and medals prior to the event, and was to receive another half dozen afterward, along with a variety of other recognitions of scholarly achievement. Outside of the circle of the faithful, poor Smith got no prizes.

In fact, from 1984 until his death seven years later, Smith ceased to enjoy the standing that his earlier contributions to learning had gained. In his last years he was generally regarded as a crank, and, by the end, little short of a crackpot. He died a figure of ridicule, lacking influence outside of his own personal sect, represented in the appendices of this book. Beyond his followers, his ideas lost all hearing; no life of Jesus, for instance, took seriously his views of Jesus as a charlatan, a homosexual, or a magician, not one. He got to write no definitive introductions, he got to edit no dictionaries or encyclopedias, he set forth no handbooks, he wrote no forewords to major, definitive bibliographies, he produced no influential textbooks, he got no honorary degrees or medals. Smith was finished. Form and substance alike, he had none of the recognitions that come to those who define their own field of learning for an entire generation of scholars.

II. Know-Nothings, Fundamentalists, and Morton Smith

Smith knew two terms of supreme abuse: know-nothing and fundamentalist. He knew whereof he cursed, for he himself was both. Smith was his own kind of fundamentalist, on the one side, and know-nothing, on the other. He was a selective fundamentalist, believing everything bad, but nothing good, about Jesus. He knew nothing about theoretical problems and cared less. He found no patience to discuss issues of method. He dismissed as wasteful all efforts at critical definition of categories. Even the definition of "parallels" at hand shows a clumsy effort at saying nothing with lots of confusing, convoluted words.

And this brings us to the points of reasoned and principled conflict between Smith and me. For, as I have already insisted, he must not be permitted after death to define the issues in the way he wanted, as a conflict of personalities, not principles. That self-indulgence no longer pertains.

First comes a conflict on historical method. Smith fervently thought that, on the basis of uncorroborated literary evidence, stories and sayings concerning a given person, without a mediating process of criticism and cultural inquiry, could be forthwith translated into historical biography. I proved beyond doubt that out of rabbinic literature that kind of history simply could not be written; stories and sayings stood for something else than things that were really done and said on some one day. He realized, before I did, that everything he had done and wanted to do was contradicted by my findings concerning the character of rabbinic literature. Specifically, that literature forms a great and rich source for history – but not the kind of history Smith had done and proposed to do.

Second is my engagement with problems of theory, for example, the theory of history of religion, the theory of the social study of religion, the theory of historical knowledge: what do we know, how do we know it, why does it matter. Smith thought that issues of method, definition of categories and examination of issues of category formation, concern for theoretical problems – these were null. "We all know what we mean," he insisted. My curiosity about what, if anything, the term "Judaism" might mean in any given context struck him as stupid: "We all know what Judaism is." In fact, Smith was a conceptual bungler. He grasped nothing of theoretical issues, and learned nothing from those who did. He had no philosophical sense at all, and he also had no patience for those of us who listened with care when thoughtful people talked about the definition of categories, the formulation of well-examined method, and the critical agenda that predominated in New Testament research of that time (and now as well).

Though fully acquainted with critical studies of Scripture, Smith honestly believed that, with the kinds of sources at hand, we may state precisely what happened, what really was said and done at a given point in times past. That is why he thought he could tell us who Jesus really was and what Jesus really said and did – as against what the Gospels said and Christianity believed. His was a fundamentalism as gullible and credulous as that of those whom he dismissed as "pseudorthodox" or merely stupid. But stupid is as stupid does: Smith was the one to treat with not serious argument but mere contempt anyone who differed from him on anything.

To be sure, Smith's fundamentalist gullibility, resting on the facticity of the stories and sayings of the Gospels (for his picture of Jesus "the magician"), rested on a certain selectivity; he believed what he wanted to believe, and, about Jesus, he wanted to believe only the worst things he could in his own mind conjure. But, selective or not, the attitude of mind that we can translate the kinds of sources at hand into narratives of things really said and done, that history of a particular, factual kind can emerge from the Gospels or rabbinic stories and sayings – that attitude marks Smith as a believer indeed.

Now, as results of mine in my *Rabbinic Traditions about the Pharisees* and *Eliezer ben Hyrcanus* emerged, and as I began to find deeply troubling issues of not only method but also category formation, I did not grasp what he immediately perceived: I had broken ranks, and I had parted company. For my part I saw nothing of the kind. He saw in my work the two matters he could not – or chose not to – address: critical historical method and concern for issues of theory. These formed critical traits of his entire life's work and continue to hobble those who accept his inheritance and value it. That is why, at the end, I append two writings on other disciples of his, who carry forward Smith's legacy of conceptual bungling and selective fundamentalism, respectively.

III. Time to Reexamine Smith's Altogether-Too-Secret "Secret Gospel"?

In this context of rereading Smith's dissertation and reevaluating his scholarship, let me propose that it is time, also, to take a second look at Smith's supposed discovery, which many now think was a forgery, of a missing paragraph in Mark's Gospel. In *The Secret Gospel: The Discovery and Interpretation of the Secret Gospel According to Mark,*[9] Smith achieved the allotted fifteen minutes of incomparable notoriety that he sought: he became principal enemy, for some few minutes, to much of Christianity. Only, in later times, Salman Rushdie outdid Smith in the olympiad of religious scandal. Islam put up two million dollars for Rushdie's murder; Christendom just yawned.

As it happens, people can make a great name for themselves by saying whatever they want to about "the historical Jesus," making the front page of the New York Times (if that is what they wish to manufacture for themselves) if what they say is sufficiently scandalous, therefore newsworthy. Announce that Jesus was precisely what the Gospels say he was – and still is – and even in churches some will yawn. But tell the world he was a homosexual magician, as Smith did, and your day is made: you get to offend and insult those you wish to provoke, and to call yourself a great scholar at the same time. In no other field of study, whether claiming historical objectivity or glorying in utter subjectivity (as in current literary criticism) can solecism pass for scholarship, and out-and-out psychosis win a hearing as a new fact.

---

[9](New York, 1975: Harper & Row).

Certainly, in what must now be declared the forgery of the century, the very integrity of the quest for the historical Jesus was breached. The very quest met its defining disgrace by Smith, whose "historical" results – Jesus was "really" a homosexual magician – depended upon a selective believing in whatever Smith thought was historical.[10] Even at the time, some of us told Smith to his face that he was an upside-down fundamentalist, believing anything bad anybody said about Jesus, but nothing good.   And no one who so rebuked him objected to the campaigns of character assassination that Smith spent his remaining years conducting; there is a moment at which, after all, truth does matter, even if, in respect to Jesus, some imagine that it does not. Still, in defense of the quest as Smith conducted it, the charge that each "biographer" of Jesus produces a Jesus in his own image is wide of the mark, since no one ever accused Smith of being a magician.

But his quest for the historical Jesus surely produced a scandal, and not only the results. As a matter of fact, Smith's presentation of the evidence for his homosexual magician, a Clement fragment he supposedly turned up in a library in Sinai in 1958, ranks as one of the most slovenly presentations of an allegedly important document in recent memory; and, to understate matters, it left open the very plausible possibility of forgery. Smith himself was an expert on such matters, having devoted scholarly essays to great forgeries in antiquity. It is no surprise that, reviewing Smith's results, the great New Testament scholar Quentin Quesnell ended his questioning of Smith's evidence with the simple colloquy: "Is there a reasonable possibility of forgery?   The answer, working only with the evidence Smith presents, seems to be clearly, yes."[11]

---

[10]Morton Smith, *Jesus the Magician,* a popularization of his findings in his *Clement of Alexandria and a Secret Gospel of Mark* (Cambridge, 1973: Harvard University Press) and *The Secret Gospel: The Discovery and Interpretation of the Secret Gospel According to Mark* (New York, 1975: Harper & Row).

[11]"The Mar Saba Clementine: A Question of Evidence," *Catholic Biblical Quarterly* 1975, 37:48-67; note Smith's reply, *CBQ* 1976, 38:196-99, and Quesnell, *CBQ* 1976 38:200-3.   Smith's replies persuaded no one; his career in New Testament scholarship ended with his "discovery," though when he was alive, fearing law suits, few expressed the widely held surmise that it was a brilliant forgery, nothing more. But the course of New Testament scholarship from the Clement fragment was completely unaffected by Smith's "discovery," which made no impact whatsoever; that represents the judgment of contemporaries while Smith was alive. Not a single "life of Jesus" portrays him as a homosexual magician, except for Smith's, and I venture to predict that none ever will. In any other historical field but this one, when others cannot replicate results, a proposed reconstruction falls by the way. But in a theological field, every possibility

Now the spectacle of the quest for the historical Jesus was exposed for all to see. What controls of rationality, objectivity, strict rules of evidence, skepticism, and criticism protected the field as such from a brilliant forgery, such as Quesnell exposed? That a field of learning should produce so grotesque a result as Smith wished reputable scholars to adopt disheartened those with the common sense to distinguish skepticism from spite, objective learning from a personal vendetta of a lapsed clergyman. It is worth dwelling on Quesnell's rather cautious indictment, to realize how open to fraud the quest had left itself, and how little, at its moment of truth, people were prepared to do in the name of the integrity of their subject. For Quesnell stood nearly alone, and to this day has yet to receive his due from those whose field he proposed to defend.

Quesnell pointed out that Smith presents photographs, but not the manuscript itself, and the photographs are unsatisfactory: "He made them himself...with a handheld camera." So, in fact, no one has ever seen the document but Smith himself. Smith claims that various experts said the text was genuine, but, Quesnell says, "Unfortunately...Smith does not include the text of the answers which the experts gave." Smith wants the primary test of authenticity to be the wording; Quesnell: "The primary test of authenticity is examination of the manuscript." That leads Quesnell to wonder whether someone might have forged the document. Now when the Dead Sea Scrolls came to light, entire academic careers were devoted to precisely the issues of validation of the manuscript itself: the ink, the medium of writing, orthography, a variety of types of physical evidence.

Solomon Zeitlin, now forgotten but once a mighty, imperial figure, called into question the early dating of the scrolls and maintained they were medieval forgeries – even in the face of the most rigorous testing of the physical evidence. Imagine the donnybrook that Smith's quaint explanation of the "disappearance" of the "original documents" would have precipitated, had a Zeitlin been around to ask the tough questions in a harsh way. Indeed, we have to imagine it, since, in the case of the historical Jesus, too little evidently was at stake to maintain rigorous standards of verification even of physical evidence. The wording indeed! How self-serving! For that, a good critical edition would have sufficed to make the forgery easy, if still a work of formidable erudition (not to say, magnificent obsession).

Smith makes much of the correctness of the fragment's vocabulary. Quesnell points out that if a Morton Smith can check the correctness of

---

endures; facts do not intervene, and tests of validation and falsification do not apply.

the letter's vocabulary and phrase construction against the 1936 critical edition of the works of Clement, any other forger could have done the same: "So could a mystifier have checked every word and phrase with the same index and successfully eliminated them [errors] from the first draft of a mystification whatever was not characteristic of Clement." So he notes, "There is no physical evidence to compel admitting a date earlier than 1936." Quesnell states matters very simply: "What Smith is able to 'authenticate,' the 'mystifier' would have been able to imitate."

Smith argued on the basis of the curious appeal to the document's "mistakes a forger would have been stupid to make." But Quesnell responds: "If Smith can construct arguments for genuineness from his insights into what a forger would not have done..., there seems to be no reason why an intelligent mystifier could not have foreseen such arguments and added some 'untypical' elements as indispensable to a successful mystification." There certainly was opportunity to introduce the volume of Clement into the library; there is no difficulty imagining a motivation. Quesnell never said in so many words that he thought Smith in particular had forged the Clement fragment, only that it is a "mystification" by a "mystifier."

He notes, "Smith tells...[that Arthur Darby Nock...] refused till the day he died to admit the authenticity of the letter, suggesting instead that it was 'mystification for the sake of mystification.'" And, Quesnell goes on, "'Secret Gospel' is written 'for the one who knows.' Who is 'the one who knows'? What does he know?" Discretion (not to mention not wanting to be sued for libel) certainly can account for Quesnell's sage reluctance to answer his own questions; but plenty of others did so privately, and the entire quest for the historical Jesus fell under a shadow for some time to come: if this, then what is impossible?

Smith disgraced New Testament studies, because he showed through his (momentary) success that the field could not defend itself from fraud. If you can say anything you want about "the historical Jesus," then Smith is as plausible as Schweitzer or Dibelius or Bultmann (to name three revered names of the field). I dwell on a memorable academic scandal of our own times not to recount the suspicions of more than a few that Smith forged the Clement fragment, but to recall the moment at which, to outsiders to the entire enterprise, the very worth of the work came under suspicion. A field of learning that cannot defend itself from forgery and fraud commands no claim on a continued place in the academy. For here we deal not merely with a naughty opinion or the thirst for scandal, but with out-and-out fakery.

Not only so, but a field of learning that validates even its existence by assuming that documents of religious faith conceal fraud – the Gospel truth is true only some of the time, and we'll find out when – surely meets its match in a secret Gospel no one is permitted to examine but everyone expected to believe. The very convention of the field – always talking about "the historical Jesus," never "Jesus Christ" – signals its a priori. But this reconsideration of Smith's Jesus as charlatan, magician, and homosexual is for others to undertake. Let us now concentrate on the task at hand.

IV. The Lesser Theses of Smith's *Tannaitic Parallels*

We come now to the concrete evidence of Smith's major intellectual failing, one that he could not overcome. I have already alluded to Smith's bungling of all manner of theoretical, methodological, and conceptual problems. Now to spell out what I mean. Smith was very clever about some things, and he wrote with enormous conviction and confidence in his own opinions. But while clever, he was not very smart. In examining seven of his eight types of parallels, I shall spell out in a number of cases evidence for a simple judgment.

It is, specifically, that Smith had no capacity at abstract, conceptual thought; he was impatient with questions of definition, theory for him held no attraction, and matters of method he resolved with the back of his hand. His intellectual ambition outran his ability; his was a second-rate mind, concealed under a veneer of furious bluster, and within a cloud of confused erudition. But a cool reading of his own words, later in this chapter and in the next, shows the sad truth about his ability: his was a rather ordinary, and in fact, quite limited, mind. His definitions as we shall now see proved intellectually coarse and uncomprehending. He made up in verbiage for what he lacked in perspicacity. Straightening out his rather convoluted thoughts yields mere commonplaces. These are severe judgments. Let me now adduce the evidence to show them moderate and factual.

We begin where Smith does not begin, with the questions of definition and program that ordinarily preface a piece of research. Showing contempt for a kind of work he could not do, Smith simply ignores all the necessary questions of method, beginning of course with rigorous definition. Smith typically begins his book *in medias res*, failing to define what he means by a parallel, why he thinks a parallel is important, what consequences he anticipates follow from his demonstration of alleged parallels, and the like. He simply states, "The primary concern of this book is rather philological than philosophical.... I have not attempted a complete classification of all possible forms of literary parallelism, which would be rather a philosophical than a philological exercise. The following chapters list only some of the more important classes, illustrating each by a number of examples." That constitutes the whole of his explanation for the work.

Repeatedly, in what is to follow, Smith sets forth a handful of examples, assuming we all know what the examples exemplify. Then, time and again, he goes on to say, of course to do the work properly, we should have to catalogue all the examples. But these are too many. So we go about our way. For a scholar who would spend the next forty years condemning all and sundry for examining only part of the evidence, Smith's self-serving excuse – I don't have to define things, and I don't have to collect all the evidence – proves sadly prophetic. He condemned in others his own faults.

This work certainly adumbrates Smith's later incapacity at conceptual matters, his impatience with questions of why and wherefore, so what and what if, in all, his hard-core, low-brow positivism. Now to the eight chapters and their main generalizations (if any).

1. *Verbal Parallels*

"Of the sorts of parallels herein after to be discussed, the simple is the verbal. One word may resemble another in one or more of several ways: semantically or grammatically or etymologically. In this chapter I shall discuss only etymological parallels, and of these, only one group." These are Semitic words in the Greek of the Gospels, and the Greek and Latin words in TL [= Tannaitic literature], "which are here considered." The upshot is this: "In respect of vocabulary, [tractate] Shabbat shows a Graeco-Roman influence far stronger than the Semitic influence shown by Mark." Much labor goes into the formation of this triviality: a work in Hebrew written in the Greek-speaking world (in which the Mishnah was written) uses more Greek words than a work in Greek written in that same language-world uses Semitic words. The upshot is, if you are writing in Hebrew among Greek speakers, you use lots of Greek words. If you are writing in Greek among Greek speakers, you do not use lots of Hebrew or Aramaic words. And then Smith ought to have found equally noteworthy the fact that the sun rose in the east this morning. On the basis of such a, to him, original and amazing demonstration, Smith could have turned himself into an astronomer.

2. *Parallels of Idiom*

"An idiom is essentially a conventional way of grouping words. Parallels of idiom therefore come next in degree of complexity after the parallels of single words. For if it proved difficult to define the term word, it will, a fortiori, prove more so to define the concept of a group of words and to determine which groups are idiomatic. Fortunately, this problem can be avoided, for this chapter will discuss only a few of the simpler and better recognized forms of idiom – those generally dealt with by grammar or singled out as 'idiomatic expressions,' for example, euphemisms..., forms of citation,...oaths...and blessings.... Only after complete lists of all the parallels between the Gospels and all the other literatures of their time and region have been drawn up, will it be possible to decide accurately the relationship between the Gospels and those literatures...." Here is Smith's flourish: announce a conclusion, but say it's too much work to prove it. His "only after" clause serves as a universal solvent, wiping out the obstacle formed by the ordinary expectation that collecting data yields plausible hypotheses. Smith takes this route again, as we shall presently see in the next chapter.

3. *Parallels of Meaning*

Of all the parallels between the Gospels and TL, those of which most has hitherto been written have been the parallels of meaning. Here I want, first of all, briefly to define the concept, parallel of meaning. In the parallelism of single words...the essential relationship lay in the form of the words, the parallelism of their meanings was merely a conditio sine qua non, for example, it would have been out of place there to discuss pairs of words which were parallel in meaning alone...and equally out of place to discuss words parallel only in external form.... The pairs of passages to be discussed in this chapter are of interest primarily because of the parallelism of their meanings, and the external form in which these meanings are expressed is of no essential importance. The concept 'meaning' I shall not attempt to define...from here on, I shall write as if I knew both, in general, the meaning of 'meaning,' and, in particular, the meanings of those sentences I shall have to discuss. Again, I shall not attempt to list all the parallels of meaning between the Gospels and TL which have hitherto been noted. The subject is too wide. Every word, from the name of the simplest thing to the name of God himself, can serve as the basis for a parallel of meaning, and on many of these parallels, of which the number is at least equal to the number of nouns and verbs in the Gospels, the standard commentators have already written. In general there are to be distinguished parallels between words referring to concrete objects...parallels between words referring to social phenomena (customs, social groups and classes, laws, etc.) and parallels between words referring to intellectual and psychological entities, the concepts of philosophy and religion. Of these groups I shall discuss only the last....

All of this verbiage evidently left Smith exhausted; here he simply collects and arranges information and passes his opinion on this and that. The chapter in fact is diffuse, confused, and pointless. The rest of this chapter is devoted to other people's mistakes on this score; by the end of the chapter, it is clear, Smith has long since forgotten why he wrote it; it has nothing to do with "parallels of meaning."

4. Parallels of Literary Form

Here Smith's intellectual incapacities come to the fore. He could not, in fact, define "literary form." And the entire enterprise of form-criticism, at which he pretends to be adept, yields stupefying banalities. In the one area in which Gospel research (along with Old Testament studies) provided Smith with fully articulated definitions and well spelled-out methods, Smith took his own route, and stumbled.

He failed because, like second-rate minds in general, in lieu of crafted and thoughtful explanation, Smith defines by example: "What are literary forms? For example: Forms of rhetoric which depend not on a single idiomatic expression nor on the grammatical peculiarities of the words, but on their meaning; forms of argument, forms of exegesis – all these are literary forms in the wider sense of the words; and in their narrower sense they refer to parables, prayers, sayings, sermons, and so on." Quite how these "examples" answer the question I do not know. Smith contents himself with not only uninterpreted examples, but then catalogues of this and that. His strongest argument is his "and so on." That is the same old claim, there are lots more data, but it's too much trouble to collect them.

Smith proceeds: "How are these parallels of literary form, which are actually parallels of meaning, to be distinguished from the parallels of meaning discussed in the chapter above? In its broad outlines, the answer is simple: above, the meanings were divided according to the subjects of knowledge – theology, philosophy, and so on; here they are divided according to literary classifications – stories, prayers, arguments, explanations, and so on. As these literary classifications hereinafter to be discussed have by general convention been called forms, it must be emphasized at once that literary form, 'the form of thought,' has no direct connection with the forms of the sentences in which the thought is expressed." This, I submit, is "writing too much," which is to say, using strings of words to say absolutely nothing that common sense does not already show.

The vacuity of Smith's "form-criticism" emerges when Smith proceeds to describe "more important parallels of literary form," and then examines in detail "parallels to be found between the sermons in the Gospels and those in TL." I am inclined to doubt that a college freshman would require Smith to reach Smith's conclusions. His form-analysis consists in the identification of these three "forms": beginning, middle, and end. For such an insight, the Hebrew University gave him a Ph.D. To an undergraduate producing such results, I would suffice with a C.

I do not exaggerate. Smith finds, for the Sermon on the Mount, [1] introductions; [2] bodies; [3] conclusions. He finds the same general structure in sermons in Tannaite literature. He concludes, "I think it clear from the above passages that TL contains forms parallel to the forms introduced in the Synoptics as sermons. It is therefore plausible to suppose that such forms of TL were also derived from the sermons customary in those days."

5. Parallels in Types of Association

"How is the material in a given book (or part of a book) associated; what principle of association can be seen in its selection and arrangement?" These are under discussion in this chapter. "Types of association" corresponds to my "logic of coherent discourse." Smith finds not parallels but striking difference: "In spite of these efforts to find parallels between the types of association found in the Gospels and those found in TL, the most striking fact remains not the parallelism of the two literatures in this respect but their difference." In a book on *Tannaitic Parallels,* what Smith shows is the opposite: the differences between the literatures. We already know that Smith will not celebrate differences or even dare to draw conclusions from them: that is the point he makes in the citation at the head of the preface of this book. In a moment, we shall see it in context.

6. Complete Parallels

"Complete passages...are parallel at once in words and in structure, in content and literary form." What Smith refers to here are sentences in the two sets of writings that say the same things in pretty much the same way. His example is Mk. 4:24, "In the measure in which you mete it shall be measured to you," and the rabbinical saying, "In the measure in which a man metes it is measured to him." Smith collects "complete" parallels. In an example of Smith's prose at its most convoluted, he concludes, "But even were all the closest parallels of these three sorts to be collected and added to the list of those which I have called 'complete,' the total would yet remain very small, especially in consideration of the fact that these parallels are collected from more than three hundred pages of Greek and from almost three thousand pages of Hebrew. If it be recalled again that these 'complete' parallels would have to be the most important element in the proof of any theory hypothecating a direct literary relationship between the Gospels and TL, then it will be seen that the most important fact demonstrated by the study of these parallels is their absence."

What Smith means by all this verbiage is that there just are not very many "complete" parallels. Two of his eight chapters prove the opposite of his thesis: Tannaitic literature is not "parallel" (whatever that is supposed to mean) to the Gospels.

7. *Parallels of Parallelism*

I reproduce this entire chapter and its appendix in Chapter Two, which follows. I offer my comments in Chapter Seven.

8. *Parallels with a Fixed Difference*

"Sometimes it is possible to draw up a fairly long list of parallels in all of which the same difference appears, and such a list must be the basis of any theory as to the development or substitution of ideas from one literature to another, and also of any philological account of the change of usage from language to language." He forthwith gives an example and leaves off defining matters. His "parallels with a fixed difference and one typical of the relationship of the literatures" encompass these cases: [1] Jesus = God; [2] Jesus = the Law. He concludes, "I think these passages suffice to show that Jesus appears in the Gospels in a number of places where the parallel passages of TL have God or the Law....A likely inference would be that Jesus occupied in the minds of the authors of the Gospels much the same place as God and the Law occupied in the minds of the authors of TL. But to make such an inference would involve an act of historical faith, for to pass from the observable similarity of words to the hypothetical similarity of ideas which the words may have been meant to express is to pass from the knowable to the unknown."

I have already made my comments on Smith's remarkable evasion. The price for a Ph.D. in Jerusalem is to repeat the mantra of Jerusalem: philology, pure and without purpose, is all that counts. Smith never again made such a statement, and everything he wrote afterward repudiated it. Further comment is not required.

V. Much Ado about Not Much

Smith's dissertation obviously had no thesis; the theme "Tannaitic parallels to the Gospels" simply defined a catch-all for whatever Smith felt he wished to address. It is an excuse for his passing an opinion on this, that, and the other thing. The dissertation provided the occasion for him to collect and arrange and free-associate about this and that. If he thought that he had made major discoveries, only in one chapter did he say so in so many words – the chapter to come. For the rest, he simply pointed to quite familiar, entirely routine phenomena, perhaps improving here and there on prior scholars' interpretation of them. Every kind of parallel he identified, except parallels of parallelism, had earlier been recognized and discussed, as Smith's presentation's footnotes demonstrate. Apart from Chapter Seven, nothing in his book would have surprised, or particularly instructed, Gospel scholars. And, as we have seen, despite his obfuscations and verbosity, Smith's definitions not only do not improve on available ones, but render needlessly complicated some perfectly clear, unexceptional points. That is what I mean by "much ado about not much."

That of course errs on the side of generosity. For to find as his great parallel of form the fact that the two sets of writings' portraits of public statements contain beginnings, middles, and endings ("[1] introductions; [2] bodies; [3] conclusions") raises the improbable possibility that Smith was joking. Only as an exceptionally subtle conceit can we imagine he really thought these commonplaces to constitute "forms" in any sense. Any pieces of writing of three or more sentences, by definition, is going to have a beginning, middle, and end. In no way does Smith's conception of "forms" correspond to the sense in which Bultmann and others used the word. Perhaps, as with the astonishing rejection of "an act of historical faith" that Smith set forth in obeisance to Jerusalem philology, Smith dissimulated, meaning only to ridicule form-criticism by trivializing its results. But nothing Smith wrote conveyed anything but perfect faith in what he was saying that minute (implying nothing about what he would say the next minute, of course), and I am inclined to think this is the best he could do. Certainly his other definitions are offered with a straight face, so this trivial and banal "definition," too, must stand for what he honestly thought made an important point.

His fifth type and sixth types of parallels prove unproductive; what he shows here is that the two sets of writings really are not parallel. A quarter of the book argues against the implicit proposition of the title: Tannaitic parallels. Here he shows the opposite: the two literatures have nothing in common. And the eighth type is simply an embarrassment. Chapter Eight is mere space filler, an effort to give weight to a very thin piece of work. So the upshot is, where Smith finds Tannaitic parallels to the Gospels, these form a collection of words and phrases. Where he finds none, they fall into the class of statements of substance and meaning.

Where Smith succeeds in his purpose, he presents commonplaces, and where success would have yielded insight into the documents and their relationships, he has nothing to say. That is precisely his confession at the end: "To pass from the observable similarity of words to the hypothetical similarity of ideas which the words may have been meant to express is to pass from the knowable to the unknown." From the perspective of Smith's later career, I find that a statement of surpassing cynicism. Nothing Smith did later on suggested he ever scrupled about passing from the knowable to the unknown; to the contrary, he is, after all, the author of *Jesus the Magician*. What he expresses here is merely the standard philologian's excuse for doing only philology, never asking philology to contribute to the study of the history, religion, literature, or theology that the texts on which philology works mean to set forth.

Smith's sole book on Judaism marks him as erudite, opinionated, and intellectually not very gifted: much ado about not much.

VI. For This, a Ph.D.?

To close, we have to ask one last question: How did Smith get away with a Ph.D. at the Hebrew University, in its day a university of high standards, for a dissertation of such surpassingly commonplace triviality, offering such exceptionally ineffable platitudes? The answer is simple. No one really could have cared very much about his work; in context, he was a curiosity, neither fish nor fowl. In Chapter Seven, I shall show that, in fact, Smith's work was ignorant and incompetent, not only because of what he did, but also because of what he failed to do. He never asked the critical question that must be addressed in any allegation that rabbinic documents relate as do the Synoptics: What about Q? Somehow Smith forgot to ask that basic question, and his teachers never knew to tell him. That proves they knew nothing of Synoptic studies, on which they presumed to direct a dissertation. How could the Hebrew University have given a doctorate for such insufficient, shoddy work?

His professor, first of all, specialized in Classics, not Semitics. The Hebrew University did not have a professor of New Testament studies; that was not a literature taken seriously. So, cleverly, Smith presented his work to scholars who either did not know much about the documents on which he claimed knowledge, or did not care about them. He found a niche for himself as an autodidact. All he really had to learn was the living Hebrew language of the place. He wanted no teachers and had none.

To his loss, Smith never had the experience he accorded to others, which was, the experience of learning, in mature years, from someone else. He had always to be the sole "best boy." That explains why, in his life as a teacher, he proved such a poor listener, so ill-equipped to learn from others, and, in his career as a scholar, alas, so incapable of civil discourse and impersonal argument. Graduate education really is designed to impart lifelong, valuable lessons about learning. Smith denied himself the opportunity to learn them, playing Gospel scholars to the specialists in Tannaitic literature, expert in Tannaitic literature and the Gospels to classicists, who knew neither. Smith's first book appears to have been read, by his *Doktorvater*, as to the footnotes, but never fully examined as to the text and the thesis. He did not work in his *Doktorvater*'s field, and his *Doctkorvater* did not contribute to his field. The entire transaction was a pretense and a fraud.

Living Hebrew then is what Jerusalem taught him. And that is what allowed him to continue to avoid the examination of people who knew, in his field, what he knew. It was only for that amazing, unique fact – he knows living Hebrew – that, when he came home, he was celebrated as – again – "the only one." His version of "best boy" was, he was the only New Testament scholar who could read Hebrew; he was the only gentile who knew anything about rabbinic literature.

So he got his Ph.D. because he was the one elephant who could dance. No one wanted to notice how poorly. Since the rabbinic scholars took no interest in the Gospels, or, for their part, the Gospel scholars in rabbinics, who was there to care? But, then, in his behalf it must be said, at that time, elephants were not the only clumsy dancers. The upshot was, Smith introduced questions he did not answer, took for granted facts that were not facts, confused his categories in a memorable display of conceptual bungling, and proved everything and its opposite in a mess of contradiction and confusion. But no one knew, or, if people knew, no one cared.

Smith went on to repeat his success at Harvard when he wrote his Th.D. dissertation in Old Testament studies. There, at the same time, our generation's scholarly giants of the field were already commencing their monumental work. But Smith ignored them. That was his way. Given his abilities, he followed mighty sound instincts. And from that point, he intimidated others from noticing the beam in his eye by proclaiming with glee the splinter he claimed to see in their eyes.

Some may conclude that this detailed inspection wastes valuable time and energy, better spent on more constructive projects. And a case can be made for that view. It is both personal and professional. The personal case is simple. Would it not be better to bypass the grave of a man who did what he could to destroy me? True Smith did what he could to discredit me, and he failed. True, within scarcely four years of my editing of his festschrift, I found myself publicly subjected to gross rudeness on his part, and within a few years afterward, I witnessed a public display of out-of-control fury that neither I nor anyone else present had ever witnessed at a national academic meeting. But since, on those occasions, at those events, no academic issues were permitted to intervene, Smith's demonstrations being eccentric and idiosyncratic in the extreme, motivation for later reflection hardly exists.

Smith deserves a civil, academic reply to his ideas. It is precisely what his conduct forestalled throughout his life. But now, were Smith to be dismissed as a crank and a crackpot, but his book to be left unread, he should enjoy an unearned posthumous victory: the substantive issues will be left merely personal after all. That is how Smith wanted matters to be defined, and not only in my case. The very personal character of his conduct of his intellectual quarrels is the strongest argument in favor of a reasoned and academic inspection of not the man but his ideas.

For, as a matter of obvious fact, Smith simply could not debate or argue; he could announce and insist, denounce and insult, hector and harry and humiliate, ridicule and demonize – but he could not sustain the kind of contention that those of us formed in the pages of the Talmud value as the sure way to truth. Indeed, it is by argument and contention that serious scholars pay their highest respect to persons and books alike. I refer readers to the tale of Simeon b. Laqish and Yohanan for a concrete statement of the ideal for life that those of us framed and shaped by the Talmud cherish and attempt to realize. Smith's knowledge of rabbinic literature did not extend to that, and similar, stories, or, if it did, he was unchanged by what he learned. He was not a tragic figure. He was just a limited one, who did the best he could with whatever gifts he had at hand. And so do we all.

Now to the shank of the book. First comes the one chapter that counts in an otherwise unremarkable collection of commonplaces and trivialities. We read *ipsissima verba*. Then, in Chapters Three through Six, we shall examine the relationships between the Mishnah and the Tosefta that Smith claims he has accurately represented. Then, in Chapter Seven, we revert, in light of those four chapters, to the allegations given verbatim in Chapter Two.

2

Parallels of Parallelism: Smith's Statement of His Thesis

[From *Tannaitic Parallels to the Gospels*, pp. 142-150]

Every literature consisting of several books – such as the Gospels or TL – makes possible the discussion of *the relationship which exists between the books*, and in the comparison of literatures it is possible to compare the relationship which exists between the books of one literature with the relationship which exists between the books of a second literature. Now both in the Gospels and in TL the most striking characteristic of this relationship is the fact of parallelism, and especially the large number of 'complete' parallels found between the different books.

Of course all the Gospels are parallel one to another in all the various manners of parallelism which have hitherto been discussed. Between Mat and Mk, for instance, there are to be found parallels of words, of idiom, of content, of literary forms, and of types of association. But scholars frequently neglect these partial parallels, depending on only one or two aspects of the material, because there are, between the two books, so many complete parallels, and these so noticeable and so important. And such is the relation of each of the synoptic Gospels to the other; and such, also, is the relationship of each one of them to Jn, for only because the synoptics are so close one to another does Jn seem far from them. As a matter of fact all of the four are very close to each other, and the more they are studied the more superficial their differences and the more important their similarities are seen to be. Such also is the state of affairs in TL: The striking fact is the large numbers of complete parallels to be found between its various books, especially between the Mishnah and Tosefta, Mekilta of R. Simon and Sifre on Deut, Sifre Zutta and Sifra, Mekilta and Sifre on

Numbers.[1]   But, apart from these pairs, there are to be found many passages common to all the midrashim.[2]

It is obvious on reflection that most European literatures do not, for the most part, consist of books thus related. In classical Greek literature, for instance, there are not many complete parallels to be found between one book and another, neither are there in classical Latin literature, nor in the better known parts of French, German or English literature. And when such relationship is found, it is found usually in works outside the normal canon of literature, such as magical texts or folk tales. Yet, in spite of these facts, scholars have paid little attention to this parallel which exists between the Gospels on the one hand and that of the books of TL on the other, viz: that in both literatures the books are related to one another chiefly by 'complete' parallelism.

On the Christian side, P. Fiebig wrote in his *Jüdische Wundergeschichten:*[3] 'Die meisten Überlieferungen liegen uns in Paralleltexten vor, die die grösste Ähnlichkeit mit den in unseren neutestamentlichen Evangelien vorhandenen Paralleltexten haben.' and when he printed the Hebrew texts which he had discussed in this book he added,[4] 'Das Studium solcher Paralleltexte ist sehr lehrreich zur Beurteilung der synoptischen Parallelen,' but gave no details whatsoever. G. Kittel, in his book, *Die Probleme des palästinischen Spätjudentums und das Urchristentum,*[5] wrote,[6] 'Das synoptische Problem, ja das ganze *Traditionsproblem* der Evangelien, ist nicht ein singuläres....Dieselbe Art der Traditionsvarianten die wir aus den Paralleltexten der Evangelien kennen, ist für die rabbinische Tradition charakteristisch....So muss man, wenn man die Überlieferung irgendeines der Rabbinen sichten will, in jedem Fall eine Synopse der Paralleltraditionen herstellen. Man erkennt dann, wie Traditionen über weite Zeitspannen hin in parallelen Kanälen laufen,' u.s.w. And he cited several examples of complete parallels found in rabbinical literature, but compared with them none of the parallels found in the Gospels.

Moreover, as against his remarks, it must be noted that the problem of parallelism is not simplified by confusion with the problem of tradition. The question, 'What are the parallels?' is a philological question which can be answered exactly by analysis and comparison of the preserved

---

[1]These are the conclusions reached by C. Albeck, *Untersuchungen über die hal. Midraschim,* Berlin, 1927, p. 154.
[2]For the material v. Albeck, idem, pp. 21 ff.
[3]Tübingen, 1911, p. 5.
[4]*Rabbinische Wundergeschichten,* Berlin, 1933, p. 3.
[5]Stuttgart, 1926.
[6]pp. 63-5.

documents. The question, 'Which theory about the nature of the tradition can best be supported by such parallels as have been preserved?' is a historical question which admits of various answers according to the various abilities and inclinations of the persons answering.

But if the Christians have done little to describe this important parallel between the Gospels and TL, the Jews have done nothing. I cannot recall even a word by any Jewish scholar remarking – for example – that the problem of the relationship between Tosefta and the Mishnah is similar to the synoptic problem, and this in spite of the fact that they are so similar as to be practically inseparable, and that any theory begun from a study of the one literature should have immediate application in the study of the other.

But if neither Jews nor Christians have written much on this parallel of parallelism which exists between the two literatures, at least both groups have written at great length on the complete parallels which exist between the books of either literature, considered singly. In particular, numberless books have been written by Christians on the synoptic problem, and the literature has been reviewed by A. Schweitzer[7] and P. Wernle;[8] it need not, therefore, be discussed here. Schweitzer reviews also the war waged throughout the nineteenth century over the question of the relationship of Jn to the synoptics. At the conclusion of this war most scholars agreed in thinking Jn a very late product of a Greek environment. Thereupon, at the beginning of the present century, came the books of Schlatter[9] and Burney[10] and gave reason to doubt the truth of this opinion. A review of the literature which they called forth is given by W. Howard in the first section of his book, *The Fourth Gospel.*[11] In all these later works, the primary interest of the authors has been historical, and there has been no discussion of the parallels between Jn and the synoptics for their own sake. Indeed, some of the authors, such as Burney, have scarcely noticed their existence. But it has been necessary to mention the variety of opinions because almost all those who have discussed the parallels have done so in order to collect material to buttress their historical theories.

To these two literatures – that on the synoptic problem and that on the relation of Jn to the synoptics – must be added a third – that of the commentators, for it is almost impossible to write a commentary on one of the Gospels without mentioning its relations to the others, and some commentators, e.g., W. Allen[12] in his commentary on Mat, have made

---

[7]A. Schweitzer, *Geschichte d. Leben-Jesu-Forschung,* 4 ed., Tübingen, 1926.
[8]P. Wernle, *Die synoptische Frage,* Leipzig, 1899.
[9]A. Schlatter, *Sprache und Heimat des vierten Evangelisten,* Gutersloh, 1902.
[10]C. Burney, *The Aramaic Origin of the Fourth Gospel,* Oxford, 1922.
[11]W. Howard, *The Fourth Gospel,* London, 1931.
[12] *The International Critical Commentary,* N.Y., 1907.

these relations the principal subject of their study. On the Jewish side the problem of the parallels between the various books of TL was not at first grasped as a single problem – undoubtedly this failure was due to the great mass of the material involved. A second cause was the fact that the material was generally considered, not as a thing in itself, but as a part of the legal tradition of which the great document was the Babylonian Talmud. At all events, the basic synopsis which will give all the parallel passages in parallel columns (not only the passages from those works I have selected as TL, but also the baraitaot of the two Talmuds and the parallel passages from the oldest of the haggadic midrashim) is still a desideratum. How complicated such a synopsis would be, can be imagined from the collection of parallel forms (and these only the ones to be found in the Babylonian Talmud) of a single tradition, printed as an example by Melamed.[13] But the lack of such a synopsis leaves only two possibilities for preliminary research: (1) the collection of parallels without critical study of them – as was done in 'Massoret Hashshas'; (2) the critical study of the parallels to a single book or group of books – as was done by the editors of the various midrashim, by Lieberman in his commentary on Tosefta,[14] Hoffmann and Albeck in their books on the halakic midrashim,[15] and Zuckermandel in his book *Tosefta, Mischna u. Boraitha.*[16]

Here, of course, it is impossible to attempt an exact answer to the questions, What are the complete parallels to be found between the books of TL, or, between the books of the Gospels? It must therefore suffice to emphasize the fact that, *as regards complete parallels, the relation between one book of the Gospels and another is similar in many details to the relation between one book and another of TL.* To illustrate this similarity I have chosen one pair of passages from the Gospels – the sermon on the mount from Mat and the parallel sermon from Lk – and one pair of passages from TL – *Peah* 1-3 and *Peah T.* 1. I know, of course, that the relation between Tosefta and the Mishnah changes from tractate to tractate, and that yet other relationships are to be found between the Mishnah and the midrashim, between Tosefta and the midrashim, and between one book and another of the midrashim. I know also that the relationship between the books of the Gospels changes not only from book to book, and not only from 'source' to 'source,' but also from passage to passage. (Thus, for example, the relation between Mat and Mk in the passion story is

---

[13]E. Melamed, *Halachic Midrashim of the Tannaïm in the Talmud Babli,* Jerusalem, 1943, p. 32.

[14]S. Liebermann, *Tosefeth Rishonim,* Jerusalem, 1937-39.

[15]D. Hoffmann, *Zur Einleitung in die hal. Midraschim,* Berlin, 1887. C. Albeck, *Untersuchungen* etc., cited above n. 1.

[16]Frankfurt a.M., 1908-9.

quite different from that between them in the stories of the Galilean ministry, although, according to the generally accepted theory, the 'source' of both these sections of Mat is Mk.) Therefore I am sure that the comparison of the two relatively small pairs of parallels here chosen will not display all the sorts of parallels of parallelism to be found between the Gospels and TL. But I think it will display a number of the more important details, and, should it do so, this will suffice. For it must be pointed out here, at the beginning, that a comparison of the relationship between the books of the Gospels with the relationship between the Mishnah and Tosefta will reveal not only important similarities, but also important differences, and only an examination of all the material, passage by passage – an examination which would require a synopsis for its undertaking and a work of several volumes for its completion – would make possible an exact review of these similarities and differences and an adequate estimation of the evidence for and against any historical theory as to the nature of the traditions behind the works studied. Any pretensions to historical significance thus specifically excluded, I can proceed to the comparison of the two pairs of parallel passages above specified. These are copied out at length in *Appendix C.* Their sections there are numbered, and from here on I shall cite them according to those numbers.

The striking parallel between 1, 2, and 4 on the one hand, and 32 and 33 on the other, is emphasized by similarity in content – all the passages contain lists of good or bad characteristics and promises of pay or punishment – and by similarity of function – all the passages serve as haggadic introductions to halakic material. But for the purposes of this chapter the interesting thing is that, to a list of blessings, Mat and the Mishnah add blessings, Lk and Tosefta, curses. 'Blessings' and 'curses' and 'add' are convenient abbreviations, but the relationship can be described abstractly without the use of terms which imply a development of the text, thus: In Mat and the Mishnah are found long lists of elements similar in one respect, in Lk and Tosefta are found short lists of these same elements together with short lists of elements antithetical to them.

The relationship between Lk. 6.20 ('poor') and Mat 5.3 ('poor in spirit'), and between Lk 6.21 ('hungering') and Mat 5.6 ('hungering... after righteousness') is very interesting, and I recall none like it between the books of TL, but the like is often found between a single Gospel and a book of TL (or a law from the Old Testament), e.g., Mat 6.6 'Give not that which is holy to the dogs,' Lk 11.44, 'Woe to you (scribes and Pharisees) for you are like unseen graves, and the men who walk over them do not know (that they have been polluted).' These passages give figurative, moral meanings to the laws about holy things and about unmarked graves: *Temurah T* 4.11 (556): 'Holy things are not to be redeemed (by substitution of their money value or of an equivalent plus a penalty) in order that they may be fed to dogs.' *Zabim T* 2.9 (678) 'What is "pollution of the depth"? (Pollution caused by a grave) of which no one anywhere (lit. at the end of the world) knew.' etc.[17]

In 3, *Peah T.* has in the midst of its list a reference to the legally fixed minimum of the peah, which is referred to in *Peah* (no. 6) after the list. It happens that this is the only instance in these chapters of a change in order between the elements in the Mishnah and those in Tosefta. And even this is not a true change in order, for in spite of the fact that in *Peah T.* the rule appears before the list of curses, yet it immediately follows the list of blessings, and so it does also in the Mishnah. Thinking in terms of the development of the text it would seem likely to guess that the Mishnah added its extra blessings before the rule, and Tosefta its curses after it, but that the position of the rule remained unchanged in both texts. As opposed to this absence of changes of order in the chapters of the Mishnah and Tosefta here cited, the passages cited from the Gospels show many such changes, not only rearrangement of adjacent passages, as of 40 and 41, but also transference over considerable intervening sections, as from 41 to 48. Moreover, whole sections of the Matthaean sermon are found in Lk outside the parallel sermon (e.g., 44 in Lk 12).

In 5, the haggadic introduction of Tosefta is extended by similar material not in the Mishnah. In the same way the introduction in Mat is extended by means of the haggadic material of 34, lacking in Lk.

In 7, the same rule is found in the two passages, and there are only slight verbal differences between them. Such is the relationship between Mat 5.39b and Lk 6.29a, and between Mat 5.42a and Lk 6.30a.

In 10 and 11 is seen a relationship typical of that which exists between Tosefta and the Mishnah. 11 is an explanation of the rule found in 10. But the rule itself is not found in the present text of Tosefta. Therefore the present text of Tosefta presupposes, here, a knowledge of the rule. And since the rule is found in the Mishnah it is a likely guess that the present text of Tosefta presupposes a knowledge of the Mishnah. (This conclusion, however, is not a necessary one, for Tosefta might presuppose a knowledge of some other text, now lost, which also contained the rule.[18] I do not think that a clear case of this sort of relationship is to be found between any passages of the two sermons cited from the Gospels in Appendix C.

---

[17]The opinion of Strack-Billerbeck in Lk 11.44 is certainly wrong. They say: 'Gräber, die als solche nicht für jedermann erkennbar waren und deshalb durch Übergiessen mit Kalktünche oder durch Aufstellen getünchter Steine gekennzeichnet werden mussten.' I think they were led into error by the parallel in Mat 23.27-8. A fine exposition of both passages is found in pp. 352-4 of the article by J. Mann, *Rabbinic Studies in the Synoptic Gospels*, HUCA, I, 323 ff.

[18]On this question see especially the preface by Prof. Lieberman to the photostatic reprint of Zuckermandel's *Tosephta*, pp. 21 ff.

Whether or not such a relationship is to be found at all between different books of the Gospels, is a much disputed question. W. Howard,[19] for example, thinks that a number of passages of Jn presuppose a knowledge by the reader of complementary passages in the synoptics - or, at least, of the content now found in those passages. But other scholars have maintained that Jn did not know the synoptics at all.[20]

As against this dubious state of affairs, there are many passages in Tosefta which would be quite incomprehensible without a knowledge of *the content* of the Mishnah (even if they do not presuppose a knowledge of the *text* of the Mishnah), and there are some passages which require a knowledge even of details of this content, and which have been miscopied by scribes who forgot for a moment such details. For example: *Maaser Sheni T* 2.11 (89), where the Erfurt Ms reads, 'R. Jose said, "If, in a box which was used both for profane things and for second tithe, coins should be found, then, if the majority put in it profane things, (the coins are to be considered) profane, and if the majority put in second tithe, second tithe." R. Simon said to him, "And do not peace-offerings contain the breast and the thigh which are prohibited to non-Israelites?"' The second sentence is explicable only by the text of the Mishnah (*Maaser Sheni* 3.2) which reads, 'It is not permitted to purchase produce from the priest's share of the crop with second-tithe money, because one who does so decreases the number of those who can eat the equivalent of the second tithe, but R. Simon permits this. R. Simon said to them, "If the more lenient opinion were adopted in the case of peace-offerings, which may be made unfit or profaned by failure to destroy the remnant or by consumption by the unclean, shall we not adopt the more lenient opinion in the case of the priest's share of the crop?" They said to him, "If the more lenient opinion

---

[19]*The Fourth Gospel,* London, 1931, pp. 149-151. He thinks Jn 3.24 presupposes Mk 1.14, Jn 6.30 ff. presupposes Mk 14.12-31, and Jn 18.24, 28, 30, 33, 40 presuppose some synoptic form of the passion story, since they refer to details found only in the synoptics.

[20]Reviews of the literature on the question of the relation of Jn to the synoptics are found in:

> T. Sigge, *Das Johannesevangelium und die Synoptiker,* Munster i.W., 1935 (*Neutestamentliche Abhandlungen* XVI, 2/3 Heft)

> H. Windisch, *Johannes und die Synoptiker,* Leipzig, 1926 (*Untersuchungen zum N.T.,* Heft 12)

Among the more recent defenders of the theory that Jn was ignorant of the synoptics is P. Gardner-Smith, *St. John and the Synoptic Gospels,* Cambridge, 1938. Such information as I have on this matter is due to the kindness of Fr. P. Benoit, who found the above books for me.

(Since the composition of this study, Jn's ignorance of the synoptics has also been maintained in a brilliant article by E. Goodenough, *John a Primitive Gospel,* JBL, 1945, pp. 145 ff.)

were adopted in the case of peace-offerings, which non-Israelites are permitted to eat, shall we adopt the more lenient opinion in the case of the priest's share of the crop, which is forbidden to non-Israelites?"' It is clear that the copyist of the Erfurt MS erred by connecting the words of R. Simon to those of R. Jose, and therefore wrote 'said to *him*' where he should have written 'said to *them*,' which, in fact, is found in the Vienna MS and in the printed editions. Such an instance, in which the text of one book is dependent on that of another so closely that neglect of the other is likely to cause error in the copying of the one, is not to be found in the Gospels.

12 contains a digression (on duties in the matter of tithes) found only in the Mishnah. Similarly, for example, 47 contains a digression found only in Mat.

13 contains rules beginning, like the rules in 40-41, with identical words, but afterwards changing, not only in words but also in content, so far that the rules found in one list are quite different from those found in the other. In the beginning of 40-41 the order of the rules is inverted in one of the parallels, a detail not found in 13. In both, the complete or almost complete parallels are found at the beginning and in the middle of the lists, but not at the end. The end of 13 is especially interesting as containing words found in the Mishnah not only in a different place, but in a different meaning. 'If ants nibbled it and if the wind or cattle broke it down' are found here as excuses for division between one field and another, whereas in 16 they appear as conditions which excuse from the duty of leaving a peah. In the same way the words 'and it shall be given you' appear in 45 after 'give,' and in 48 after 'ask,' carrying quite different meanings. In this latter instance, however, it can be supposed that it was only by accident that the two editors of the Gospels used the same words, but as against this supposition it must be remembered that J. Hawkins[21] drew up a considerable list of 'words used with different applications or in different connexions, where the passages containing them are evidently parallel.' The example under discussion is not in Hawkins' list, perhaps because the two passages in which the words are found are not 'evidently parallel'; but the list suffices to prove that the parallels between the Gospels show a number of instances in which the same words are used with different meanings. Moreover, in 23 a single end of a sentence is found attached to two quite different sentences – exactly the use of 'and it shall be given you' in 45 and 48.

The relationship between Mat 5.40 and Lk 6.29 is famous, and I recall no instance in which exactly the same relationship is found between

---

[21] *Horae Synopticae*, 2 ed., Oxford, 1909, p. 67. The most striking example in his list is Mat 3.5: 'There went out to him.... all the vicinage of the Jordan.' / / Lk 3.3: 'He came into all the vicinage of the Jordan.'

different sayings in TL. However, contradictions between Tosefta and the Mishnah are very frequent. To take an example from Peah: *Peah T.* 2.16 (20) gives all the spikes of grain found in ant-holes to the land-owner, *Peah* 4.11 divides them – those in the area where the grain is still standing go to the land-owner, those behind the reapers are again divided – the upper go to the poor, the lower to the land-owner. But the curious thing in the relation of these vss. of Mat and Lk is that there is no contradiction as to the general rule, only a reversal in the order of examples.

In 14, 15 and 16 is found a large section of legal material, present in the Mishnah and absent in Tosefta. So Mat twice includes large sections of legal material lacking in Lk, secs. 36-9 and 42. In 17-24 the two texts contain rules for the most part different, but concerning similar subjects – again like 40-41 and the beginning of 45. Thereafter 25-8 contains another legal section found in the Mishnah but lacking in Tosefta, like the passages of Mat mentioned above.

The last of these laws, that found in 28, is interesting because it serves as a transition to a new subject. The question is, What is the smallest area of land on which one is obliged to leave a peah. The Mishnah cites a number of opinions, last among them that of R. Akiba who says that any piece of land, however small, lies under the obligation of peah. Thereafter, in 29-31, appear 3 laws dealing with 'any piece of land, whatsoever' and without any relation to peah. The last two of these laws are found in Tosefta, in spite of the fact that the first of them, and the opinion of R. Akiba which served as a transition to the subject of 'any piece of land,' and the argument in which the opinion of R. Akiba was cited, – all these are lacking in Tosefta; i.e., Tosefta lacks the transition, but contains the material to which the transition leads, in spite of the fact that this material is altogether out of place in the tractate, except as conclusion of the missing transition. In the case of the Gospels, it is possible that such a transition as this was lost from the sermon in Lk 6, but exactly what it contained cannot be determined. One of the most noticeable instances in which one Gospel contains a transition lacking in another is Mat 14.12-13 which parallels Mk 6.29-32. After Herod killed John the Baptist, according to Mat, 'His disciples....buried him and, coming, brought the news to Jesus. And Jesus, hearing, went away.' In Mk this transition is lacking and Jesus' journey is introduced as if without relation to the death of John.

Yet one more detail: In 30 both texts cite the opinion of R. Jose as to the case in which 'a man signs away his possessions to his sons and signs over to his wife any (piece of) land, whatsoever.' There is no contradiction between the two opinions, but that in Tosefta is so worded as to give an impression favorable to the wife, that in the Mishnah so worded as to give an impression favorable to the sons. The best known example of this sort of relationship as found in the Gospels is that of Mk 9.40: 'He who is not against us is for us.' and Mat 12.30 (= Lk 11.23): 'He who is not with me is against me.' One half of another example is found in the sermon on the mount, in Mat 6.22-3, which begins, 'The light of the body is the eye,' and concludes, 'If then the light in you be darkness, how great is the darkness?', whereas Lk 11.34-6, though it begins with the same words, concludes, 'Beware then lest the light in you be darkness. If then your body be all light, having no dark part, it will be all light, as when the lamp with its shining illumines you.'

To sum up, briefly: It has been found that the relations between the complete parallels found between *Peah* 1-3 and *Peah T.* 1 are very similar to the relations between the complete parallels found between the sermon on the mount in Mat and its equivalent in Lk. This parallelism extends even to many details. However, there are very important differences. The differences in the order of the elements between one Gospel and another are more frequent than those between the Mishnah and Tosefta. The Gospels do not contain passages in which it is unmistakably clear that the understanding of one Gospel depends on a knowledge of the content, if not of the text, of another, but the understanding of Tosefta often depends on a knowledge of the Mishnah. From such facts it would be easy to develop a historical theory to the effect that the relation of Tosefta to the Mishnah was closer than that of one Gospel to another because of the different ways in which written sources had been used. But either the demonstration or the refutation of such a theory would require a complete examination of the material.

Appendix C

[From *Tannaitic Parallels to the Gospels*, pp. 185-197]

	Peah	**Peah T.**
1	I.1 These (are) things which have no (legally fixed) limit: the peah and the first-fruits and the visiting (of the temple) and returning kindnesses and study of the Law.	I.1 Things which have no (legally fixed) limit: The peah and the first-fruits and the visiting (of the temple) and returning a kindness and study of the Law.
2	These (are) things (of) which a man eats the fruits in this world and the principal remains for him for the world to come: Honoring father and mother and returning kindnesses and	

Peah	**Peah T.**
bringing peace between a man and his fellow, and study of the Law is the equivalent of them all.	

3   (See 6)

Peah has a (legally fixed) limit from below and does not have a (legally fixed) limit from above. (But if) one makes all his field a peah it is not a peah.

4

.2 For these things they exact penalties from the (average) man in this world and the principal remains for him in the world to come: For idolatry and for incest and for bloodshed, and for slander as the equivalent of them all.

5

Merit has a principal and has fruits, for it is said....

.3 Transgression has a principal and does not have fruits, for it is said....How, (maintaining this, can) I establish (the text), 'And they shall eat of the fruit of their way, of their plans shall they be satiate.'? But a transgression which bears fruits has fruits and (one) which does not bear fruits has no fruits.

.4 A good thought is conjoined by God (*lit.* the Place) to practice, an evil thought is not conjoined by God (lit. the Place) to practice, for it is said....Behold! How, (maintaining this, can) I establish, etc.

6   .2 They do not give less for peah than (one part) from sixty, and (this) in spite of the fact that they said, 'Peah has no (legally fixed) limit.' Everything (is) according to the size of the field and according to the number of the poor and according to the greatness of the poverty (*or* yield, *sc.* of the field, *or*

cp. 3.

Peah	*Peah T.*
humility, *sc.* of the giver).	

7 .3 They give peah from the beginning of the field and from its middle. R. Simon says, 'And provided only that he will give in the end according to the (legally fixed minimal) limit.' R. Judah says, 'If he left one stalk (at the end) he can join (what he left in other parts of the field) to it as peah, and if not he gives (what he gives in other parts of the field) only as abandoned property.'

.5 A man gives peah from the beginning of the field and in the middle and in the end. If he gave, whether in the beginning or in the end, he satisfied (his obligation). R. Simon says, 'If he gave, whether in the beginning or in the end, see, this is peah; and, (nevertheless), it is necessary that he should give in the end according to the (legally fixed minimal) limit.' R. Judah says, 'If he left one stalk (at the end) he can joint (what he left in other parts of the field) to it (and so is) giving as peah, and if not he gives (what he gives in other parts of the field) only as abandoned property.)'

8 R. Judah said, 'With what (reference are these) things said? With (reference to) an instance in which one gave the peah and wishes to add (to it). If one did not give...

9 R. Simon said, 'Because of four things the Law said a man shall not give peah except in the end of his field, because of robbery of the poor and because of the loss of time of the poor and because of appearances and because of cheats. Because of robbery of the poor: How?...

10 .4 They stated a rule in (regard to) peah: 'Everything which is good and is kept watch over and grows from the ground and is harvested (all) at once and is taken in for storage, is liable to peah.' And grain and peas are in (the class defined by) this rule.

Peah	Peah T.

Peah

.5 And among the trees the sumach and the carobs and walnuts and the almonds and the grapevines and the pomegranates and the olives and the palms are liable to peah.

11

Peah T.

.7 Truck, in spite of the fact that it is harvested (all) at once, is not taken in for storage; and figs, in spite of the fact that they are taken in for storage, nevertheless they are not harvested (all) at once. R. Jose bar Judah says, 'Juicy dates are free from peah, for the first does not wait for the last.' (i.e., the first rots before the last ripens, so they cannot be harvested all at once.) R. Elazar bar Zadok says, 'Jujubes are liable to peah.' Others say also white figs and puffy figs.

12 .6 A man may give (an area of his field) as peah and (be) free from (the duty of paying) tithes (on that area), at any time until (the produce) is heaped up (to be tithed)....If a priest or Levite bought (the content of) the threshing floor, the tithes are theirs (provided they made the purchase) before (the produce) be heaped up. He who dedicates (his harvest) and (then) redeems (it) is liable for the tithes (if he redeemed it) before the assessor (of tithes) heaped it up.

13 II.1 And these (things) limit (fields, etc.) for (the purpose of) peah (so that if two parts of a property be separated by one of these things a separate peah must be given for each part): a ravine and a pool and a private road and a public road and a private path fixed in summer and in the rainy season and a cistern and fallow land and a different

.8 These (things) limit (fields, etc.) for (the purpose of) peah (so that if two parts of a property be separated by one of these things a separate peah must be given for each part): a ravine and a pool and a private road and a public road and a private path fixed in summer and in the rainy season, a cistern and fallow land and a different

Peah

crop. 'And one who cuts for fodder limits (the field).' (These are) the words of R. Meir, and the Sages say, 'He does not limit (it) unless he plough.'

.2 (If there be) a channel of water (so broad) that (the produce on either side) cannot be cut at the same time, R. Judah says (this) limits (the field.)

And (as for) all hills which can be hoed with a hoe, in spite of the fact that oxen cannot get over (them) with a plough, one gives a single peah for all.

cp. 16 (.7)

14 .3 All (these things) are limits for sown crops, and nothing is a limit for trees but a fence, and if the branches of the trees touch (across the fence, then even) this does not serve as a limit, but (the owner) gives one peah for all. .4 And for carob trees (he gives one peah for) all which can be seen one from another. Rabban Gamliel said, 'My father's household were accustomed...

15 .5 If a man sow his field with one kind (of seed), then in spite of the fact that he makes two threshing floors...

Peah T.

crop. And one who cuts for fodder and three furrows' (space) of opening (i.e., of unplanted land.)

And, (if there be) a channel of water (so broad) that (the produce on either side) cannot be cut at the same time, R. Judah says, if (the reaper has to) stand in the middle and cut first on one side and then on the other, (this) limits (the field), and if not it does not limit (it).

(If *hagab* locusts ate an area, (or if) *gobai* locusts ate it, and (if) ants nibbled it, and if the wind or cattle broke it (down), everybody admits that if he plough (the wasted area) (that) limits (the field), and if not it does not limit (it).

Peah	**Peah T.**
.6 (There is) a story (to the effect that) R. Simon of Mizpah...	

16 .7 A field which Samaritans reaped, robbers reaped, ants nibbled, the wind or cattle broke down, is free (from peah). (If the owner) reaped half of it and robbers (later) reaped (the remaining) half of it, it is free, for the liability to peah (went) with the standing grain.

.8 (If) robbers reaped half of it and (the owner later) reaped (the remaining) half of it, he gives peah from what he reaped. (If) he reaped half of it and sold half of it, the purchaser gives peah for the whole. (If) he reaped half of it and dedicated half of it, whoever redeems it from the assessor gives peah for the whole.

17   .9 (If) he cut half of it and sold what was cut (or) cut half of it and dedicated what was cut, he gives (peah) from the remainder for the whole.

18   (If he planted on) terraces ten handbreadths high, he gives a peah from each one. If the ends of the rows ran together he gives a peah from one for the whole (planting).

cp. 19.

19 III.1 (In the case of) beds of grain between olive trees, the house of Shammai say, 'A peah from each one'; the house of Hillel say, 'From one for the whole.' And it is admitted that if the ends of the rows ran together he gives a peah from one for the whole.

cp. 18.

Peah	*Peah T.*
20	He who follows the rows (of the garden bed, to pick out only a few vegetables) is liable when he begins and when he stops.
21 .2 He who cleans out patches of his field and leaves some green stalks, R. Akiba says...And the Sages say... .3 He who takes out bunches of green onions for the market and leaves dry ones for the storehouse, gives a peah for these by themselves and for those by themselves; and so in (the case of) peas and so in (the case of) a vineyard.	
22	.10 If (a man) had four or five grapevines and (was) picking the grapes (as he needed them) and taking them (straight) into his house, he is free from the duty of leaving grapes which he happens to drop or which he did not at first notice, but he is bound to leave the gleanings. If he left, (to vintage time, a small crop which he had not taken for table use) he gives (peah etc.) from what is left for what he left.
23 One who thins out (vegetables) gives (a peah) from what is left for what he left; and if he takes (all) from one place he gives from what is left for all (the original planting).	And one who thins out (vegetables) gives (a peah) from what is left for what he left. R. Judah said, 'With what (reference are these) things said? With (reference to) one who thins out to (take the thinnings to) market. But in (the case of) one who thins out (and keeps the thinnings for food) inside his own household, he gives from what is left for the whole (original planting).'
24	.11 If a man cut (produce as he needed it) and brought it (straight) into his house, even (though in this way he

	Peah	*Peah T.*

<table>
<tr><td></td><td></td><td>gradually denuded) all his field, (he would be) free from the (requirement to leave) gleanings, a 'forgotten' sheaf, and peah, but liable for the tithes.</td></tr>
<tr><td>25</td><td>.4 Onions kept for seed are liable to peah, but R. Jose declares (them) free.</td><td></td></tr>
<tr><td>26</td><td>As for beds of onions between (other) vegetables, R. Jose says....And the Sages say....</td><td></td></tr>
<tr><td>27</td><td>.5 Brothers who divided (a property) give two peot....</td><td></td></tr>
<tr><td>28</td><td>.6 R. Eliezer says, 'A (piece of) land (sufficient for sowing) a quarter (kab of seed) is liable to peah. R. Joshua says...
R. Tarefon says...
R. Judah ben Beterah says...
R. Akiba says, 'Any (piece of) land whatsoever is liable to peah and to firstfruits and (is sufficient to satisfy the requirement) for writing a prozbul and for the acquisition, together with itself, of movable property'...</td><td></td></tr>
<tr><td>29</td><td>.7 (In the case of a man who) lying sick, signs away his property, (if) he left (for himself) any (piece of) land whatsoever, his gift is a (valid) gift...</td><td></td></tr>
<tr><td>30</td><td>(If) a man signs away his property to his sons and signs over to his wife any (piece of) land whatsoever, she has lost her dowery. R. Jose says, 'If she agreed to (it), in spite of the fact that he did not sign (it) over to her, she lost her dowery.'</td><td>.12 (If) a man signs away his property to his sons and retain for his wife any (piece of) land whatsoever, she has lost her dowery. R. Jose said, 'With what (reference are these) things said? With (reference to) an instance in which she agreed to (it) as (an equivalent for her) dowery. But (if) she did not agree to (it) as (an equivalent for her) dowery, what he gave he gave (validly) and (beside that) she may</td></tr>
</table>

Peah	***Peah T.***

<table>
<tr><td></td><td></td><td>collect her dowery from the rest of the property.'</td></tr>
<tr><td>31</td><td>.8 (If) a man sign away his property to his slave, (the slave) is (thereby) freed. (If) he left (for himself) any (piece of) land whatsoever, (the slave) is not freed. R. Simon says, 'He is always freed unless (the master) say, "Behold, all my property is given to so-and-so my slave except for one ten-thousandth part of it. "'</td><td>.13 (If) a man sign away his property to his slave, (the slave) is thereby freed. If he left (for himself) any (piece of) land whatsoever, (the slave) is not freed. R. Simon says, 'He is always freed unless (the master) say, "I have given all my property to so-and-so my slave except for one ten-thousandth part of it." (Such a statement) says nothing at all. (But if he said,) "Except for such-and-such a city," "Except for such-and-such a field," in spite of the fact that he have nothing but that field or that city, the servant acquired the right to possessions (and so) acquired himself as a free man.' And when they said (these) things before R. Jose he said, 'Every man shall kiss his lips who answers rightly.'</td></tr>
</table>

Mat	***Lk***

<table>
<tr><td>32</td><td>5.3 Blessed are the poor in spirit, for theirs is the kingdom of Heaven.</td><td>6.20 Blessed are the poor, for yours is the kingdom of God.</td></tr>
<tr><td></td><td>.4 Blessed are the mourners, for they shall be comforted.</td><td>see 21b</td></tr>
<tr><td></td><td>.5 Blessed are the meek, for they shall inherit the earth.</td><td></td></tr>
<tr><td></td><td>.6 Blessed are those who hunger and thirst after righteousness, for they shall be filled.</td><td>.21 Blessed are those who hunger now, for you shall be filled.</td></tr>
<tr><td></td><td></td><td>.21b Blessed are those who weep now, for you shall laugh.</td></tr>
<tr><td></td><td>.7 Blessed are the merciful, for they shall receive mercy.</td><td></td></tr>
<tr><td></td><td>.8 Blessed are the pure in heart, for they shall see God.</td><td></td></tr>
<tr><td></td><td>.9 Blessed are the peacemakers, for they shall be called the children of God.</td><td></td></tr>
</table>

Mat	Lk
.10 Blessed are those persecuted because of righteousness, for theirs is the kingdom of Heaven.	
.11 Blessed are you when you shall be reviled and persecuted and everything bad shall be said against you falsely for my sake.	.22 Blessed are you when men shall hate you and when they shall ostracize you and revile you and cast out your name as bad, for the sake of the Son of Man.
.12 Rejoice and be glad, for your pay is great in the heavens; for thus they persecuted the prophets before you.	.23 Rejoice in that day and jump for joy, for behold, your pay is great in heaven, for their fathers acted in these same (ways) toward the prophets.

33

.24 But woe to you, the rich, for you have your consolation.
.25 Woe to you, who are filled now, for you shall hunger; woe (to you) who laugh now, for you shall mourn and weep.
.26 Woe, when all men speak you well, for their fathers acted in this same way towards the prophets.

34 .13 You are the salt of the earth..
.14 You are the light of the world...

35 .17 Do not think that I came to destroy the Law...

36 .21 You have heard that it was said...
.22 But I say to you...(murder)

37 .27 You have heard that it was said...
.28 But I say to you...(adultery)

38 31 And it was said...
.32 But I say to you...(divorce).

39 .33 Again you have heard that it was said...
.34 But I say to you...(oaths)

40 .38 You have heard that it was said, 'An eye for an eye'...
.39 But I say to you not to resist evil.

	Mat	**Lk**

Mat

.39b But whoever strikes you on the right cheek, turn him the other also.   see .29

.40 And to one who wishes to go to law with you and take your shirt, give your coat also.   see .29

.41 And whoever compels you to carry his burden a mile, go with him two.

.42 Give to the one who asks you, and do not turn away the man who wants to borrow from you.   see .30

41 .43 You have heard that it was said, 'You shall love your neighbor and hate your enemy.'

.44 But I say to you, 'Love your enemies and pray for those who persecute you.'

Lk

.27 But I say to you, to those who hear, 'Love your enemies, do good to those who hate you,

.28 bless those who curse you, pray for those who outrage you.

see .39

see .40

.29 To one who strikes you on the cheek, turn the other also; and to him who takes your coat, do not deny your shirt also.

see 42

.30 Give to everyone who asks you, and do not ask your property back from the one who takes it.

see 7.12

.31 And as you wish that men should treat you, so treat them.'

.45 In order that you may become children of your father in the heavens, for he makes his sun rise on the evil and the good and sends rain on the just and the unjust.   see .35, end.

46 For if you love those who love you, what pay have you? Do not even the tax-collectors do the same?   .32 And if you love those who love you, what sort of grace is there for you; for even the tax-collectors love those who love them.

.47 And if you greet your brothers only what do you do more (than usual)? Do not even the gentiles do the same?   .33 And if you do good to those who do good to you, what sort of grace is there for you? Even those who are lax about their religious observances (*lit.*

Mat	Lk
	the sinners) do the same.
	.34 And if you lend (to those) from whom you hope to receive, what sort of grace is there for you? Even the lax (*v.s.*) lend to the lax in order that they may receive in turn the like (favors).
	.35 But love your enemies and do good and lend hoping for nothing in return, and your pay will be great and you will be children of the Highest, for He Himself is good to the thankless and wicked.

.48 Be you, then, perfect, as your heavenly Father is perfect.

.36 Become merciful, as your Father is merciful.

42 6.1 Take care not to give alms publicly, so as to be seen...
.2 When, therefore, you give alms...
.5 And when you pray...
.16 And when you fast...

43 .19 Lay not up for yourselves treasures on earth...
.24 You cannot serve God and mammon.

44 .25 Therefore I tell you, 'Take no thought for your life...nor for your body...
.34 Sufficient unto the day is the evil thereof.'

45 7.1 Judge not, that you be not judged.
.2 For by what judgment you judge, you shall be judged.

.37 And judge not, and you shall not be judged.
37b And do not condemn, and you shall not be condemned. Release and you shall be released.

See .7
.2b And in what measure you mete it shall be measured to you.

.38 Give and it shall be given you...
.38b For in what measure you mete it shall be measured back to you.
.39 And he told them a parable, 'Can one blind man lead another? Will not both fall into a ditch?

Mat	**Lk**
	.40 A pupil is not above his teacher. Fully trained, each will be as his teacher.

46 .3 Why do you see the straw in your brother's eye? And do you not notice the beam in your eye?

.4 Or how will you say to your brother, 'Let me take the straw out of your eye.' and see, the beam is in your eye?

.5 Hypocrite! Take first, from your eye, the beam and then you will see clearly to take the straw from the eye of your brother.

.41 Why do you see the straw in your brother's eye? And do you not notice the beam in your own eye?

.42 How can you say to your brother, 'Brother, let me take out the straw which is in your eye.' not seeing, yourself, the beam in your eye? Hypocrite! Take first the beam from your eye, and then you will see clearly to take out the straw which is in your brother's eye.

47 .6 Give not that which is holy to the dogs...

48 .7 Ask, and it shall be given you; seek, and you shall find; knock, and it shall be opened to you.

.8 For everyone who asks, gets...

.9 Or what man among you, whose son asks for bread, will give him a stone?

.11 ...If, then, you, being wicked, know how to give good gifts to your children, how much more so your Father in heaven...?

.12 Therefore, all such things as you may wish that men might do to you – you also do thus to them, for this is the law and the prophets.

see .38

see .41

49 .13 Enter through the narrow gate, for broad is the gate and easy the road which leads to destruction....

50 .15 Beware of false prophets...

51 .16 From their fruits you shall know them. Are grapes gathered from thorns, or figs from thistles?

Mat	**Lk**
.17 Thus every good tree gives good fruits and the rotten tree gives bad fruits.	see .44
.18 A good tree cannot bear bad fruits, nor a rotten tree bear good fruits.	.43 For there is no fine tree giving rotten fruit, nor rotten tree giving fine fruit.
.20 So, then, from their fruits you shall know them.	.44 For every tree is known from its own fruit. For figs are not gathered from thorns, nor is the grape plucked from the briar.
see .16	.45 The good man, from the good treasure of his heart, brings forth good...

52   .21 Not everyone who says to me, 'Lord, Lord.' shall enter into the kingdom of Heaven, but he who does the will of my Father...

.22 Many will say to me in that day, 'Lord, Lord, did we not prophesy in thy name?'...

.46 And why do you call me, 'Lord, Lord,' and not do what I say?

53   .24 Therefore, whoever hears these words of mine and does them, will be likened to a wise man who built his house on bedrock.

.25 And the rain came down and the rivers came and the winds blew and attacked that house and it did not fall, for it was founded on bedrock.

.26 And everyone hearing these words of mine and not doing them shall be likened to a foolish man who built his house on the sand.

.27 And the rain came down and the rivers came and the winds blew and struck that house and it fell, and its fall was great.

.47 I shall show you what anyone coming to me and hearing my words and doing them is like:

.48 He is like a man building a house, who dug and went deep and put a foundation on bedrock. And when there was a flood, the river ran against that house and was not able to shake it because it was well built.

.49 But one hearing and not doing is like a man building a house on dirt without a foundation, (a house) which the river ran against and, straightway, it fell, and the breakup of that house was great.

3

The Character of the Tosefta

The Tosefta is Judaism's definitive writing, because the Tosefta forms the bridge between the Mishnah and the two Talmuds, and that is a statement well substantiated in all that follows. In terms of its own time, the Tosefta was compiled sometime after the conclusion of the Mishnah in ca. 200 but before the formation of the Talmud of the Land of Israel, ca. 400, and my guess is that it is a work of the third century, 200-300. A small fraction of its contents could have reached final formulation prior to the closure of the Mishnah, but most of the document either cites the Mishnah verbatim and comments upon it, or can be understood only in light of the Mishnah even though the Mishnah is not cited verbatim, and that is sound reason for assigning the whole to the time after the Mishnah was concluded.

But in substance the document's claim proves still stronger. For the Tosefta's materials, incoherent and cogent not among themselves but only in relationship to the Mishnah, serve as the Mishnah's first commentary, first amplification, and first extension – that is, the initial Talmud, prior to the one done in the Land of Israel by ca. 400 and the one completed in Babylonia by ca. 600. No important commentary to the Mishnah after the two Talmuds (and there were not very many in any event) read the Mishnah out of phase with the two Talmuds (particularly the Babylonian one), and the really perspicacious commentators appealed first of all to the Tosefta. So in these pages we really find out where it all began.

But that does not mean the Tosefta is a very accessible document. The opposite is the case. And the reason derives from the Tosefta's very character as a document of mediation, expansion, and extension of another piece of writing. If Judaism can be defined and described only in relationship to the Mishnah and two Talmuds, joined as they are by the Tosefta, the Tosefta, for its part, makes sense only in relationship to the

Mishnah. That is so not only for its program and order, which are defined by the Mishnah, but also for its individual compositions. Each completed unit of thought of the Tosefta is to be understood, to begin with, in relationship with the Mishnah: Is it a citation of and commentary to the Mishnah passage that forms its counterpart? Is the passage fully to be comprehended on its own or only in relationship to a counterpart passage of the Mishnah? Or is the passage free-standing? The answers to these three questions define the first step in making any sense at all of a passage of the Tosefta.

That explains why the Tosefta is a problem in the unfolding of the writings of Judaism, since its importance lies in its relationship to three other documents, the Mishnah, which came earlier, and the Talmud of the Land of Israel and the Talmud of Babylonia, which were completed later on. The Tosefta does not present a system of its own, as does the Mishnah, nor does it present both an inherited system and one of its own, as do both Talmuds. Rather, like a vine on a trellis, the Tosefta rests upon the Mishnah, having no structure of its own; but it also bears fruit nourished by its own roots. The character of this introduction is dictated by the traits of the document. What I aim in this and the next three chapters to do is set forth important parts of the Tosefta and explain what they mean and how they guide us to an understanding of the document in its canonical setting in Judaism.

My goal of documentary representation for the purposes of testing Smith's allegations is accomplished by translations of, and commentaries upon, important passages of the Tosefta, always in relationship to the Mishnah for the reason given above. The purpose of the translations of course is to provide as close a counterpart in English to not only the sense but also the syntax of the Hebrew of both the Tosefta and the Mishnah. The purpose of the commentary is to explain what seems to me to require attention and to set forth the relationship between a given passage of the Tosefta and its counterpart in the Mishnah. So this presentation of the document takes its program from the character of the document that is being introduced. Smith did no consequential work of this kind in his Appendix C, on which his Chapter Seven is based.

The Tosefta is not a free-standing document, presenting its own viewpoint, propositions, and even system. Luke and Matthew are free-standing documents, each with its own beginning, middle, and end. The Tosefta by contrast is secondary, derivative, dependent. That is not because it is a commentary upon the Mishnah, the Mishnah's first Talmud. For the criterion for knowing a free-standing from a contingent document is not the form; a commentary may, in fact, present in the form of a tradition and augmentation what is in fact a quite fresh and original system of its own; a fair part of the Yerushalmi, and an even larger component of the Bavli, fit the description of a systemic statement in commentary form.

The dependent status of the Tosefta derives from the simple fact that, for most of the document – my estimate is in excess of 80 percent of the whole – we cannot understand a line without first consulting the Mishnah's counterpart statement. Once a text derives its first level of meaning from some other document, we no longer can maintain that we have a free-standing statement, let alone a systemic one. But we can understand Matthew without reading Luke, and Luke without reading Matthew.

The reader will soon perceive, the Tosefta not only depends for structure, order, and sense upon the Mishnah, but, in general, the materials assembled in the Tosefta set forth no viewpoint other than that of the Mishnah's counterpart materials, clarified, refined, and improved. There is no introducing a commentary apart from its base text, and that accounts for the character of this introduction: an extended presentation of a document, in its own terms, of which many have heard, but few have direct and immediate knowledge. After working through these pages, readers will know precisely what the Tosefta is, how it works, why it is important, and where and when its authorship made the massive contribution to the formation of Judaism that won for them pride of place in the formative centuries of Judaism. Of these matters, Smith says nothing – because about them, he knew nothing. As is often the case in Smith's books and in many of his articles, what there is to say is simply: *iqqar haser min hassefer:* to which I offer three distinct translations, among which readers may choose the one they prefer. All apply. They are: the book misses its own point, does not make the point it intends, lacks a point altogether.

I. Purpose and Redactional Character of Tosefta

The Tosefta, meaning "supplement," is a corpus of materials correlative to the Mishnah. Standing apart from the Mishnah, the greater part of the Tosefta's materials is incomprehensible gibberish, bearing no autonomous meaning to be discovered wholly within the limits of a discrete passage. The Tosefta's units relate to corresponding ones in the Mishnah in one of three ways:

1. the Tosefta cites the Mishnah verbatim and then supplies glosses or further discussions of the Mishnah's rules;

2. the Tosefta complements the Mishnah without directly citing the corresponding passage;

3. the Tosefta supplements the Mishnah with information relevant to, but in theme and meaning autonomous of, the principal document.

The first sort of relationship characterizes about half of the pericopae of the document, the second about another third, and the last, about a sixth. the Tosefta's aggregations of materials normally are grouped in accord with their respective relationships to the Mishnah. A sequence serving a given chapter of the Mishnah, for example, may begin with pericopae in which the Mishnah is cited, then proceed to another set in which the Mishnah is complemented, and finally, present materials in which the Mishnah is given supplementary but essentially separate materials. The formulary traits of the Tosefta run parallel to those of the Mishnah in the first, and, to a lesser extent, the second sort of materials. But in the main the Tosefta in language is a far less formalized document than the Mishnah. The Mishnah's redaction tends to produce aggregates of materials characterized by a common formulary pattern and a common theme. So far as the Tosefta may be divided into sizable groups of materials, by contrast, it is redacted primarily in accord with a single relationship to the Mishnah exhibited by a sequence of otherwise formally and thematically discrete units. In size, the Tosefta is approximately four times larger than the Mishnah.

The Tosefta is important within rabbinical literature for two reasons. First, pericopae of the Tosefta (or versions of pericopae, attributed to authorities of the first and second century, strongly resembling those now found in the Tosefta) commonly form the foundation of the treatment, by both Palestinian and Babylonian Talmuds, of the corresponding pericopae in the Mishnah. Indeed, the Tosefta supplement to the Mishnah often stands at the outset, and generates the two Talmuds' analyses of that same Mishnah. Second, the entire exegetical tradition of the Mishnah in later times depends upon the Tosefta's original exegesis of that document at all points at which the Tosefta is available and cited. If, therefore, one wants to understand how the Mishnah has been interpreted for nearly eighteen centuries, the place to begin is in the Tosefta. It hardly needs saying that the Tosefta, separate from its importance within the other principal documents of Rabbinic Judaism, contains innumerable sayings which bear considerable value of their own. For the period after the redaction of the Mishnah and before the conclusion of the Talmuds, from ca. 200 to ca. 600, the Tosefta, and, especially, formulations of sayings which ultimately found their way into the Tosefta, constitutes a document of paramount importance.

II. Origin and Development

We do not know who compiled and redacted the Tosefta or when the work reached its present form. On this matter we presently rely upon the judgment of M.D. Herr:

> Very often a baraita quoted in the Talmud in a corrupt form is found in the Tosefta in its original coherent form. Furthermore, very often there is a discussion in the Talmud about the exact meaning of the words of a certain tanna (either in the Mishnah or in the baraita), while the parallel statement as found in the Tosefta is manifestly clear. It would therefore seem obvious that the Tosefta in its present form was not edited before the end of the fourth century C.E. and cannot therefore be identified with any of the...earlier collections of beraitot. It is certain that the Tosefta was composed in Erez Israel, since the beraitot which it contains resemble more those of the Jerusalem Talmud than those of the Babylonian Talmud.[1]

The many textual problems of the Tosefta itself, however, leave room for other interpretations of the data to which Herr makes reference, not to mention quite different theories of the character of the sayings themselves and the interrelationships of their diverse versions. For the present purpose it suffices to note that the Tosefta reaches its present shape some time between the redaction of the Mishnah, about A.D. 200, and that of the Palestinian Talmud, two and a half centuries later, about A.D. 450, I think by 360. These are no more than guesses.

III. Text

We know little about the transmission of the Tosefta thereafter. Most of the pericopae of the Order of Purities are cited by Samson of Sens (ca. 1150-1230), in his commentary to the Mishnah of the present Order, and many are quoted by Maimonides in his Mishneh Torah (1180), principally in the Book of Cleanness.[2] The first modern text was that of M.S. Zuckermandel (1881), following the Erfurt Manuscript. For our Order in particular, the preferred text is the version of the Vienna Manuscript, edited by Karl Heinrich Rengstorf.

My translation is based upon Lieberman's text for the first four divisions of the Mishnah and the Tosefta, Zeraim, Moed, Nashim, and Neziqin, Zuckermandel's for the fifth, and Rengstorf's for the sixth,[3] but also includes pericopae in the version of Samson of Sens. The extant text

---

[1]*Encyclopaedia Judaica* 15:1283-1285.
[2]The Code of Maimonides. Book Ten. The Book of Cleanness, translated from the Hebrew by Herbert Danby (New Haven, 1954: Yale University Press).
[3]Karl Heinrich Rengstorf, Die Tosefta. Text. Seder VI: Toharot (Stuttgart, 1967: Kohlhammer).

is further revised, in my translation, in the light of the exegetical study of the text and of its problems by Saul Lieberman, *Tosefeth Rishonim. A Commentary Based on Manuscripts of the Tosefta and Works of the Rishonim and Midrashim in Manuscripts and Rare Editions*. III. *Kelim-Niddah* (Jerusalem, 1939: Bamberger and Wahrmann) and IV. *Mikwaoth-Uktzin* (Jerusalem, 1939: Mossad Rabbi Kook Press). I cite this commentary as TR. Among commentaries systematically consulted are Isaac Pardo (1718-1790), *Hasdé David. IV. Tohorot* (Jerusalem, 1970), and Elijah ben Solomon Zalman ("Elijah Gaon," "Vilna Gaon," cited as GRA), (1720-1797), printed in the Mishnah, ed. Romm (Vilna, 1887).

An exegesis of each pericope, together with an explanation of both the text as translated and its meaning, is found for each tractate in the relevant volumes of my *History of the Mishnaic Law*. There is no need to extensively annotate each pericope because the requisite information on the relationship of each pericope to the Mishnah's counterpart, textual problems and emendations, and the meaning of the given passage is supplied there. The unavoidable length of such annotation would greatly increase the size of this introduction.

IV. Who Stands Behind the Tosefta?

The Tosefta came to closure about two centuries after the Mishnah, one may guess at about 300. Accordingly, the Tosefta is a Talmud, an Amoraic document. That is to say, the circles that produced the Talmud of the Land of Israel, a systematic commentary to thirty-nine of the Mishnah's sixty-three tractates, as well as compositions of scriptural exegesis for the Pentateuch, also stand behind the Tosefta. But all of the authorities appearing in the Tosefta bear the names of figures who also appear in the Mishnah. Accordingly, the Tosefta also appears to constitute a Tannaitic document, in that (if the attributions are to be believed) its materials derive from the same sages who created the Mishnah.

It is difficult to establish criteria for evaluating whether the Tosefta is a pseudepigraphic document, written by later figures but claiming the authority of earlier ones, or a collection of statements, external to those preserved in the Mishnah, deriving from the Mishnah's framers themselves. At this point nothing is to be taken for granted. We may assume neither the authentic, nor the pseudepigraphic, character of the Tosefta's attributions of its materials, and, with them, of the Tosefta's origin: alongside but slightly after the Mishnah, on the one side, or in the aftermath of two centuries of Mishnah exegesis among Talmudic authorities, on the other.

We may identify passages of the Talmuds, both of the Land of Israel and of Babylonia, which appear to take up (or, at least, correspond to) the intellectual program originating in the Tosefta. More obviously, many passages of the Talmuds treat the exegesis, not of the Mishnah directly, but of the Tosefta's exegesis of the Mishnah. Accordingly, such passages follow the program of (1) citing the Mishnah, then (2) citing the Tosefta's amplification of the Mishnah, and, finally, (3) analyzing and unpacking that secondary amplification – a neat progression. If it could be demonstrated that the bulk of the two Talmuds consists of discourse following that sequence of documents, we should reliably conclude that the Tosefta stands at the midpoint, between the closure of the Mishnah, on the one side, and the construction of the Talmud of the Land of Israel, and, in its wake, the Talmud of Babylonia, on the other side. But we stand a considerable distance from a systematic inquiry into the matter.

What we may say with certainty is simple. The Tosefta contains three types of materials, two of them secondary to, therefore assuredly later than, the Mishnah's materials, the third autonomous of the Mishnah and therefore possibly deriving from the same period as do the sayings compiled in the Mishnah.

The first type of materials contains a direct citation of the Mishnah, given in this translation in italics, followed by secondary discussion of the cited passage. That type of discourse certainly is post-Mishnaic, hence by definition Amoraic, as much as sayings of Samuel, Rab Judah, and R. Yohanan are Amoraic.

The second sort of materials depends for full and exhaustive meaning upon a passage of the Mishnah, although the corresponding statements of the Mishnah are not cited verbatim. That sort of discussion probably is post-Mishnaic, but much depends upon our exegesis. Accordingly, we may be less certain of the matter.

The third type of passage in the Tosefta stands completely independent of any corresponding passage of the Mishnah. This is in one of two ways. First, a fully articulated pericope in the Tosefta may simply treat materials not discussed in a systematic way, or not discussed at all, in the Mishnah. That kind of pericope can as well reach us in the Mishnah as in the Tosefta, so far as the criterion of literary and redactional theory may come to apply. Second, a well-constructed passage of the Tosefta may cover a topic treated in the Mishnah, but follow a program of inquiry not dealt with at all in the Mishnah. What the statements of the Tosefta treat, therefore, may prove relevant to the thematic program of the Mishnah but not to the analytical inquiry of the framers of the Mishnah. Such a passage, like the former sort, also may fit comfortably into the Mishnah. If any components of the received Tosefta derive from the second century, that is, the time of the framing of the Mishnah, it would be those of the third type.

In proportion, a rough guess would place less than a fifth of the Tosefta into this third type, well over a third of the whole into the first. In all, therefore, the Tosefta serves precisely as its name suggests, as a corpus of supplements – but of various kinds – to the Mishnah.

V. The Tosefta and the Mishnah

The Tosefta depends upon the Mishnah in yet another way. Its whole redactional framework, tractates and subdivisions alike, depends upon the Mishnah's. The Mishnah provides the lattice, the Tosefta, the vines. Since there is no understanding of the Tosefta out of the context of the Mishnah, I give the Mishnah passage alongside, and before, each Tosefta passage in this book. Accordingly, the rule (though with many exceptions) is that the Tosefta's discussion will follow the themes and problems of the Mishnah's program, much as the two Talmuds' treatments of the passage of the Mishnah are laid out along essentially the same lines as those of the Mishnah. The editorial work accordingly highlights the exegetical purpose of the framers of both the two Talmuds and the Tosefta. The whole serves as a massive and magnificent amplification of the Mishnah. In this regard, of course, the framers of the Tosefta may claim considerably greater success than those of the two Talmuds, since the Tosefta covers nearly all the tractates of the Mishnah, while neither Talmud treats more than two-thirds of them (and then not the same two-thirds).

But the Tosefta's redactors or arrangers tend to organize materials, within a given tractate, in line with two intersecting principles of arrangement. First, as I said, they follow the general outline of the Mishnah's treatment of a topic. Accordingly, if we set up a block of materials in the Tosefta side by side with a corresponding block of those of the Mishnah, we should discern roughly the same order of discourse. But, second, the Tosefta's arrangers also lay out their materials in accord with their own types. That is to say, they will tend (1) to keep as a group passages that cite and then comment upon the actual words of the Mishnah's base passage, then (2) to present passages that amplify in the Tosefta's own words opinions fully spelled out only in response to the Mishnah's statements, and, finally, (3) to give at the end, and as a group, wholly independent and autonomous sayings and constructions of such sayings. I stress that that redactional pattern may be shown only to be a tendency, a set of not uncommon policies and preferences, not a fixed rule. But when we ask how the Tosefta's editors arranged their materials, it is not wholly accurate to answer that they follow the plan of the

Mishnah's counterparts. There will be some attention, also, to the taxonomic traits of the units of discourse of which the Tosefta itself is constructed. That is why two distinct editorial principles come into play in explaining the arrangement of the whole.

When we turn from the definition of the Tosefta and of its editorial and redactional character to the contents of the document as a whole, the Mishnah once more governs the framework of description. For the Tosefta, as is already clear, stands nearly entirely within the circle of the Mishnah's interests, rarely asking questions about topics omitted altogether by the Mishnah's authors, always following the topical decisions on what to discuss as laid down by the founders of the whole. For our part, therefore, we cannot write about the Tosefta's theology or law, as though these constituted a system susceptible of description and interpretation independent of the Mishnah's system. At the same time, we must recognize that the exegetes of the Mishnah, in the Tosefta, and in the two Talmuds, stand apart from, and later than, the authors of the Mishnah itself.

Accordingly, the exegetes systematically say whatever they wish to say by attaching their ideas to a document earlier than their own, and by making the principal document say what they wish to contribute. The system of expressing ideas through reframing those of predecessors preserves the continuity of tradition and establishes a deep stability and order upon the culture framed by that tradition. But it makes the labor of teasing out the ideas of the later generations parlous. Describing what is particular to the exegetes and distinctive to their layer of the continuous enterprise of thought demands protracted and subtle inquiry.

VI. A Sample Passage

If the readers were to take up this writer's six-volume English translation of the Tosefta and begin reading on page one, by page three they would close the book and declare it unintelligible, a complete mishmash with no order, sense, proposition, or meaning. They would be justified to conclude that the document served as a mere scrapbook of this and that, lacking all focus, sense, and purpose, a kind of *genizah* within the covers of a book. But when they realize – by reading the Tosefta side by side with the corresponding Mishnah paragraphs and chapters – that the framers did follow a principle of organization, which we can define and demonstrate to have applied throughout, then they can no longer dismiss the Tosefta as a mere scrapbook, essentially unintelligible in its own terms. Once we recognize that the authorship has carefully and thoughtfully organized matters, we understand that they are accomplishing a highly sophisticated literary purpose.

That conclusion should hardly be surprising, since even the most superficial traits of the document – its organization in close correspondence with the Mishnah, by the Mishnah's tractates, by the Mishnah's tractates' chapter divisions, by the Mishnah's tractates' chapter divisions' subdivisions – demonstrate the same fact. Indeed, the authorship of the Tosefta was made up of literary craftsmen of the highest order, with remarkable skills of organization. Theirs, after all, was not a (mere) commentary, since without printing, arranging a commentary around a text in the middle of the page is not very easy; and, more to the point, the Mishnah was published orally, not in writing but through processes of memorization, so that, by definition, printing or no, the commentary form of literary formulation and expression was simply not available. They solved their problem in the very odd way that we now discern.

But the character of the Tosefta governs the possibilities of presenting here a sample in such a way that the traits of the document, not merely a few lucid sentences, may be set forth. To see how the Tosefta fits into the sweep of the rabbinic literature extending from the Mishnah, ca. 200, through the Tosefta, ca. 200-300, to the Talmud of the Land of Israel or Yerushalmi, ca. 400, we follow a single passage. This allows us to place the Tosefta into its larger context. What is important, we shall observe, is how the Tosefta receives the Mishnah and transmits it forward; in the passage before us, the first of the two Talmuds address not so much the Mishnah as the Mishnah as transmitted by the Tosefta. (The second Talmud follows suit but will not detain us.) When we see in great detail precisely how the Tosefta adds its amplification and explanation to the Mishnah, and then how the Yerushalmi and the Bavli in sequence take up the Tosefta's reading of the Mishnah, we shall grasp how profoundly the whole of rabbinic literature in its formative age focuses upon not the Mishnah but the Tosefta, the kind of hub of the whole.

The following pages present a chapter of the Mishnah, Mishnah-tractate Berakhot Chapter Eight in relationship to the Tosefta to that chapter. There follow the Yerushalmi's and finally the Bavli's treatment of the same chapter. We shall see how the Tosefta precipitates discourse, which then proceeds in quite unanticipated directions. In this way we get a good sense of proportion and balance: where the Tosefta matters, where it is left behind as the later authorities develop new interests altogether. The main point we shall observe is the position of the Tosefta in relationship to the Mishnah before and the first of the two Talmuds afterward. That we see when we follow the words of the Mishnah as these are augmented and revised in the Tosefta, then the words of the Tosefta as these are explained and made the starting point for further discussion in the two Talmuds. From a certain point in each case, the exposition of the Mishnah as the Tosefta reads the Mishnah falls away and other interests come to the fore; I give only the passages in which the Tosefta figures prominently as the Mishnah's first, and authoritative, exposition.

I. Mishnah-tractate Berakhot Chapter Eight

I

8:1   A.   These are the things which are between the House of Shammai and the House of Hillel in [regard to] the meal:

         B.   The House of Shammai say, "One blesses over the day, and afterward one blesses over the wine."
And the House of Hillel say, "One blesses over the wine, and afterward one blesses over the day."

8.2   A.   The House of Shammai say, "They wash the hands and afterward mix the cup."
And the House of Hillel say, "They mix the cup and afterward wash the hands."

8:3   A.   The House of Shammai say, "He dries his hands on the cloth and lays it on the table."
And the House of Hillel say, "On the pillow."

8:4   A.   The House of Shammai say, "They clean the house, and afterward they wash the hands."
And the House of Hillel say, "They wash the hands, and afterward they clean the house."

8:5   A.   The House of Shammai say, "Light, and food, and spices, and *Habdalah.*"
And the House of Hillel say, "Light, and spices, and food, and *Habdalah.*"

         B.   The House of Shammai say, "'Who created the light of the fire.'"
And the House of Hillel say, "'Who creates the lights of the fire.'"

8:6   A.   They do not bless over the light or the spices of gentiles, nor the light or the spices of the dead, nor the light or the spices which are before an idol.

         B.   And they do not bless over the light until they make use of its illumination.

8:7   A.   He who ate and forgot and did not bless [say Grace] –

         B.   the House of Shammai say, "He should go back to his place and bless."
And the House of Hillel say, "He should bless in the place in which he remembered."

         C.   Until when does he bless? Until the food has been digested in his bowels.

8:8   A.   Wine came to them after the meal, and there is there only that cup –

         B.   the House of Shammai say, "He blesses the wine, and afterward he blesses the food."
And the House of Hillel say, "He blesses the food, and afterward he blesses the wine."

C.   They respond *Amen* after an Israelite who blesses, and they do not respond *Amen* after a Samaritan who blesses, until hearing the entire blessing.

The Mishnah chapter goes over rules on the conduct of meals, first for Sabbaths and festivals, then in general, with special concern for preserving the cultic purity of the meal. That means the people at the meal keep the laws of cultic cleanness set forth in the book of Leviticus, as these are interpreted by the sages of the Torah. The details are explained in the Tosefta, Yerushalmi, and Bavli, and we do well to allow the course of rabbinic thought and writing to carry us into the matter. Here is how the Tosefta confronts the same themes and also cites some of the passages verbatim.

Tosefta to Mishnah Berakhot Chapter Eight

5:21 (ed. S. Lieberman, p. 28, lines 41-42)

They answer *Amen* after a gentile who says a blessing with the Divine Name. They do not answer *Amen* after a Samaritan who says a blessing with the Divine Name until they have heard the entire blessing.

5:25 (Lieberman, p. 29, lines 53-57)

A.   [The] things which are between the House of Shammai and the House of Hillel in [regard to] the meal:

B.   The House of Shammai say, "One blesses over the day, and afterward he blesses over the wine, for the day causes the wine to come, and the day is already sanctified, but the wine has not yet come."

C.   And the House of Hillel say, "One blesses over the wine, and afterward he blesses over the day, for the wine causes the Sanctification of the day to be said.
"Another explanation: The blessing over the wine is regular [= always required when wine is used], and the blessing over the day is not continual [but is said only on certain days]."

D.   And the law is according to the words of the House of Hillel.

5:26 (Lieberman, pp. 29-30, lines 57-61)

A.   The House of Shammai say, "They wash the hands and afterward mix the cup, lest the liquids which are on the outer surface of the cup be made unclean on account of the hands, and in turn make the cup unclean."

B.   The House of Hillel say, "The outer surfaces of the cup are always deemed unclean.
"Another explanation: The washing of the hands must always take place immediately before the meal.

C.   "They mix the cup and afterward wash the hands."

5:27 (Lieberman, p. 30, lines 61-65)

A. The House of House of Shammai say, "He dries his hand on the napkin and leaves it on the table, lest the liquids which are in the napkin be made unclean on account of the cushion, and then go and make the hands unclean."

B. And the House of Hillel say, "A doubt in regard to the condition of liquids so far as the hands are concerned is resolved as clean.

C. "Another explanation: Washing the hands does not pertain to unconsecrated food.

D. "But he dries his hands on the napkin and leaves it on the cushion, lest the liquids which are in the napkin be made unclean on account of the table, and they go and render the food unclean."

5:28 (Lieberman, p. 30, lines 65-68)

A. The House of Shammai say, "They clean the house, on account of the waste of food, and afterward they wash the hands."

B. The House of Hillel say, "If the waiter was a disciple of a sage, he gathers the scraps which contain as much as an olive's bulk.

C. "And they wash the hands and afterward clean the house."

5:29 (Lieberman, p. 30, lines 68-72)

A. The House of Shammai say, "He holds the cup of wine in his right hand and spiced oil in his left hand."
He blesses over the wine and afterward blesses over the oil.

B. And the House of Hillel say, "He holds the sweet oil in his right hand and the cup of wine in his left hand."

C. He blesses over the oil and smears it on the head of the waiter. If the waiter was a disciple of a sage, he [the diner] smears it on the wall, because it is not praiseworthy for a disciple of a sage to go forth perfumed.

5:30 (Lieberman, pp. 30-31, lines 72-75)

A. R. Judah said, "The House of Shammai and the House of Hillel did not dispute concerning the blessing of the food, that it is first, or concerning the *Habdalah*, that it is at the end.
"Concerning what did they dispute?
"Concerning the light and the spices, for –
"the House of Shammai say, 'Light and afterward spices.'
"And the House of Hillel say, 'Spices and afterward light.'"

5:30 (Lieberman, p. 31, lines 75-77)

B. He who enters his home at the end of the Sabbath blesses the wine, the light, the spices, and then says *Habdalah*.

C. And if he has only one cup [of wine] he leaves it for after the meal and then says all [the liturgies] in order after [reciting the blessing for] it.

5:31 (Lieberman, p. 31, lines 81-85)

A. If a person has a light covered in the folds of his garment or in a lamp, and sees the flame but does not use its light, or uses its light but does not see its flame, he does not bless [that light]. [He says a blessing over the light only] when he both sees the flame and uses its light.

As to a lantern – even though he had not extinguished it (that is, it has been burning throughout the Sabbath), he recites a blessing over it.

B.   They do not bless over the light of gentiles. One may bless over [the flame of] an Israelite kindled from a gentile, or a gentile who kindled from an Israelite.

5:32 (Lieberman, p. 31, lines 80-81)

In the house of study –
the House of Shammai say, "One [person] blesses for all of them."
And the House of Hillel say, "Each one blesses for himself."

Clearly, the Tosefta has a variety of materials. Some of the materials are free-standing, but some simply cite and gloss the Mishnah. We see in the following comparison just how these things come to the surface. I add in italics the amplificatory language of the Tosefta. That is where the Tosefta's character as a set of glosses to, and an elaborate, secondary development of, the Mishnah emerges.

The Tosefta and the Mishnah to Mishnah-Tractate Berakhot
Chapter Eight Compared

		Mishnah		Tosefta
8:1	A.	These are the things which are between the House of Shammai and the House of Hillel in [regard to] the meal:	5:25	[The] things which are between the House of Shammai and the House of Hillel [as regards] the meal:
	B.	The House of Shammai say, "One blesses the day, and afterward one blesses over the wine." And the House of Hillel say, "One blesses the wine, and afterward one blesses over the day."		The House of Shammai say, "One blesses the day, and afterward one blesses over the wine, *for the day causes the wine to come, and the day is already sanctified, but the wine has not yet come.*" And the House of Hillel say, "One blesses over the wine, and afterward one blesses the day, *for the wine causes the Sanctification of the day to be said. Another matter: The blessing of the wine is continual, and the blessing of the day is not continual.*" And the law is according to

8:2 A.   The House of Shammai say, "They wash the hands and afterward mix the cup." And the House of Hillel say, "They mix the cup and afterward wash the hands."

5:26   *the words of the House of Hillel.*
The House of Shammai say, "They wash the hands and afterward mix the cup, *lest the liquids which are on the outer surfaces of the cup may be made unclean on account of the hands, and they may go back and make the cup unclean.*" The House of Hillel say, "*The outer surfaces of the cup are perpetually unclean.*" *Another matter: The washing of the hands is only [done] near [at the outset of] the meal.* "They mix the cup and afterward wash the hands."

8:3 A.   The House of Shammai say, "He dries his hands on the napkin and lays it on the table." And the House of Hillel say, "On the cushion."

5:27   The House of Shammai say, "He dries his hand on the napkin and lays it on the table, *lest the liquids which are in the napkin may be made unclean on account of the pillow, and they may go and make the hands unclean.*"
The House of Hillel say, "*A doubt in regard to the condition of liquids so far as the hands are concerned is clean.*" *Another matter: Washing the hands does not pertain to unconsecrated food. But he dries his hands on the napkin and leaves it on the cushion lest the liquids which are in the pillow may be made unclean on account of the table, and they may go and render the food unclean.*

8:4 A. The House of Shammai say, "They clean the house and afterward wash the hands." And the House of Hillel say, "They wash the hands and afterward clean the house."

5:28 The House of Shammai say, "They clean the house *on account of the waste of food"* and afterward wash the hands." The House of Hillel say, "*If the waiter was a disciple of a sage, he gathers the scraps which contain as much as an olive's bulk.* They wash the hands and afterward clean the house."

8:5 A. The House of Shammai say, "Light, and food and spices, a n d *Habdalah."* And the House of Hillel say, "Light, and spices, and food, and *Habdalah."*

5:30 R. Judah said, "*The House of Shammai and the House of Hillel did not dispute concerning the blessing of the food, that it is first, and concerning the* Habdalah *that it is the end. Concerning what did they dispute? Concerning the light and the spices, for* the House of Shammai say, 'Light and *afterward* spices,' and the House of Hillel say, 'Spices and *afterward* light.'"

B. The House of Shammai say, "'Who created the light of the fire.'" And the House of Hillel say, "'Who creates the lights of the fire.'"

[NO EQUIVALENT.]

8:8 A. Wine came to them after the meal, and there is there only that cup –

5:30 (Lieberman, p. 31, lines 75-77).

A. *He who enters his home at the end of the Sabbath blesses over the wine, the light, the spices, and then says* Habdalah.

B. the House of Shammai say, "He blesses over the wine and afterward he blesses over the food." And the House of Hillel say, "He blesses over the food and afterward he blesses over the wine." [If wine came to them after the meal and] there

B. *And if he has only one cup* [of wine], *he leaves it for after the meal and then says them all in order after* [blessing] *it. If he has only one cup* [of wine] [he leaves if for after the meal and then says them all in order, thus:] Wine, then food.

is there only that cup House of Shammai say, "He blesses the wine and then the food." (House of Hillel say, "He blesses the food and then the wine.")

8:6 A. They do not bless the light or the spices of gentiles, nor the light or the spices of the dead, nor the light or the spices which are before an idol.

B. And they do not bless the light until they make use of its illumination.

5:31 B They do not bless the light of gentiles. *A n Israelite who kindled* [a flame] *from a gentile, or a gentile who kindled from an Israelite – one may bless* [such a flame].

5:31 (Lieberman, p. 31, lines 81-85).

A. *If a person has a light covered in the folds of his garment or in a lamp, and he sees the flame but does not use its light, or uses its light but does not see its flame, he does not bless.* [He blesses only] *when he both sees the flame and uses its light.*

8:8 C. They respond *Amen* after an Israelite who blesses, and they do not respond *Amen* after a Samaritan who blesses, until one hears the entire blessing.

5:21 (Lieberman, p. 28, lines 41-42). *They answer "Amen" after a blessing with the Divine Name recited by a gentile.* They do not answer *Amen* after a Samaritan who blesses *with the Divine Name* until they hear the entire blessing.

The pattern is clear. We simply cannot understand a line of the Tosefta without turning to the Mishnah. That means that the Tosefta passage before us must have been composed after the Mishnah was in hand, that is, after 200 C.E., and that the authorship of the Tosefta had in mind the clarification of the received document, the Mishnah.

THE TOSEFTA AND THE TWO TALMUDS: When we examine the two Talmuds' reading of the Mishnah, we shall see how both Talmuds' compositions' authors have cited the Tosefta passage and formed a commentary to that. So without access to the indicated passages, we cannot grasp what the Talmuds want to know about the Mishnah –

which in this case is, the sense of the Tosefta's wording in the Tosefta's commentary to the Mishnah. In this context the Talmuds form secondary expansions of the Tosefta, rather than commentaries directly upon the Mishnah. But, of course, we shall presently see that the two Talmuds accomplish their own goals, not only serving the purposes of the compilers of the Tosefta.

We come now to the first of the two Talmuds, the Talmud of the Land of Israel, a.k.a. the Yerushalmi. To understand what follows we must know that the Yerushalmi will address a chapter of the Mishnah by citing the Mishnah in small blocks, not reading it whole but only in phrases and clauses. Our special interest is in the place of the Tosefta in the Yerushalmi's structure. What we shall see is that the Yerushalmi is consecutive upon not the Mishnah but the Tosefta's reading of the Mishnah. I abbreviate the parts of the Yerushalmi's chapter that do not pertain to our problem, indicating cuts by an addition of three dots. What is important in what follows is the form of the document, and we shall not be detained with an elaborate explanation of the details. What we want to see is the sequence, from the Mishnah, through the Tosefta, to the Talmud. Since that is the purpose of this abbreviated abstract, I facilitate matters by underlining the passages of the Yerushalmi at which the Tosefta defines discourse.

IV. Yerushalmi to Mishnah Berakhot Chapter Eight

8:1   The House of Shammai say, "One blesses the day and afterward
          one blesses over the wine."
          And the House of Hillel say, "One blesses over the wine and
          afterward one blesses the day."

I.   A.   *What is the reason of the House of Shammai?*
            The Sanctification of the day causes the wine to be brought, and the
            man is already liable for the Sanctification of the day before the
            wine comes.
            What is the reason of the House of Hillel?
            The wine causes the Sanctification of the day to be said.
            Another matter: Wine is perpetual, and the Sanctification is not
            perpetual. [What is always required takes precedence over what is
            required only occasionally.]
      B.   R. Yosé said, "[It follows] from the opinions of them both that with
            respect to wine and *Habdalah*, wine comes first."
            "*It is not the reason of the House of Shammai* that the Sanctification of
            the day causes the wine to be brought, and here, since *Habdalah*
            does not cause wine to be brought, the wine takes precedence?"
            "*Is it not the reason of the House of Hillel that* the wine is perpetual and
            the Sanctification is not perpetual, and since the wine is perpetual,
            and the *Habdalah* is not perpetual, the wine comes first?"
      C.   R. Mana said, "From the opinions of both of them [it follows] that
            with respect to wine and *Habdalah*, *Habdalah* comes first."

"Is it not the reason of the House of Shammai that one is already obligated [to say] the Sanctification of the day before the wine comes, and here, since he is already obligated for *Habdalah* before the wine comes, *Habdalah* comes first?"

Is it not the reason of the House of Hillel that the wine causes the Sanctification of the Day to be said, and here, since the wine does not cause the *Habdalah* to be said, *Habdalah* comes first?"

D. R. Zeira said, "From the opinions of both of them [it follows] that they say *Habdalah* without wine, but they say the Sanctification only with wine."

E. *This is the opinion of R. Zeira, for* R. Zeira said, "They may say *Habdalah* over beer, *but they go from place to place* [in search of wine] *for the Sanctification."*

II. A. R. Yosé b. Rabbi said, "They are accustomed there [in Babylonia], where there is no wine, for the prayer leader to go before the ark and say one blessing which is a summary of the seven, and complete it with, 'Who sanctifies Israel and the Sabbath Day.'"

B. *And thus the following poses a difficulty for the opinion of the House of Shammai: How should one act on the evenings of the Sabbath?*

He *who was sitting and eating on the evening of the Sabbath,* and it grew dark and became Sabbath evening, and there was there only that one cup – [the House of Shammai say, "Wine, then food," and the House of Hillel say, "Food, then wine," so Mishnah 8:8].

Do you say he should leave it for the end of the meal and say all of them [the blessings] on it?

What do you prefer?

Should he [first] bless the day? The food takes precedence.

Should he bless the food? The wine takes precedence.

Should he bless the wine? The day takes precedence.

C. *We may infer* [the answer] *from this:*

If wine came to them after the meal, and there is there only that cup –

R. Ba said, "Because it [the wine's] is a brief blessing, [he says it first, for] perhaps he may forget and drink [the wine]. But here, since he says them all over the cup, he will not forget [to say a blessing over the wine in the cup]."

D. What, then, should he do according to the opinion of the House of Shammai?

Let him bless the food first, then bless the day, and then bless the wine.

E. *And this poses difficulty for the opinion of the House of Hillel: How should one act at the end of the Sabbath?*

If he was sitting and eating on the Sabbath and it grew dark and the Sabbath came to an end, and there is there only that cup –

do you say he should leave it [the wine] for after the meal and say them all on it?

What do you prefer?

Should he bless the wine? The food comes first.

Should he bless the food? The light comes first.

Should be bless the light? The *Habdalah* comes first.

F. *We may infer* [the solution to the impasse] *from this:* R. Judah said, "The House of Shammai and the House of Hillel did not differ concerning the blessing of the food, that it comes first, nor concerning *Habdalah*, that it comes at the end.
"Concerning what did they differ?
"Concerning the light and the spices, for:
"The House of Shammai say, 'The spices and afterward the light.'
"And the House of Hillel say, 'The light and afterward the spices.'"

G. R. Ba and R. Judah in the name of Rab (said), "The law is according to him who says, 'Spices and afterward light.'"]

H. What should he do according to the opinion of the House of Hillel? Let him bless the food, afterward bless the wine, and afterward bless the light.

III. A. As to [the beginning of the] festival day which coincides with the end of the Sabbath –
R. Yohanan said, "[The order of prayer is] wine, Sanctification, light, *Habdalah*."
Hanin bar Ba said in the name of Rab, "Wine, Sanctification, light, *Habdalah*, *Sukkah*, and season."
And did not Samuel rule according to this teaching of R. Hanina.

B. R. Aha said in the name of R. Joshua b. Levi, "When a king goes out and the governor comes in, they accompany the king and afterward bring in the governor."

C. Levi said, "Wine, *Habdalah*, light, Sanctification."...

8:2 **The House of Shammai say, "They wash the hands and afterward mix the cup." And the House of Hillel say, "They mix the cup first and afterward wash the hands."**

I. A. *What is the reason of the House of Shammai?*
So that the liquids which are on the outer side of the cup may not be made unclean by his hands and go make the cup unclean.
What is the reason of the House of Hillel?
The outer side of the cup is always unclean [so there is no reason to protect it from the hands' uncleanness].
Another matter: One should wash the hands immediately before saying the blessing.

B. *R. Biban in the name of R. Yohanan* [said], *"The opinion of the House of Shammai is in accord with R. Yosé and that of the House of Hillel with R. Meir, as we have learned there* [Mishnah Kel. 25:7-8]:
"[In all vessels an outer part and an inner part are distinguished, and also a part by which they are held.]
"R. Meir says, 'For hands which are unclean and clean.'
"R. Yosé said, 'This applies only to clean hands alone.'"

C. R. Yosé in the name of R. Shabbetai, and R. Hiyya in the name of R. Simeon b. Laqish [said], "For *Hallah* [dough-offering] and for washing the hands, a man goes four miles [to find water]."
R. Abbahu in the name of R. Yosé b. R. Hanina said, "This is what he said, '[If the water is] before him [that is, on his way, in his vicinity, or near at hand, he must proceed to it and wash]. But if it is behind him [that is, not on his way], they do not trouble him [to obtain it and wash].'"...

8:3   **The House of Shammai say, "He dries his hands on the napkin and puts it on the table."**
And the House of Hillel say, "On the cushion."

I.   A.   The Mishnah deals with either a table of marble [which is not susceptible to uncleanness] or a table that can be taken apart and is not susceptible to becoming unclean.

        B.   *What is the reason of the House of Shammai?*
So that the liquids which are on the napkin may not become unclean from the cushion and go and render his hands unclean.
And what is the reason of the House of Hillel?
The condition of doubtful uncleanness with respect to the hands is always regarded as clean.
Another reason: The [question of the cleanness of] hands does not apply to unconsecrated food [which in any case is not made unclean by unclean hands which are unclean in the second remove].

        C.   *And according to the House of Shammai,* does [the question of the cleanness of] hands [indeed] apply to unconsecrated food?...

8:4   **The House of Shammai say, "They clean the house and afterward wash the hands." And the House of Hillel say, "They wash the hands and afterward clean the house."**

I.   A.   *What is the reason of the House of Shammai?*
        B.   Because of the waste of food.
        C.   *And what is the reason of the House of Hillel?*
        D.   If the servant is clever, he removes the crumbs which are less than an olive's bulk, and they wash their hands and afterward they clean the house.

8:5   **The House of Shammai say, "Light, and food, and spices, and** *Habdalah.*** And the House of Hillel say, "Light, and spices, and food, and** *Habdalah.*** The House of Shammai say, "'Who created the light of the fire.'" And the House of Hillel say, "'Who creates the lights of the fire.'"**

I.   A.   <u>It was taught:</u>
        B.   <u>R. Judah said, "The House of Shammai and the House of Hillel did not differ concerning the [blessing for] the meal, that it comes at the beginning, or concerning *Habdalah*, that it comes at the end. And concerning what did they differ? Concerning the light and spices, for the House of Shammai say, 'Spices and light.' And the House of Hillel say, 'Light and spices.'"</u>
        C.   <u>R. Ba and R. Judah in the name of Rab [said], "The law is in accord with him who says, 'Spices and afterward light.' [That is, Judah's House of Shammai.]"</u>
        D.   <u>The House of Shammai say, "The cup [should be] in his right hand, and the sweet oil in his left hand. He says [the blessing for] the cup and afterward says the blessing for the sweet oil."</u>
        E.   <u>The House of Hillel say, "The sweet oil [should be] in his right hand and the cup in his left hand, and he says [the blessing for] the sweet oil and rubs it in the head of the servant. If the servant is a disciple</u>

of a sage, he rubs it on the wall, for it is not fitting for a disciple of a sage to go forth scented in public."....

L.   **[The House of Shammai say, "'Who created....'"]**

M.   According to the opinion of the House of Shammai, [one should say as the blessing for wine], "Who created the fruit of the vine" [instead of "who creates...," as actually is said].

N.   According to the opinion of the House of Hillel, [one should say,] "Who creates the fruit of the vine" [as is indeed the case].

O.   [The Shammaite reply:]

P.   The wine is newly created every year, but the fire is not newly created every hour....

This truncated passage serves to show how heavily the Yerushalmi's compositions' authors have relied upon the Tosefta's reading of the Mishnah. Stated simply: Without the Tosefta, there would have been no Talmud – at least, at the present passage of the Mishnah. The same characterizes the second Talmud's approach to the same Mishnah paragraphs. It would not materially advance the program of this book to proceed to examine that document in detail. It suffices to make only one observation.

The Bavli's authorship appeals directly to the Tosefta, without addressing the program of the Yerushalmi. While, therefore, both Talmuds are organized as commentaries to the Mishnah, they are entirely autonomous of one another. The Babylonian Talmud does not expand upon the earlier one but forms its own discussions in accord with its own program. While the Bavli treats the Mishnah in the same way as does the Yerushalmi, in addition, the authorship of the second Talmud moved in a direction all its own, systematically commenting in large and cogent compositions upon not only the Mishnah but also Scripture, that is, on both the Oral and the Written Torahs.

4

The Facts of Mishnah-Tosefta Relationships [1]: The Tosefta as a Commentary to the Mishnah

The passages of the Tosefta presented in this section cite verbatim and then explain passages of the Mishnah and can be understood only in the context of the Mishnah. These examples clearly contradict Smith's claim, since in these cases the Tosefta cites the Mishnah verbatim and then glosses it. Smith does not allege that one Gospel cites and glosses the other. I give both the Mishnah and then the Tosefta passage in its case. The Mishnah, when cited in the Tosefta, is given in italics, and this shows in a very graphic way how the latter document has cited and then glossed the former. In these passages – filling up approximately half of the volume of the Tosefta over all – there can be no doubt that the formulation of the Tosefta's statements took place after the Mishnah's statements were wholly in place and recognized as authoritative, and that must mean, after the Mishnah had reached closure and probably after the document had assumed that position of authority that required commentary, extension, clarification, and application. The passages given here time and again treat the Mishnah as decided law and clarify its points of reference and the application of its law.

In order to provide access to the context, I include some passages that properly belong in Chapter Five. Where the predominant interest is in Mishnah exegesis narrowly construed, I classify a passage in the present part. Where the interest is in the expression in an autonomous framework of a passage that serves to expand and clarify the sense of the Mishnah and that can be understood only in the context of the Mishnah, I classify the passage in Chapter Five. Any other arrangement would have denied the reader access to the Tosefta, in relationship to the Mishnah, in its own terms. But we grasp the Tosefta only in relationship to the Mishnah, and hence it seemed to me best to present as a single set an entire composite of the Tosefta, defined by a common reference point in a given Mishnah passage. This leads to some small measure of unclarity in the organization of this introduction, but it does provide a very clear entry into the Tosefta, and that is my main purpose in this pages.

In seeing groupings of Tosefta paragraphs, all part of a sequence and all referring, or at least relevant, to a single Mishnah paragraph, readers will soon observe an interesting principle of organization. The framers of the Tosefta will be seen to have followed this order in setting forth their paragraphs: [1] passages that cite and gloss a Mishnah paragraph; [2] passages that do not cite a Mishnah paragraph verbatim but that amplify or clarify or otherwise extend and expand the sense of the same Mishnah paragraph that to begin with is cited; [3] passages that compile materials relevant to the theme or subject matter of a Mishnah paragraph, but that do not cite that paragraph verbatim or even pursue its proposition. We shall notice, therefore, a very clear-cut principle of editing, in which the different types of Tosefta paragraph, differentiated by reference to their relationship to the corresponding Mishnah paragraph, are set forth in a fixed order.

Since, we know, we deal here with the first talmud, prior to the Talmud of the Land of Israel, which was the second, and the Talmud of Babylonia, the third and final one, these observations require reconsideration of a widely circulated, but utterly false, proposition. It is that the Talmud (people ordinarily mean by that imprecise term, the Talmud of Babylonia) is a mess. They see no order, no purpose, no structure, no beginning, middle, or end. But that judgment only tells us that those who repeat it have no grasp of the highly articulated order, purpose, structure of the Talmud of Babylonia; and the same is to be said for the first and second talmuds as well.

If the Tosefta's framers have structured their document with such precision, in relationship to the Mishnah, and order, in relationship to the three types of materials they had in hand, what shall we say of the two Talmuds to follow? Even the superficial survey, given in Chapter Three, of the treatment of Mishnah-tractate Berakhot Chapter Eight in the Tosefta, Yerushalmi, and Bavli, permits us to identify the types of discourse and the order of those types. It would lead us far afield to dwell on that point. It suffices here only to insist that this, the most confusing and confused of all rabbinic writings of the formative age, demonstrably is made up of three distinct types of discourse, and ordinarily sets forth those three types of discourse in a fixed order. Any novice in the study of the Bavli knows even from first impressions that the same is so there, and, it goes without saying, a sustained inquiry into the Yerushalmi will produce the same result. The fault that has produced the false and contrary impression is simple. People are used to seeing these documents in their smallest whole units of thought, meaning, sentence by sentence (if not word by word); and then they are used to free-associating. Having no sense of the paragraphs, let alone the chapters, they deny themselves a view of the whole. But that perspective, seeing the whole all at once and all together, gives us a glimpse of the aesthetic power of these remarkable writings.

Mishnah-tractate Kelim 25:7-8

A. All utensils have outer parts and an inner part, and they further have a part by which they are held (BYT SBY'H) [that is, a finger-hold sunk into the edge of the vessel which does not become unclean in the outer or inner part of the utensil].
B. R. Tarfon says, "[This distinction in the outer parts applies only] to a large wooden trough."
C. R. Aqiva says, "To cups."
D. R. Meir says, "To the unclean and the clean hands."
E. Said R. Yosé, "They have spoken only concerning clean hands alone." [Danby: "If a man touched the outer part with unclean hands, he does not render the holding part unclean and vice versa; or if clean hands touched one of the parts and the other part was unclean, the hands do not become clean (= D). According to R. Yosé it is only for this latter case that provision is made in distinguishing an outer part and a holding part."]

M. Kel. 25:7 (Y. Hag. 3:1, Y. Ber. 8:2; B. Hag. 22b, B. Ber. 52a)

F. [Yosé continues:] "How so (KYSD)?
G. "[If] one's hands were clean, and the outer parts of the cup were unclean, [and] one took [the cup] with its holding part, he need not worry lest his hands be made unclean on the outer parts of the cup."
H. [If] one was drinking from a cup, the outer parts of which are unclean, one does not worry lest the liquid which is in his mouth be made unclean on the outer parts of the cup and go and render the [whole] cup unclean.
I. A kettle [unclean on the outside] which is boiling – one does not worry lest the liquids go forth from it and touch its outer parts and [having become unclean in the first degree] go back to the inside [and make it unclean].

M. Kel. 25:8

Before us are two generations' glosses of A. We now are told that in utensils we distinguish three, not two parts. In addition to the inside and the outside, we also differentiate a holding part.

In B-C Tarfon and Aqiva differ as to the objects which are going to be subject to the distinctive rule of the holding place. Tarfon says this applies to a large wooden trough, but not to small utensils. Aqiva says the rule applies to cups. If the outer part of the cup is made unclean, one can still drink via the holding place and the liquid will not be unclean; this "holding place" seems to form some kind of spout. That ends the Yavnean's gloss. Now the Ushans will introduce a gloss developing Aqiva's notion.

Meir says the distinction regarding cups is made in respect to clean and unclean hands. He therefore introduces two cases. There is a distinction between the holding place and the outer part in this regard: If one's hands were unclean, and the outer side of the cup was clean and if there was a little liquid on the outer part of the cup, one holds the cup with the holding place and does not have to be concerned that the liquid on the outer part of the cup will be made unclean by the unclean hands and then render the whole cup unclean.

Yosé says that *unclean* hands will not enjoy that kind of lenient ruling. But clean hands are protected by the rule. Then 25:8 explains the meaning of "clean hands" in this context. (It seems to me Yosé's view is consistent with B. Bekh. 38a.)

F introduces the whole. While the pericope is linked to Yosé's saying, explaining his view, G in fact will apply to Meir's as well, for he agrees that the matter concerns clean hands: the hands are clean but also wet; the outer part of the cup is unclean. If one holds the holding part, the outer part of the cup is unclean. If one holds the holding part, the outer part of the cup is deemed *not* to affect the liquids on his hands. Or further, if the outer part is unclean, the person relies on the holding place and does not have to worry about the liquids being made unclean on the outer part of the cup.

H presents a new rule. If one is drinking from a cup with unclean outer parts, one does not have to worry about the effect of that uncleanness on the liquid in his mouth. The liquid will not be made unclean and make the cup unclean on the inside. Aqiva (T. Kel. B.B. 3:9) gives a pertinent rule. I then gives us the same lenient ruling. The whole depends on Joshua's opinion (M. Yad. 3:1), that liquids render the utensil unclean. The sages hold only a utensil made unclean by a Father of uncleanness made the hands unclean. It would be difficult to show a more perfect progression of rules than the set going from Joshua through Aqiva to Meir + Yosé.

A.   Said R. Aqiva, "They made mention of the holding place only for cups, so that one may not drink and [it result that] each drop render the next unclean (WR'SWN R'SWN MTM').

B.   "Unclean liquids which were put in the holding place of a cup, and which a clean load touched –
      "the loaf is made unclean.

C. "Clean liquids which were put at the holding place of the cup, and which an unclean loaf touched –
"the liquids are made unclean.

D. "Unclean liquids which were put on the ground, and a cup, the outer sides or holding place of which are clean, touched them –

E. "the outer parts of the cup are made unclean.

F. "The clean liquids which were put on the ground, and a cup, the outer sides or holding place of which are clean, touched them –
"the liquids are made unclean."

G. R. Meir says, "*For unclean hands:*

H. "*How so?*

I. "It is not possible to say [that we are dealing with dry hands], for hands do not render unclean when they are dry. It is not possible to say [the hands render unclean] when full of liquids. For before one can touch them, the liquids [already] were made unclean.

J. "It therefore follows that if one's hands were unclean, and the outer parts of the cup were clean, and liquid was dripping on the outer parts of the cup, one holds it [the cup] on its holding place and does not take account lest the liquids which are on the outer parts of the cup be made unclean on account of his hands and go and make the cup unclean."

T. Kel. B.B. 3:9

L. R. Yosé says, "*Concerning clean hands:*
"*How so?* [If] one's hands were clean and on them was some moisture and the outer parts of the cup were unclean, one takes it [the cup] with its holding place and does not worry lest the liquids which are on his hands be made unclean on account of the cup and go and make his hands unclean."

T. Kel. B.B. 3:10 (T. Reng., p. 77, lines 7-26)

M. R. Tarfon says, "A large trough of wood has a holding place.

N. "This is general rule: If one takes it with one [hand], its holding place is with one [finger]. If one takes it with two, its holding place measures two [fingers]. The place at which one takes hold of it – there is its holding place."

O. R. Judah says, "A utensil which has a rim and an ear and a handle has no holding place [for it does not need one].

T. Kel. B.B. 3:11 (T. Reng., p. 78, lines 1-4)

T. develops and explains the enigmatic remark of Aqiva. "For cups" is now linked to M. 25:8H. M. has held that if one is drinking from a cup with unclean outer parts, one does not have to worry that the liquid in his mouth become unclean on the outer parts of the cup and go and make the cup unclean.

Sens interprets as follows: Aqiva in A holds, contrary to M., that that *is* a serious consideration. The holding place is important because one should drink from that place and so avoid the unclean outer part of the cup. But *Mishnah Aharonah* explains Aqiva's saying in accord with M., as follows: Aqiva is concerned that we not produce uncleanness for the liquid. Drinking from the cup invariably brings the lips into contact with the outer part of the cup, and the liquid will then be made unclean. Then Aqiva's point in T. is that, if we do not distinguish that which is unclean in the first degree, that liquid unclean in the first degree will render [the whole cup] unclean, as in A. Lieberman *TR* III, p. 80, which says *MA* is correct.

Saul Lieberman (Personal Letter, July 15, 1973) explains A as follows: "R. Aqiva's view is that the rabbis distinguished between the back of the vessel and its holding place, because, if we take the holding place as part of the back, which is usually wet and impure, then the holding place is always considered impure as well. When the man drinks, it often happens that the fluid overruns the brim and goes into the holding place and then back into his mouth; the fluid which overruns the rest of the back of the vessel slips down and does not return. Therefore, argues R. Aqiva, the holding place was legally separated from the rest of the back of the vessel and considered pure, in order that each drop of fluid in the process of drinking should not become impure. This law applies only to the case of the holding place which was pure, although the rest of the back was impure. But, on the contrary, if the holding place was impure, and a loaf of bread touched the back of the vessel, the loaf is impure, because in that case the back of the vessel is not separated from the holding place. Similarly, when the holding place is full of fluids and at that time an impure loaf touched the back of the vessel, the loaf is impure. And likewise when impure fluids on the ground touched the holding place only, the whole back of the vessel becomes impure. See HD p. 151." The passage of HD to which Lieberman refers us interprets Aqiva's saying as follows: The lenient rule, distinguishing the thickness of the holding place from the remainder of the outer part of the utensil, does not apply indiscriminately, but solely to the matter explained in the Mishnah which follows Aqiva's saying [M = H]. "And this also is what is taught here: One who drinks from a cup, the outer parts of which are unclean, and puts the holding place in his mouth need not fear lest that which is unclean in the first degree, which he is drinking, render unclean the liquid which is on the outer parts of the cup, so that he may end up drinking unclean liquid. Specifically in this matter we do not take account [of that fact]...but if unclean liquids are found on the holding place and a clean loaf touched the outer part of the cup, even though it did not touch the holding place, the loaf is made unclean...."

B goes on to say this rule applies in respect to the cited case. But unclean liquid on the holding place of the cup *will* make a loaf unclean. And C gives the contrary case. In D-E, the outer part of the cup or holding place which touches unclean liquids is going to be made unclean. Lieberman preserves the reference in Zuckermandel to the holding place, and gives the following: "Clean liquids which were placed on the ground, and a cup whose outer parts were unclean or [the unclean] holding place [of which] touched them – the liquids are made unclean." I have followed his view in my translation. Accordingly, in B, C, D, or E, the holding place and the outer parts of the cup produce equivalent effects. So B-E explain the limits of A, the whole in accord with M.

Meir's explanation of the law then follows (G-J). Meir first of all excludes the possibility that the lenient ruling about distinguishing the holding place from the outer part of the cup applies to a situation where dry hands touch an unclean cup. If the hands are dry, they will not make anything unclean. The hands therefore are to be regarded as moist. So, J continues, we deal with a case in which the hands were unclean (that is, G), and the outer part of the cup was clean *and* wet. If with *unclean* hands one holds the cup on the holding place, one does not have to worry about the effect of the hands upon the liquid of the cup, therefore about contaminating the cup through the liquid. That is a perfectly clear explanation of Meir's original saying. But M. has represented Meir as speaking of both unclean and clean hands. It is *Yosé* in M. who speaks of unclean hands alone.

Now Yosé's position is explained – that is, Meir's in M.! If the hands are clean and wet and the outer part of the cup unclean, the holding place may be used. Then the liquids on the hand will not be made unclean on account of the cup, etc.

The important difference between Meir and Yosé therefore is whether the lenient rule pertains primarily to the cup or primarily to the hands. If it speaks of the cup then G-J follow, that is, Meir's position in T. = Yosé in M. If it speaks of the person's hands, then L may also be stated, that is, the lenient ruling is given to protect person's hands, not the cup alone.

M. gives up Tarfon in M. Kel. 25:7B. N then expands the ruling and explains how it is to be applied.

O stands entirely apart from the foregoing. The converse is a very broad rule: A utensil which has no rim, ear, or handle is going to have a holding place and this without regard to whether it is solely a cup, as Aqiva had said, is a trough, as in Tarfon's view, or a cup in accord with the views of Yosé and Meir. I should suppose this very lenient conception is what is limited by the Yavneans and their successors.

A-B stand by themselves. Vessels used for Holy Things are in a different category from all others (which proves beyond doubt that nearly the entire tractate deals with vessels used in ordinary everyday life). The foregoing distinction does not apply. The Temple vessels are not divided. And when immersed, each must be immersed by itself, not inside any other utensil.

D explains C, and the point is clear. The completion of the manufacture of a utensil may be marked by a person's intention. If someone has decided to use a utensil, even though it is not entirely done, it is subject to uncleanness. But if one has decided to change the purpose or use of a vessel or to rework a completed utensil so that it will not be subject to uncleanness, he must actually carry out some action in that connection. A good example is a ring; if it is for an animal, it is clean, but if it is for a man, it is unclean. Merely deciding to use a man's ring for an animal does not suffice to make it insusceptible. One can still change his mind until he actually makes it into a new utensil.

> A. Utensils used for Holy Things have no outer part or inner part and have no holding place, and they do not immerse utensils in the midst of [other] utensils for Holy Things.
> B. Said R. Yosé, "This is redundant (LSWN KPWL): Whatever has outer parts and an inner part has a holding place, and [whatever] does not have outer parts and an inside [obviously] does not have a holding place.
> C. "In this respect, the Holy Things of the sanctuary and the Holy Things of the provinces are governed by the same rule."
>
> T. Kel. B.B. 3:12 (T. Reng., p. 78, lines 5-9)

B gives Yosé's comment on A (= M. 25:9A), a good gloss. One does not have even to allude to a holding place in this context.

> A. All utensils descend to their uncleanness with [mere] intention, but do not ascend from their uncleanness except with an act which changes them (AYNWY M^cSH).
> B. R. Judah says, "An act which changes them *for the worse* (LQLQWL)."
>
> T. Kel. B.B. 3:13 (T. Reng., p. 78, lines 10-12; B. Shab. 52b)

The same pattern recurs. B comments on M. 25:9D. Judah's opinion is that the change cannot involve merely repairing a utensil.

The following is part of a much larger case in which the Tosefta systematically cites and glosses statements of the Mishnah.

Mishnah-tractate Niddah 1:3-5

> A. R. Eliezer says, "Four women [who do not regularly have a flow (= M. 1:1G) (Maimonides)] fall into the category of those for whom the time [of first seeing blood] suffices [Danby: that they be deemed unclean only from their time of suffering a flow]:

B.   "(1) the virgin, (2) the pregnant woman, (3) the nursing mother, and (4) the old lady."

C.   Said R. Joshua, "I heard only [that this rule applies to the] virgin."

D.   But the law is in accord with the opinion of R. Eliezer.

M. 1:3

E.   Who is (1) *the virgin?*

F.   Any girl who never in her life saw a drop of [menstrual] blood, even though she is married.

G.   (2) *A pregnant woman?*

H.   Once it is known that the foetus is present [= three months].

I.   (3) *A nursing mother?*

J.   Until she will wean her son [= twenty-four months, M. Git. 7:6].

K.   [If] she gave her son to a wet nurse, weaned him, or he died –

L.   R. Meir says, "She conveys uncleanness [to everything she touched] during the preceding twenty-four hours."

M.   And sages say, "Sufficient for her is her time." ["It is enough for her that she be deemed unclean only from her time of suffering a flow."]

M. 1:4

N.   (4) Who is *an old woman?*

O.   Any woman for whom three periods have gone by without a flow near to the time of her old age [menopause].

P.   R. Eliezer (MS, M, P, PB, L: Eleazar [see *Nussah*, p. 1176]) says, "Any woman [not only an old lady] for whom three periods have passed without her suffering a flow – sufficient for her is her time."
["It is enough for her that she be deemed unclean only from her time of suffering a flow."]

Q.   R. Yosé says, "A pregnant woman and a nursing mother for whom three periods have passed [without their suffering a flow] – sufficient for them is their time."

M. 1:5 (Y. Nid. 1:3, 4)

The present unit is devoted to the exposition of Eliezer's opinion, M. 1:3A. As noted, he has his dispute with Shammai, M. 1:1A, all women versus four women; or with M. 1:1G. His point is clear. In these four cases, he holds, a drop of blood signifies the onset of the menstrual cycle. But all other women who have a regular flow are unclean retroactively. Eliezer does not specify the extent of the retroactivity. Perhaps Meir supplies the limits of his opinion. Since retroactivity is a concession, it should be the shorter of the two intervals, twenty-four hours or the period from the last examination (M. 1:1D-F), and I take it that Meir selects the former as the shorter. The main point in all four instances is that the appearance of blood is unusual, in which case we depend upon the first appearance to delimit the start of the capacity to effect contamination. Joshua's dispute, along the lines of his sayings at M. Par. 1:1 (Part IX, p. 23), has to do with what he claims is an oral tradition. D is of course a gloss; it certainly is logical to assign the decided law to the party whose opinions are now carefully to be spelled out, not bypassed.

M. 1:4K-M supply an Ushan gloss to Eliezer's opinion, explaining the matter of the status of the nursing mother. Sages say that for the first twenty-four months, during which time the woman is in the status of the nursing mother, the leniency applies, even though the actual nursing is no longer done by her.

M. 1:5N-Q then take up a separate matter, the old woman. This category is first defined, O. P-Q are added because of the reference to the passing of three periods without menstrual blood. Eliezer/Eleazar, P, does not wish to limit the rule to a woman near menopause, so he differs from O. The same applies to anyone, not only to the woman near old age. Yosé disagrees with Eliezer/Eleazar, P; limiting the matter to a pregnant woman and a nursing mother, as against *any woman* of O and P. Do Eliezer/Eleazar and Yosé disagree with Eliezer of M. 1:3A? It is difficult to say, since their sayings stand quite separate from Eliezer's at A. That is, M. 1:3A's Eliezer says four women fall into the present category, as against any woman who has missed three periods – not exactly to the point. Yosé then limits matters, as I said, to the pregnant woman and nursing mother, two of Eliezer of M. 1:3's four categories – again, not quite precisely the terms of M. 1:3's Eliezer, but clearly the terms of M. 1:5's Eliezer/Eleazar.

Accordingly, I am inclined to see the last dispute, P-Q, as autonomous of the original matter, generated by M. 1:5N-O, but secondary and peripheral to M. 1:3A-B. Does Yosé disagree with M. 1:4G, I? On the surface, he surely does, since M. 1:4 says that a pregnant woman and a nursing mother fall into the category of those for whom the moment of discovery begins the period of uncleanness, without retroactive contamination, and Yosé says that is the case only if we have three months in which the period is missed. But, in redactional context, Yosé is made to disagree with Eliezer/Eleazar, and we shall have to follow the redactor in interpreting his opinion in the setting of P, although, as is clear, it can be read as a disagreement with the articulation of M. 1:4. The difference is trivial.

A.   *R. Eliezer says, "Four women – sufficient for them is their time: a virgin, a pregnant woman, a nursing mother, and an old woman."*

B.   *Said R. Joshua, "I heard only the virgin."*

C.   Said to him R. Eliezer, "They do not say to him who has not seen the new [moon] to come and give testimony, but to him who has seen it.

"You have not heard, but we have heard.

"You have heard one, but we have heard four."

D. All the days of R. Eliezer the people followed the rule laid down by him. After R. Eliezer died, R. Joshua restored the matter to its former status.

E. *And the law is in accord with R. Eliezer.*

T. 1:5, p. 223, lines 5-12 (B. Nid.
7b, Y. Nid. 1:2, B. Er. 41a)

A-B = M. 1:3A-C; E = M. 1:3D. What is supplied is C and D. See *Eliezer* I, pp. 323-324, and, on other versions of D, *TR* III, p. 257.

A. *Who is a virgin?*

B. *Any girl who has never seen a drop of blood in her life,*

C. and even if she is married and had children, I call her a virgin, until she will see the first drop [of menstrual blood].

D. It comes out that they did not refer to virgin in respect to the tokens of virginity but a virgin in respect to menstrual blood.

T. 1:6, p. 223, lines 13-16 (Y. Nid.
1:3, B. Nid. 8b)

A-B = M. 1:4E-F. C-D supplement M.

A. *Who is a pregnant woman?*

B. *Once the presence of the foetus is recognized –*

C. [Zuckermandel, p. 642, 1. 1, Lieberman, *TR* III, p. 257, Y. Nid. 1:3, B. Nid. 8b: *Said Sumkhos in the name of R. Meir:*] three months, as it is said, *And it came to pass at the end of three months* (Gen. 38:24).

D. [If] she was in the presumption of being pregnant and saw a drop of blood and afterward she miscarried something which is not a human foetus – [B. Nid 8b: she is still presumed to be pregnant and] sufficient for her is her time.

E. And even though there is no scriptural proof of the matter, there is scriptural allusion to the matter: *We were with child, we writhed, we have as it were brought forth wind* (Isa. 26:18).

T. 1:7, p. 223, lines 17-21 (Y. Nid.
1:3, B. Nid. 8b)

A-B = M. 1:4G-H. D is an important addition, because it gives a liberal definition of those pregnant women subject to M. 1:3A's lenient ruling. Y. gives D in the name of Judah.

A. A girl who did not reach her time for seeing blood and who saw a drop of blood –

B. at the first and at the second appearance of the blood, sufficient for her is her time.

C. [But when she sees] the third drop of blood, she imparts uncleanness [to what she touched] during the preceding twenty-four hour period.

D. [If] she missed her flow for three periods and then saw a drop of blood, sufficient for her is her time.

E. And once [a girl] has reached her time for seeing blood and she saw a first drop [*TR* III, p. 257:] sufficient for her is her time, and [after she saw] a second, she imparts uncleanness during the preceding twenty-four hour period.

F.   And at the third [period] – sufficient for her is her time.

G.   [If] she missed three periods and then she saw a drop of blood, she imparts uncleanness during the preceding twenty-four hour period. [B. Nid. 9b: If she missed three periods and again observed a discharge, sufficient for her is her time.]

T. 1:8, p. 224, lines 1-6 (B. Nid. 9b)

H.   And from what time is a girl likely to see [a drop of blood]?

I.   From the time that she will produce two pubic hairs.

J.   Said R. Eleazar, McSH B: "A young girl in Hairalu (Y.: cYYTLW) whose time has come to see blood and who missed three periods, and the case came before sages, and they said, 'Sufficient for her is her time [of actually observing a flow].'"

K.   They said to him, "It was an interim ruling [and not meant as established law]." [Y. Nid. 1:4: "You were a minor, and a minor has no right of testimony."]

T. 1:9, p. 224, lines 7-10 (Y. Nid.
1:1,4; B. Nid. 9b)

T. now supplies secondary materials, pertinent to M. 1:3B1, the virgin. How do we legislate for the passage of a girl from the one status, a virgin, for whom the time of the appearance suffices to delimit the period of presumed contamination, to that of a woman, who, Eliezer holds, contaminates for the preceding twenty-four hours (or presumably, for less than that time if there have been intervening examinations)? A-D spell out the stages in the progress to womanhood. In the case of a girl before puberty, we rule as follows: At the first and second appearance of blood, the girl remains a virgin (in the present sense). At the third, she is deemed to be like all other women. E then introduced a second problem. What happens if a girl has reached puberty? Then it is expected that she will menstruate regularly. Therefore, once the girl has reached puberty, the first drop leaves her in the former status, but the second confirms her new status as a woman. G brings us to M. 1:5P, a woman who has missed three periods. There Eliezer/Eleazar had told us that sufficient for her is her time.

H picks up the matter of E, at what point do we impose the distinction fundamental to A/E. J-K raise a further issue. What if a girl reaches puberty and does not menstruate? Sages are alleged by Eleazar to say that she falls into the category of a woman who has had a period and then misses it for three successive months. His position is therefore the same as the Eleazar/Eliezer of M. 1:5P and is assigned to sages. K rejects the precedent.

A.   R. Yosé and R. Simeon say, "A pregnant woman and a nursing
     mother – her time is not sufficient for her until she will miss three
     periods.
B.   "And the days of her pregnancy join together with the days of her
     nursing."

T. 1:10, p. 224, lines 11-13 (Y. Nid.
1:4, B. Nid. 10b, 36a)

Yosé (+ M. 1:5Q) and Simeon do not agree with Eliezer, M. 1:3B2 + 3.
They demand evidence that the menstrual cycle has been interrupted. B
further qualifies the matter. B is explained at B. Nid. 10b: "In what
manner? If there was a break of two periods during her pregnancy and of
one during her nursing, or two during her nursing and one during her
pregnancy, or of one and a half during her pregnancy and one and a half
during her nursing, they are all combined into a series of three periods.

A.   [If] an old lady missed three periods and then saw a drop of blood –
     sufficient for her is her time [for she is assumed to have entered
     menopause].
B.   [If] she [again] missed three periods and saw a drop of blood, [still]
     sufficient for her is her time.
C.   [If] she [again] missed three periods and saw a drop of blood, lo,
     she is equivalent to all other women. She renders unclean for the
     preceding twenty-four hours or from one examination to the next.
D.   Not [only] that she has settled on a fixed period, but even if she has
     diminished [or] she had added to it.
E.   If she missed three of them and saw a drop of blood, sufficient for
     her is her time.
F.   If she [again] missed the three of them and saw a drop of blood,
     sufficient for her is her time.
G.   If she [again] missed the three of them and saw a drop of blood, lo,
     she is like all other women and conveys uncleanness for the
     preceding twenty-four hour period or from one examination to the
     next.
H.   But that she has established a period for herself.

T. 1:11, p. 224, lines 13-19, p. 225,
lines 1-2 (Y. Nid 1:5, B. Nid. 9b)

T. carries forward the issue of M. 1:5. We have said that an old
woman, for whom the time of flow suffices to define the period of
contamination, is one who has missed three periods near the time of
menopause. But what happens if there is a renewed flow? A-B hold that
for a period of six months – missing the flow three periods, then seeing it,
two such sequences in succession – the woman remains in her
established status. But if this then happens in a third three-period
sequence, the old woman falls into the category of normal women, as at
C. She has established a regular period, F, but if she again misses it, she
conveys uncleanness retroactively (*TR* III, p. 258). B. Nid. 9b's version of

C is, "This is the case not only where she observed it at successively decreasing intervals or increasing intervals." Following Rashi, Slotki (p. 60, n. 10) comments, "Irrespective of whether (a) the first interval extended over ninety-three days, the second over ninety-two, and the third only over ninety or (b) the first extended over ninety-one days, the second over ninety-two, and the third over ninety-three days."

A.   *The four women* concerning whom they have said, "Sufficient for them is their time" – how so?
B.   [If] she saw a bloodstain and afterward saw a drop of blood – sufficient for her is her time [and the stain is not deemed equivalent to blood].
C.   [If] she missed three periods between one appearance and another appearance of blood and did not see a drop of blood and afterward saw a drop of blood – sufficient for her is her time.
D.   [If] she missed three periods during the days of her purifying and did not see a drop of blood, and afterward saw a drop of blood, sufficient for her is her time.

T. 1:12, p. 225, lines 3-7 (Y. Nid. 1:4, B. Nid. 36a)

A = M. 1:3A. Now we have an illustrative case, parallel to M. 1:2. The stain is distinct from the drop of blood. The point of the set is the same as at T. 1:8 for the young girl who missed three periods, and T. 1:11 for the old lady. Missing the periods does not remove the woman from the present category.

A.   "A nursing mother whose infant died during the twenty-four months of nursing imparts uncleanness within the preceding twenty-four hour period.
B.   "Therefore if she goes on and nurses her infant, even during a period of five years, sufficient for her is her time," the words of R. Meir.
C.   R. Judah and R. Yosé and R. Simeon say, "Sufficient for her is her time only during the twenty-four months in which it is normal to nurse the infant.
D.   "Therefore if she goes on and nurses her infant even for five years, only the twenty-four months apply to her, during which she falls under the rule of the nursing mother."

T. 2:1, p. 225, lines 9-14 (B. Nid. 9a)

E.   "[A nursing mother] whose husband died – lo, she should not be betrothed nor should she be wed until twenty-four months have been completed," the words of R. Meir.
F.   And R. Judah says, "Eighteen months."
G.   And R. Jonathan b. Joseph says, "The House of Shammai say, 'Twenty-four months,' and the House of Hillel say, 'Eighteen months.'"

H. Said Rabban Simeon b. Gamaliel, "In accord with the opinion of the one who says, 'Twenty-four months,' she is permitted to be wed in twenty-one months. In accord with the opinion of the one who says, 'Eighteen months,' she may be wed in fifteen months, for the milk deteriorates only after three months [of conception]."

T. 2:2, p. 225, lines 15-19, p. 226, lines 1-3 (B. Ket. 60a-b)

I. "An infant continues to suckle all twenty-four months. From that point onward, he is like one who sucks [from] an abomination," the words of R. Eliezer.

J. And R. Joshua says, "The infant continues to suck even for five years. If he is separated from the nipple and returned after twenty-four months, lo, this is he who is like one that sucks from an abomination.

T. 2:3, p. 226, lines 4-7 (Y. Ket. 5:6, Y. Nid. 1:4, B. Ket. 60a)

K. A woman is obligated to care for her child for twenty-four months. The same rule applies whether it is her own child or whether she is given a child to suckle.

L. The woman to whom a child is given to suckle should not do [additional] work [while caring] for him and should not suckle another child with him.

T. 2:4, p. 226, lines 8-10 (B. Ket. 59b, 60b)

M. An infant who recognizes his mother – they do not give him to a wet nurse because of the danger to life.

N. An infant sucks from the gentile woman and from the unclean cow, and from any of them does he suck, and even on the Sabbath. If he was weaned, it is prohibited.

O. Abba Saul says, "We would suck from the clean animal on the festival."

T. 2:5, p. 226, lines 11-14 (B. Yev. 14a)

P. Three kinds of women have intercourse with a *mokh* [contraceptive device]: a girl under age, a pregnant woman, and a nursing mother.

Q. A girl under age – lest she become pregnant and die.

R. What is a girl under age? From eleven years and one day until twelve years and one day.
One younger than that or older than that – one has intercourse in the normal way.
Therefore one has intercourse in the normal way and does not scruple.

S. A pregnant woman – lest she make the foetus into a sandal.

T. A nursing mother – lest she kill her infant.

U. For R. Meir did say, "The entire period of twenty-four months one winnows inside and scatters [seed] outside."

And sages say, "One has intercourse in the normal way, and the Omnipresent will look out for him, as it is said, *The Lord guards the innocent* (Ps. 116:6)."

> T. 2:6, p. 226, lines 15-23 (B. Yev. 12b)

V.   A man should not marry a woman made pregnant by his fellow or one who is nursing the child of his fellow, as it is said, *Do not remove an ancient landmark or enter the fields of the fatherless* (Prov. 23:10).

> T. 2:7, p. 227, lines 1-3

The interests of the composite are quite separate from those of M. The sole point of intersection is at T. 2:1, which goes over the ground of M. 1:4K-M. T. rephrases the dispute, giving each party two clauses. But the "reason" is based upon the opinion. M.'s sages are now identified. E-F go on to a second dispute on the nursing mother. Jonathan gives the same opinions to the Houses, with Meir equivalent to the Shammaites, Judah to the Hillelites. Simeon b. Gamaliel then observes that for three months after remarriage the breast-feeding may continue.

It suffices to conclude with a simple observation. At no point does Luke's version of the Sermon on the Mount cite and gloss Matthew's, or Matthew's, Luke's. That is not how the two Gospels relate to one another. Smith's fundamental allegation proves contrary to the facts.

5

The Facts of Mishnah-Tosefta Relationships [2]: The Tosefta as a Complement to the Mishnah

The passages of the Tosefta presented in this section do not cite verbatim, but do serve to explain passages of the Mishnah and can be fully and exhaustively understood only in the context of the Mishnah. Because the relationships between the Mishnah's and Tosefta's compositions of this classification most closely approximate those Smith alleges he perceives between Matthew's and Luke's materials, I give a sizable sample of sources.

I give both the Mishnah and then the Tosefta passage in its case. In order to provide access to the context, I include some passages that properly belong in Chapter Four, above. Where the interest is in the expression in an autonomous framework of a passage that serves to expand and clarify the sense of the Mishnah and that can be understood only in the context of the Mishnah, I classify the passage here. Where the predominant interest is in Mishnah exegesis narrowly construed, I classify a passage in Chapter Four. Now only so, but readers may well consider that my classification is not compelling and may prefer a different way of seeing things. That is surely a quite proper response to the problem. It remains to observe that the three types of relationship between a Mishnah passage and a Tosefta passage ordinarily follow a fixed order: [1] commentary, [2] complement, [3] compilation of pertinent but autonomous materials.

Mishnah-tractate Miqvaot 2:1-2

A.   The [indubitably] unclean person who went down to immerse –

B.   it is a doubt whether he immersed or whether he did not immerse,

C.   and even if he did immerse –
D.   it is a doubt whether there are forty seahs [of rainwater] in it, or whether there are not [forty seahs in it] –
E.   two immersion pools, in one of which there are forty seahs, and in one of which there are not forty seahs –
F.   he immersed in one of them and does not know in which one of them he immersed –
G.   his matter of doubt is deemed unclean.

M. 2:1 (B. Er. 35b)

A.   An immersion pool which was measured and found lacking [forty seahs] –
B.   all things requiring cleanness which were made depending on it, [Danby: "any acts requiring cleanness that had theretofore been done following immersion therein"]
C.   retroactively,
D.   whether in private domain or whether in public domain,
E.   are unclean.
F.   Under what circumstances?
G.   With reference to a major uncleanness.
H.   But with reference to a minor uncleanness:
I.   [Katsh #129, M, N, C, PB, Pa lack:] for example,
      (1) [if] one ate [a half-loaf of] unclean foods,
      (2) drank [a quarter-qav of] unclean liquids,
      (3) one's head and the greater part of one's body came into drawn water,
      (4) or three logs of drawn water fell on one's head and the greater part of one's body –
J.   and he went down to immerse –
K.   it is a matter of doubt whether he immersed or did not immerse –
L.   and even if he immersed,
      it is a matter of doubt whether there are forty seahs [of rainwater] in it or there are not [forty seahs] in it –
M.   two immersion pools, in one of which there are forty seahs, and in one of which there are not –
N.   one immersed in one of them and does not know in which one of them he immersed –
O.   his matter of doubt is deemed clean.
P.   R. Yosé declares unclean,
Q.   for R. Yosé says, "Everything which is in the assumption of being unclean always remains in its [Pa: *uncleanness and;* Katsh #129, M, Maimonides, C: its *uncleanness*] unfitness until it will be known that it has been cleaned [without regard to whether it is a major or minor source of uncleanness].
R.   "But its matter of doubt, when it pertains to its becoming unclean and [or] conveying uncleanness is clean."

M. 2:2 (A-E: B. Qid. 79a, which
lacks C; B. Git. 31b, Y. Git. 3:8)

Let us begin our consideration of the unit with Maimonides' account (*Immersion Pools* 10:6), as follows:

If one who is unclean goes down to immerse himself and it is in doubt whether or not he has immersed himself; or if, even though he did immerse himself, it is in doubt whether the pool contains forty seahs or not; if there are two pools, one containing forty seahs but not the other, and he immerses himself in one of them and it is not known in which of them he has immersed himself, he is deemed unclean, since one who is unclean is presumed to be still unclean until it is known that he has immersed himself properly.

So, too, if an immersion pool is measured and found wanting, whether the pool is in a public domain or in a private domain, any acts requiring conditions of cleanness which have hitherto been performed following immersion therein are deemed to have been performed in uncleanness, until the time becomes known as to when it was measured and was not wanting.

This applies if the immersion was for a grave uncleanness; but if a man immersed himself for a lesser uncleanness – for example, if he has eaten unclean foodstuffs or drunk unclean liquid, or if his head and the greater part of his body have come into drawn water, or if three logs of drawn water have fallen on his head and the greater part of him – since the principle set forth regarding these things rests only on the authority of the scribes, he is deemed to be clean....

And even if it is in doubt whether a man (of less uncleanness) has or has not immersed himself, or if the immersion pool is afterward found to lack the prescribed quantity, or if there are other doubts such as these, he is deemed to be clean.

M. 2:1, standing by itself, makes the simple point that since the person is certainly unclean, A, we do not declare that his status has changed until he is certainly made clean by a suitable immersion. The pericope is stated in apocopated phrases, most clearly in evidence at E, which continues to develop the problem before the first unit has been concluded, for example, by *unclean.*

What is interesting is the relationship between M. 2:1 and M. 2:2. M. 2:2F-I form the counterpart of M. 2:1A's the unclean person, and then, at M. 2:2K-O we have a point-by-point reversion to M. 2:1B-G:

M. 2:1		**M. 2:2**	
B.	doubt whether he immersed or whether he did not immerse	K.	doubt whether he immersed or whether he did not immerse
C.	and even if he did immerse	L.	and even if he did immerse doubt whether or not there are forty seahs
D.	doubt whether or not there are forty seahs		
E.	two immersion pools, one with forty seahs and one without	M.	two immersion pools, one with forty seahs, and one without
F.	immersed in one and does not know in which	N.	immersed in one and does not know in which

	he immersed		he immersed
G.	doubt deemed *unclean*	O.	his matter of doubt is deemed *clean*
		P.	R. Yosé declares unclean

The contrast is between M. 2:1A and M. 2:2F-J:

M. 2:1		**M. 2:2**	
A.	*The unclean person* (who) went down to immerse	F.	(Under what circumstances)
		G.	with reference to a major uncleanness
		I.	but with reference to a major uncleanness (+ 1, 2, 3, 4)
		J.	(and he) went down to immerse

Accordingly, M. 2:2F-J establish a contrast to M. 2:1, and the purpose of the entire set is to lead us to Yosé's opinion (as with Simeon's M. 1:1-3, 6). M. 2:2Q explains M. 2:1, and, as we saw, the point of M. 2:1 is simply that what is indubitably unclean is assumed to remain unclean until we know for sure that it is clean, without reference to the source of uncleanness. M. 2:2F-J wish to make a distinction of importance, holding that that is the case with reference to a major uncleanness – for example, someone unclean by a Father of uncleanness – but with reference to a minor uncleanness, the matter of doubt is deemed clean.

Yosé does not accept the distinction of M. 2:2G-I. He distinguishes, rather, between two kinds of doubt, not two kinds of uncleanness. If we have a matter of doubt about something and we do not know whether the thing itself is clean or unclean, then we assume it is clean. It follows that if we do not know whether it has imparted uncleanness to something else, we assume it has not done so. But when we are sure that something is unclean, there is no doubt about its remaining so until we are sure that it is clean. The dispute therefore is between the view that we distinguish major from minor uncleanness by reference to doubts about immersion pools, and the view that we distinguish between doubts about the condition of an object (or a person), and, when we are in doubt that something is unclean and also in doubt that the thing has been properly immersed, then the doubt is deemed clean. Accordingly, sages propose to make distinction in accord with the status of that *to which* uncleanness is imputed or imparted. Yosé holds that the distinction depends upon the effect, *upon other things,* of that to which uncleanness is imputed. Sages distinguish among doubts in terms of the uncleanness suffered by the object. Yosé makes his distinction in terms of the uncleanness imparted by the object: doubts about the status of the object, in respect to its remaining unclean, are deemed unclean, but doubts about the status of the object, in respect to other things – therefore, in respect to its becoming unclean itself – are deemed clean. Perhaps Eleazar of M. Toh. 2:7 would find affinity with the position of sages, and sages of M. Toh. 2:3-5+6 would discover grounds for agreement with Yosé. For, as we recall, Eleazar stresses that sources of uncleanness are equal to one another, differentiated only in terms of that to which uncleanness is imparted. Sages distinguish among the effects *upon other objects* of sources of uncleanness of varying degrees of sanctification.

M. 2:2A-E appear to form a completely autonomous unit, inserted whole into the large set of Meir and Yosé. The qualifying materials of M. 2:2F-R on the face of it have nothing to do with M. 2:2A-E and do not propose a distinction in respect to the retroactive uncleanness of the pool which was measured and found lacking. In that matter, whether in reference to a major or a minor uncleanness, whatever has been immersed in the pool is *retroactively* unclean, the issue being retroactivity. The rule of M. 2:2A-E, read as a distinct unit, poses no problems. Now we have a true case of doubt. The pool was measured and satisfactory. People used it. Then, sometime later, it was measured and found lacking in forty seahs. Whatever has been immersed in the pool between the time that it was satisfactorily filled and the time that it was found lacking is declared unclean.

If we ask Yosé his view of this matter, he surely will agree. Why? Because things are assumed unclean until appropriately immersed; we know that the things immersed in the pool were unclean, and they remain so. What will Meir have to say? Will he persist in his distinction between minor and major uncleanness? I cannot see any reason for him to change his mind. The qualifying materials of F-O do apply as much to M. 2:2A-E as to M. 2:1, in which case the redactor who has inserted them meant to tell us that Meir's view applies to both M. 2:1 and M. 2:2A-E. How, after all, are they different? At M. 2:1 we have an unclean person and doubt about either whether he immersed, or whether the pool in which he immersed was valid; and at M. 2:2A-E the doubt is whether the pool in which the immersion of an unclean object took place was valid. Accordingly, the redactor who has given us M. 2:2A-E as a prologue to M. 2:2F-O, inserting a quite distinct item into the construction, has excellent reasons for doing so.

The net result is a dispute, M. 2:2F-O versus M. 2:2P-R, on both M. 2:2A-E and M. 2:1. The dispute quite properly is expressed by the joining language of F-H+J+O, which is the operative language for B.'s Meir. Yosé's language, M. 2:2P-R, by contrast serves M. 2:1, but is hardly necessary at M. 2:2A-E, which declare the matter unclean in any event.

That strongly suggests the interpolation of M. 2:2A-E comes after the completion of the unit, M. 2:1+2:2F-R.

We shall now see that T. treats M. 2:2A-E as a quite separate item. But now Simeon wishes to introduce a still further distinction, in addition to those of Yosé and Meir (accepting B.'s attribution), namely, public versus private domain. Had M. preserved his opinion on its parallel pericopae, M. 2:1 and M. 2:2ff., it could have given us yet a third opinion, in place of M. 2:2G-N: "Under what circumstances? With reference to private domain [M. 2:1's *unclean*]. But with reference to public domain, the unclean person who went down to immerse [= M. 2:1A, 2:2J] – it is a matter of doubt...and even it...two immersion pools...his matter of doubt is deemed clean." Simeon's opinion therefore could have been phrased for the purposes of M. just as readily as have been those of Yosé and Meir. Instead, it is preserved by T. as a gloss of M. 2:2A-B, cited verbatim.

A. An immersion pool which was measured and found lacking – all the acts requiring cleanness which were carried out depending upon it –
B. whether this immersion pool is in the private domain, or whether this immersion pool is in the public domain – [supply: *are unclean*.]
C. R. Simeon says, "In the private domain, it is unclean [Sens: *they suspend*].
"In the public domain, it is clean."

T. 1:16, p. 262, lines 6-9

D. Said R. Simeon, "M^cSH B: The water reservoir [Sens: MGW-RH. See Lisowsky, p. 293, N. 135] of Disqus in Yavneh was measured and found lacking.
E. "And R. Tarfon did declare clean, and R. Aqiva unclean.
F. "Said R. Tarfon, 'Since this immersion pool is in the assumption of being clean, it remains perpetually [in this presumption of] cleanness until it will be known for sure that it is made unclean.'
G. "Said R. Aqiva, 'Since this immersion pool [Sens: *this unclean person*] is in the assumption of being unclean, it perpetually remains in the presumption of uncleanness until it will be known for sure that it is clean.'

T. 1:17, p. 262, lines 10-15

H. "Said R. Tarfon, 'To what is the matter to be likened? To one who was standing and offering [a sacrifice] at the altar, and it became known that he is a son of a divorcée or the son of a *halusah* [one who has been released from leviratical marriage by *halisah*] –
"'for his service is valid'
I. "Said R. Aqiva, 'To what is the matter to be likened?
"'To one who was standing and offering [a sacrifice] at the altar, and it became known that he is disqualified by reason of a blemish –

"'for his service is invalid.'

T. 1:18, p. 262, lines 16-18, p. 263,
lines 1-2

J.   "Said R. Tarfon to him, 'You draw an analogy to one who is blemished. I draw an analogy to the son of a divorcée or to the son of a *halusah*.

K.   "'Let us now see to what the matter is appropriately likened.

L.   "'If it is analogous to a blemished priest, let us learn the present law from the case of the blemished priest. If it is analogous to the son of a divorcée or to the son of a *halusah*, let us learn the law from the case of the son of the divorcée or the son of a *halusah*.'

T. 1:19, p. 263, lines 3-6

M.   "R. Aqiva says [*sic*] (1) 'The unfitness affecting an immersion pool affects the immersion pool itself, and the unfit aspect of the blemished priest affects the blemished priest himself.

N.   "'But let not the case of the son of a divorcée or the son of a *halusah* prove the matter, for his matter of unfitness depends upon others.

O.   (2) "'A ritual pool's unfitness [depends] on one only, and the unfitness of a blemished priest [depends] on an individual only, but let not the son of a divorcée or the son of a *halusah* prove the matter, for the unfitness of this one depends upon ancestry [Lit.: the house].'

P.   "They took a vote concerning the case and declared it unclean.

Q.   "Said R. Tarfon to R. Aqiva, 'He who departs from you is like one who perishes [Lit.: departs from his life].'"

T. 1:20, p. 263, lines 7-12 (A-C: B.
Qid. 79a. Nid. 2b; D-Q: Y. Ter. 8:2,
B. Qid. 66b)

M. 2:2A-E are treated by T. as separate from the remainder of the pericope. M. 2:2A-B, D-E = T. 1:16A-B. We should expect B to end, *are unclean*. M.'s interest in the retroactive decision now is omitted, because it is going to be obvious and is the primary focus of the rest of the story, D-Q. Simeon wishes, at C, to introduce the distinction of private and public domain, the distinction explicitly rejected by M.

M. clearly summarizes the result of the following story by its inclusion at C, *retroactively*, that is, the position of Aqiva. The issue of E can only be the status of objects immersed in the pool before the pool was lacking. F-G simply lay out the framework of the argument. The real issue is H versus I; thus each party has a valid analogy. Tarfon draws the matter of the analogy clearly – thus playing into Aqiva's hands and setting the stage for Q. Aqiva clearly has the better part of the argument – in fact, he has two arguments and Tarfon only one. Tarfon is not given a chance to reject Aqiva's analysis. The proper comparison, Aqiva says, is between the blemished priest and the immersion pool, for in both cases we deal with something directly affecting that which is found unfit. But nothing the son of the divorcée or of the *halusah* has done explains his status; it is what his mother has done which makes him unfit. P is curious. Since Tarfon has not stated a contrary argument, why do we need a vote? Q is standard in Aqiva-Tarfon disputes, continuing O and irrelevant to P; in any event it is clearly tacked on.

Self-evidently, M. has nothing to do with this dispute. It records the outcome at M. 2:2C, as I said, and that is the sole point at which T.'s interesting pericope is alluded to. Otherwise the clear point in common is the dispute between Simeon and the position of M., to which the issue of retroactivity is irrelevant.

What is still more curious is why Simeon should cite the debate of Tarfon and Aqiva. The issue of whether or not we deal with private or public domain is not specified. Simeon should want to deal with public domain. All parties agree that the matter in private domain yields a decision of uncleanness. Yet the point of the story is that the objects are retroactively *unclean.* Even if we assume that we have public domain (and the specification of the owner of the reservoir suggests we deal with private domain), then the precedent does *not* support Simeon's position. Simeon should want to have Tarfon win the argument, in which case he might extend the decision of cleanness to his issue – but even that would be farfetched. As it stands, the precedent clearly supports those who hold that the objects are retroactively deemed unclean, *without regard to domain,* just as M. says and as Simeon denies. Accordingly, we should want to ask Simeon exactly what he intended to prove by citing this precedent. Even if all Simeon introduced were the dispute at D-E, without the debate, all the more so the vote and Tarfon's concession, he still would find himself invoking the name of Tarfon against that of Aqiva, and, at Usha, it is difficult to see how much he would have gained thereby.

It goes without saying that Yosé will find much support for his position in Aqiva's ruling – the presumption of uncleanness persists until we know for sure that the person, object, or pool is clean. He, not Simeon, then should cite the story. But compare Mishnah Aharonah (MA) to M. 2:2.

Mishnah-tractate Miqvaot 2:3

A.   A doubt about drawn water which sages have declared clean –

B.   it is a matter of doubt whether they [three logs of drawn water] fell or did not fall.

C.   [And] even if they did fall,
it is a matter of doubt whether there are forty seahs in it [the immersion pool's waters] or whether there are not –

D.   two immersion pools in one of which there are forty seahs and in one of which there are not –

E. it [drawn water] fell into one of them, and one does not know into which one of them it fell —

F. its [the pool's] matter of doubt is deemed clean,

G. because it has something upon which to depend [Danby: "since there is that whereon to rely (in deeming it clean)"].

[Segal, p. 430, N. 1: *viz.*, that the three logs did not fall in at all; or that the *mikweh* did contain forty seahs; or, finally, that the three logs fell into the *mikweh* containing forty seahs.]

H. [PB, Pa lack H-J] [If] both of them were less than forty seahs, and if [drawn water] fell into one of them and one does not know into which of them it fell —

I. its [the pool's] matter of doubt is deemed unclean,

J. for it has nothing upon which to depend.

[Maimonides, *Immersion Pools* 10:2: "Since they have nothing on which to rely: for if they have fallen into one, it will have become invalid, and if they have fallen into the other, the other will have become invalid."]

M. 2:3

The articulation of doubts at M. 2:1 and 2:2 now shifts, the subject of B being the drawn water. The parallels to the foregoing are close, and the group should be regarded as a cogent unit spelled out in accord with a single agendum and formulary pattern. Now we speak about drawn waters, declared clean at M. Toh. 4:7: "These are matters of doubt which sages have declared clean: A doubt concerning drawn waters [which have fallen] into the immersion pool." The point is that we do not know whether the drawn water has fallen into the immersion pool in sufficient measure to render the pool unfit by reason of an excess of such water. An immersion pool which contains forty seahs can absorb any amount of drawn water. But if an immersion pool contains less than forty seahs, and the forty seahs are completed by the addition of drawn water, the pool is unfit.

In the present case, therefore, three logs of drawn water may have fallen into an immersion pool which lacks forty seahs of suitable water. The first doubt is B. In point of fact we are not sure that the water has fallen in. If they have fallen in, we are not sure that the pool actually was lacking forty seahs (C). D gives us a separate case. We have two pools, one with the requisite volume of water, one without, and we do not know into which of them the drawn water has fallen. The doubt is deemed clean. The result is that we may add suitable water to the immersion pool which lacks the requisite volume and thus bring it up to the necessary volume. F-G make the point that in the present case there is a possibility of genuine doubt, for we are not sure that something has taken place to render the immersion pool unfit. But H gives us an example in which there is no doubt. Whatever actually has happened, one of the pools certainly has been made unfit.

MA again observes that even Yosé will agree with the present rule (G), for, while we deem something unclean to remain unclean until definitely purified, we also deem the immersion pool valid until it is proved invalid (T. 2:1C).

A. An immersion pool which one left empty and came and found full is fit,

B. because it involves a matter of doubt concerning drawn water in an immersion pool,

C. and the assumption concerning immersion pools is that they are fit.

T. 2:1, p. 263, lines 14-15

M. Toh. 3:5, doubts in matters pertaining to uncleanness are adjudged in accord with the state of affairs upon discovery, is set aside in favor of M. Toh. 4:7, as at M. 2:3. The illustration is simpler than those of M. 2:3, however. We simply assume that we have rainwater and not drawn water. C gives us a still further reason. The pericope serves as a prologue to an entire chapter of T. devoted to the present problem, repeatedly introducing considerations treated at M. Toh., Chapters Five and Six.

A. A water duct which is pouring water into an immersion pool, and a mortar is set at its [the duct's] side –

B. and it is a matter of doubt whether it [water] is [pouring] from the water duct to the immersion pool [and is fit], or whether it is [pouring] from the mortar into the immersion pool [and is unfit] –

C. it is unfit, because the matter of unfitness is demonstrable.

D. And if the greater part [of water] in the immersion pool is fit,

E. [supply: *it is fit*] because this is a matter of doubt concerning drawn water in connection with an immersion pool.

T. 2:2, p. 263, lines 16-19

We continue to illustrate the main principle of M. 2:3, that matters of doubt concerning drawn water in an immersion pool are deemed clean. At A-C, we can show that there is an invalidity. Why? The water duct is right before us, and we can tell that some of the water may flow from the duct into the mortar, en route to the pool. On the other hand, if the pool is composed chiefly of suitable water, then the doubt has to do with the status of the pool, not merely the flow of water. The pool is confirmed in its assumed status.

A. Two immersion pools which do not contain forty seahs [of rainwater] –

B. and three logs of drawn water [into one of them] –

C. and it *is* known into which of them it has fallen –

D. and afterward, a second [quantity of three logs of drawn water] fell –

E. but it is not known into which of them they have fallen –

F.   lo, I am able to attribute [the matter], saying,

G.   "To the place into which the first [three logs of drawn water] have fallen, there have the second ones fallen [as well]."

T. 2:3, p. 264, lines 1-5

A.   Three logs [of drawn water] fell into one of them, and it is not known into which of them they fell,

B.   and afterward a second [quantity of three logs of drawn water] fell, and it is known into which of them they fell –

C.   one cannot attribute [the matter], saying,

D.   "Into the place into which the second ones have fallen, there did the first ones fall [as well]."

E.   In one [of the immersion pools] there are forty seahs [of rainwater], and in one of them there are not [forty seahs of rainwater] –

F.   lo, I declare, "Into the one containing forty seahs of rainwater have they fallen."

G.   One [pool] is [comprised of] drawn water and one of fit water – lo, I declare, "They have fallen into the drawn water."

T. 2:4, p. 264, lines 6-11

The cases augment M. 2:3's interest in whether we have a basis for declaring the pool fit. If we do, then we rely upon that same basis in a case of doubt. But if we do not, then we admit that whatever has happened, both pools are unfit. At T. 2:3 we know which of the two pools is unfit, namely, that into which the three logs of drawn water have fallen; when two further ones fall, and we do not know where, we suppose that what happened before has happened again (G), and, in consequence, deem the pool already unclean to remain unclean. But the other remains clean. At T. 2:4, by contrast, we do not know which pool has been invalidated. Then two further logs of drawn water fall, and we do know into which they have fallen. We do not know for sure which one of the pools is invalid. We therefore cannot state that the second logs have fallen into the same one (D). T. 2:4E-F conclude the problem. If one of the pools is valid and one is not, then I assume that the one which is valid has received the unfit water and nullified its impairing effects. G is disjunctive.

The main principle established in the present unit predominates through the end of the chapter of Tosefta, namely, if we have good reason to come to a lenient decision and attribute an impairment to what is already impaired, or uncleanness to what must in any event be unclean, we indeed come to that lenient decision. The exercise moves from impairment of the unfit immersion pool to contamination of food which is unclean with a major uncleanness. But the complications in the application of the present principle occupy much attention as well, and matters are not going to be so simple as they presently appear.

A.   Two immersion pools which do not contain forty seahs [of rainwater],

B.   and three logs [of drawn water] have fallen into one of them, and it is not known into which of them they have fallen –

C.   and afterward rain came, and they [the two pools] were filled up [with suitable water] –

D.   R. Yosé says, "They say to him that he should not immerse in [either] one of them.

E.   "But if he did immerse in one of them and prepared things requiring cleanness,

F.   [supply: *they are deemed clean*] "because this is a matter of doubt concerning drawn water in respect to an immersion pool.

G.   "To what is the matter likened?

H.   "To a person, one of whose hands has been made unclean, and it is not known which of them [is unclean].

I.   "They say to him that he should not prepare things requiring cleanness with either one of them.

J.   "But if he did prepare clean things requiring cleanness with one of them,

K.   "they are clean, because it is a matter of doubt involving the hands."

T. 2:5, p. 264, lines 12-19

A-C set up a condition in which we have one suitable pool, and one which is unfit. Why? Because one of the pools has been made unfit by the presence of three logs of drawn water before the two pools were filled with suitable water (M. 2:4). The opinion of Yosé, D, brings us back to M. 2:2P. That is, we have now reproduced the case of M. 2:2M-N. We tell the man not to immerse in either. This is parallel to saying, "His matter of doubt is deemed unclean" (M. 2:2P). But if he *did* immerse, what is our ruling? Then we hold that the matter of doubt concerns drawn water in an immersion pool, and we deem the doubt to be clean. The parallel, H-K, is clear as stated. M. 2:2R is what is spelled out. We have a matter of doubt about conveying uncleanness to something else, and, in such a case, deem that which may or may not have received uncleanness to be clean. What T. gives us, therefore, is the basis of Yosé's qualification.

Sens quite reasonably assigns all the foregoing to M. 2:3, and what is to follow is cited by him at M. 2:2. Because of the obvious redactional care with which Tosefta Chapter Two has been redacted, I prefer to present the entire set in its established sequence, even though this requires us now to turn back to M. 2:1-2, and, in particular, to M. 2:2's distinction between contamination by a major source of uncleanness and by a minor one. For our chapter of T. arranges its pericopae in ascending order of conceptual complexity (and difficulty), much as does T. Par. 6:4-8/M. Par. 7:1-5. T. 2:5 forms the transition from the issue of M. 2:3 to that of M. 2:2, working back via Yosé. Now we turn to the matter of varying degrees of uncleanness.

A.	Two immersion pools –
	one containing forty seahs [of rainwater] and one not containing [forty seahs of rainwater] –
B.	one immersed in one of them on account of a condition of uncleanness deriving from a major source of uncleanness and prepared things requiring cleanness –
C.	[he immersed] in the first and prepared [things requiring cleanness] –
D.	[he immersed] in the second and prepared [things requiring cleanness] –
E.	[if] these and those are lying [before him] –
F.	the first are held in a state of suspense, and the second are held to be clean.
G.	Under what circumstances?
H.	When we deal with a condition of uncleanness deriving from a major source of uncleanness.
I.	But if we deal with a condition of uncleanness deriving from a minor source of uncleanness, these and those are clean. [We assume he first immersed in the suitable pool.]

T. 2:6, p. 265, lines 1-5

Sens's version of the same pericope varies the cases of A-D. We had best consider his entire picture of T. 2:6 before proceeding:

A.	Two immersion pools –
B.	in one of them there are forty seahs [of rainwater] and in one of them there are not –
C.	one immersed in one of them on account of uncleanness deriving from a major source of uncleanness –
D.	and he prepared things requiring cleanness –
E.	they are suspended.
F.	[If] he immersed in the second and prepared [things requiring cleanness],
G.	they are clean [for he has certainly immersed in a fit pool before preparing the food].
H.	[If he immersed] in the first and did not prepare [things requiring cleanness], [then immersed] in the second and prepared [things requiring cleanness] – they are clean [for the same reason].
I.	[If he immersed] in the first and prepared [things requiring cleanness], [and then immersed] in the second and prepared [things requiring cleanness] –
J.	[if] these and those are lying [before him] –
K.	the first are suspended, and the second are clean.
L.	Under what circumstances?
M.	In the case of uncleanness deriving from a major source. But in the case of uncleanness deriving from a minor source, these and those are clean [for we hold that he immersed the first time in the fit pool].

T. 2:6 following Sens

A.   [If] he immersed in one of them on account of a condition of uncleanness deriving from a minor source of uncleanness and prepared things requiring cleanness –

B.   they are clean.

C.   [If] betweentimes he was made unclean by a [Lisowsky: *major*] [Sens + *TR* IV, p. 8] *minor* source of uncleanness, and he immersed in the second [pool] and prepared [things requiring conditions of cleanness] –

D.   [if] these and those are lying [before him] –

E.   lo, these prove [the condition of one another and both are kept in a state of suspense].

      [If, in a mixture, the status of one part is certain, it proves or establishes the status of the remainder. Since one part is certainly unclean, both are suspended. This explains why the first is suspended, since in any event the second is suspended. If he had not prepared the first, the second would have been clean. Now, however, one is assuredly unclean. Both are kept in suspense because of doubt (*TR* IV, pp. 8-9).]

F.   [If] the first were eaten, and [or] made [definitely] unclean, of [if] they perished before the second were prepared –

G.   the second are deemed clean.

H.   [If this took place] after the second were prepared, the second are held in a state of suspense [as before, E].

T. 2:7, p. 265, lines 6-10

A.   [If] he immersed in one of them on account of a condition of uncleanness deriving from a major source of uncleanness and prepared things requiring cleanness, they are suspended [= T. 2:6A-D (Sens)].

B.   [If] he was made unclean in the meantime by a minor source of uncleanness,

C.   and he immersed in the second [pool] and prepared things requiring cleanness –

D.   [Sens lacks:] they are deemed clean [since now there has been proper immersion on account of A's case, and B's is deemed clean because of doubt].

E.   [And if] these touched the others,

F.   the first are held in a state of suspense, and the second are burned.

G.   [If] he immersed in one of them on account of a condition of uncleanness deriving from a minor source of uncleanness,

H.   and prepared clean things,

I.   they are deemed clean.

J.   [If] he was made unclean in the meantime by a major source of uncleanness and immersed and prepared things requiring cleanness,

K.   they are held in a state of suspense.

L.   [And if] these touched those,

M.   the second are held in a state of suspense, and the first are burned.

T. 2:8, p. 265, lines 11-17

T.'s substantial set goes over the ground of M. 2:1, 2G-R. M. 2:1 has told us that if we have two immersion pools, one valid and one not, and we have a doubt about the immersion, the doubt is deemed unclean. But this, M. 2:2G has told us, concerned uncleanness deriving from a major source of uncleanness. If it is a minor source, the matter of doubt is deemed clean. The variable introduced by T. is parallel to M. Toh. 5:3-4, in which we have a case of two paths. A person walked in one, prepared clean things, was purified, walked in the second and prepared clean things. The second are deemed clean, because we assume the first to have been unclean. But if the first still are in hand, both are suspended, one is surely unclean. If the man walked in one path, prepared things requiring cleanness, then walked in the other without an intervening process of purification, the first now are held in suspense, and the second are burned as indubitably unclean. T. Toh. 6:3 introduces the language of M. Miq. 2:3, namely, whether we have a mitigating factor on which basis to declare one set to be clean. Thus T. links the two autonomous units of M., M. Toh. 5:3-4 and M. Miq. 2:1-3. This brings us to the present major unit.

At T. 2:6 we have doubt about the suitability of immersion of someone who has been made unclean with a major source of uncleanness. We know from M. 2:1 that the matter of doubt is deemed unclean. The case unfolds at C-D of Lisowsky's version = I of Sens's. The man immersed in the first pool and prepared clean things, then he immersed in the second and did likewise. Both sets of food are in hand. How do we rule? If the man had immersed and prepared clean things, they would have been suspended. But with the complication that both pools have been used, one set of food surely is clean, and we do not know which it is. We hold that if the first is held in a state of suspense, the second is deemed clean. I then adds the qualification of M. 2:2G-O, in the view of sages. Why are both clean? Because even if we had doubt about one, in any event it would have been clean.

The next phase of the problem is at T. 2:7, with the complication at B as to the diverse reading at T. 2:7C, since T. 2:7A has *minor*, T. 2:8A+B *major* + *minor*. The substance of the case, moreover, requires *minor*. If we read *major*, why, at T. 2:7E, should both be held in suspense, and, in particular the first set? For the second set in any event is suspended. Even if the man had not prepared the first set, we have no "proof" of the status of the other. The two in fact are equivalent. If the man had not prepared the first set of food, the second would have been clean. But since he prepared both, and since among them one is certainly unclean, both are kept in a state of suspension because of the doubt (*TR* IV, pp. 8-9).

Let us now turn to the case of T. 2:7 as a whole. The man originally was unclean because of a minor source of uncleanness. B's point is as stated at M. 2:2M-P. But in betweentimes, he was made unclean by a minor source, and *then* he immersed in the second pool and prepared things requiring cleanness. We have both sets of food in hand. As at T. Toh. 6:3, we introduce the notion that what we do in the case of one determines the status of the other. So, too, at T. 2:7E, we hold that the condition of one determines that of the other. Have we treated the first immersion as fit or unfit? We have said it is a matter of doubt, but, under the circumstances of A, have determined that the doubt produces a decision of cleanness. But if the doubts are of equivalent weight, both are suspended (E).

But if we have lost the first set of food, the second is now treated as fit. F spells this out. If we do not have the first in hand or we know the first indeed was unclean or the first set of food perished before the second was prepared, the second is deemed clean. Why? Because the first is assumed definitely to have been unclean. If both are before us (H), the second is held in a state of suspense, which goes over the case of D-E.

Lieberman, *TR* IV, p. 9, explains T. 2:8E-F as follows: If the first pool was fit and the man was made clean on account of contamination by a major source of uncleanness, then the second pool was unfit. The man therefore remains unclean by reason of the minor source of uncleanness, and the second set of food is unclean and to be burned. But if the first pool was unfit, then the one who immersed in it remains unclean by reason of a major source of uncleanness. He has made the first set of food requiring cleanness unclean, and it renders the second set unclean. But the first set of food requiring cleanness remains in its doubt. Why? Perhaps the first pool *was* fit, and the one who immersed was purified. The second set of food requiring cleanness, made unclean by a man who is unclean by reason of a minor source of uncleanness, then does not render the first set of food unclean. T. 2:8G-M then reverse the pattern. The man immersed after contamination by a minor source of uncleanness and prepared clean things. If the first pool was fit, then the second was unfit, and the man is now unclean by reason of a major source of uncleanness. When the two sets of food touch, the second set renders the first unclean, and M follows. On the other hand, if the first pool was unfit, then, while the man was made unclean by a major source of uncleanness and prepared things requiring cleanness, he in the meantime immersed in a valid pool. The second set of food is therefore fit. The first is definitely unclean and is burned. As at T. Toh. 6:4ff., once the two have been in contact, if one remains in suspense, the other cannot be clean. The contact here is equivalent to not having an intervening process of purification at T. Toh. 6:4ff.

T. 2:9-10 will now present us with a further variable. Until now one of the pools has been fit and the other unfit. In the following set, one of the pools is fit, but the other, filled with drawn water, not only is unfit but, because a person whose head and the greater part of whose body entered into drawn water is deemed unclean, imparts uncleanness to the one who dips in it. T. 2:11 concludes this part of the work with a further variable.

A.   Two immersion pools of forty seahs each –

B.   one containing drawn [water], and one containing suitable [water] –

C.   and one immersed in one of them on account of a condition of uncleanness deriving from a major source of uncleanness and prepared things requiring cleanness –

D.   they are held in a state of suspense.

E.   [If he immersed] in the second and prepared things requiring cleanness –
[following Sens:] *they are clean.*
[GRA: We surmise that he first immersed in drawn water, then in suitable water, so he was perfectly clean before preparing the second.]

F.   [If he immersed] in the first and did not prepare things requiring cleanness, then immersed in the second and prepared things requiring cleanness –

G.   [if he immersed] in the first and prepared [things requiring cleanness], [then immersed] in the second and prepared [things requiring cleanness] –

H.   if these and those are lying [before him] –

I.   the first are suspended and the second are clean.
[They first are held in suspense because of doubt about a major source of uncleanness, but prove nothing about the status of the second (*TR* IV, p. 9), because the status as to uncleanness of the one is not comparable to the status as to uncleanness of the other, by contrast to L, below.]

J.   Under what circumstances?

K.   In the case of a condition of uncleanness deriving from a major source of uncleanness.

L.   But in the case of a condition of uncleanness deriving from a minor source of uncleanness, these and those are held in a state of suspense.
[*TR* IV, p. 9: Now the doubt affecting both is of the same order. One is surely unclean. It establishes the condition of the other – meaning that both are suspended.]

T. 2:9, p. 265, lines 18-19, p. 226,
lines 1-4. Text translated by Sens

With the additional complication of the drawn water, we face the problems familiar in the earlier pericopae, and the principles behind the decision are not very different. At C we have a doubt about uncleanness in respect to a major source. The food is held in a state of suspense, as expected. Then at E, the man has immersed in the second pool. We hold the food is clean. Why? We attribute the suitable immersion to the second such action, as GRA explains. And the same consideration explains F. The man immersed in both pools. The problem comes at G. One immersion has been because of a major source of uncleanness. What is the further doubt? It is whether the man has immersed in drawn water – a minor source of uncleanness. Accordingly, the status of the one does not prove anything about that of the other, because the uncleanness under consideration at the first immersion is at a different level from that in mind at the second. But, J-L add, if the two immersions concern uncleanness of a minor sort – (1) a minor source of contamination to begin with, or, equivalently, (2) immersion in drawn water – then we do hold they prove the status of one another, and, in the present case, both are suspended. The importance of the variable is to distinguish the case of uncleanness at two different levels – major, minor – from the one in which uncleanness is at the same level – minor, minor – in respect to proving or establishing the condition of the one upon the basis of the status of the other.

Mishneh LaMelekh (*ML*) to *Immersion Pools* 10:7 points out that after the immersion in the second pool, there is the possibility that the man has immersed in drawn water. But, *ML* points out, having immersed in both pools, he surely has been cleansed of the major uncleanness. On account of the doubt about having become unclean because of a minor source of uncleanness – the drawn water – we are not going to rule other than we do at I.

A.   [If] two people went down and immersed in the two of them [the pools of T. 2:9],

B.   one unclean with a condition of uncleanness deriving from a major source of uncleanness, and one unclean on account of a minor source of uncleanness –

C.   he who immerses on account of a major source of uncleanness is unclean [the doubt is deemed unclean, as at M. 2:2].

D.   And the one who immerses on account of uncleanness deriving from a minor source of uncleanness is clean [for the same reason].

E.   One who is unclean with uncleanness deriving from a major source of uncleanness and one who immerses to cool himself –

F.   he who immerses on account of uncleanness deriving from a major source of uncleanness is unclean, and the one who immerses to cool himself is clean.
[The doubt affecting the latter is because of a minor source of uncleanness – drawn water.]

G.   One who is unclean with uncleanness deriving from a minor source of uncleanness, and one who immerses to cool himself –

H.   both of them are kept in a state of suspense. [Now the two are unclean for a minor cause and prove the case of one another, just as at T. 2:9J-L.]

I.   To what is the matter likened?

J. To two paths, one unclean and one clean, and there were two who went in the two of them and prepared things requiring cleanness.

K. In the case of one there is sufficient intelligence for interrogation, and in the case of the other there is not sufficient intelligence for interrogation –

L. in the case of the private domain, both of them are kept in a state of suspense.

M. In the case of public domain, the one who has intelligence for interrogation is deemed, in a matter of doubt, to be unclean.

N. And the one who does not have intelligence for interrogation in a state of doubt is deemed clean.

T. 2:10, p. 266, lines 5:15

The problem of A-D is, To which party do we assign immersion in the suitable pool? The answer is at D. We assume that one party must have immersed in the suitable pool, and it is the one whose uncleanness derives from a minor source of uncleanness. The other is assumed to have immersed in the drawn water and to remain unclean (C). The principle of Meir, M. 2:2, is applied by extension.

E begins a new problem. One of the people is unclean because of a major source of uncleanness, and the other is a clean person who immerses merely to cool himself. Following the foregoing pattern, we assume the one who is clean has immersed in the suitable pool, and the other immersed in the drawn water. We do not imagine that the clean person has immersed in drawn water. On the other hand, at G-H, both are possibly unclean because of a minor source of uncleanness. The one who immerses to cool himself off now is not facing a matter of doubt appreciably different from the one who is unclean because of a minor source of uncleanness. Since the doubt is of equivalent weight, both are kept in a state of suspense, just as at T. 2:9. The analogy at the end, I-N, treats the one who can be interrogated as equivalent to the immersion pool containing drawn water, and the one who cannot be interrogated is the analogue to the suitable immersion pool. In private property, both are suspended. We cannot declare one clean without declaring the other clean. In the case of public domain, however, we invoke the principle that matters concerning one who can be interrogated are deemed unclean, just as is the case with the drawn water, as I said.

A. Two immersion pool, each containing twenty seahs,

B. one with drawn water, and one with suitable water –

C. one immersed to cool himself in one of them and prepared things requiring cleanness –
they are clean.

D. [If he then immersed] in the second, and prepared things requiring cleanness –
they are burned.

E.   [If one immersed] in the first and did not prepare [things requiring cleanness], [and then immersed] in the second and prepared [things requiring cleanness] –
they are burned.

F.   [If one immersed] in the first and prepared things requiring cleanness, and [then immersed] in the second [and prepared, etc.] –

G.   if these and those are lying before him –

H.   the first are deemed clean,

I.   and the second are to be burned.

T. 2:11, p. 266, lines 16-20

In the final case, we deal with a single person, and his intent was to immerse only to cool off. The opening case, A-C, again gives the benefit of doubt to the one who immerses only to cool himself. He is deemed clean. But if he then immerses in the second, food prepared is unclean and is burned. It surely is unclean. In the case of E we have a certainty that the man has immersed in drawn water. We do not know in which order he has done so. We do not give him the benefit of the doubt. At F-I we say that the first are clean, just as at C, in which case the second definitely are unclean. The second would be unclean even if the man did not prepare food requiring cleanness after the first immersion and before the second, and the second therefore are burned in any event (*TR* IV, p. 10). There is no problem about the differentiation as to the source of uncleanness; the man is unclean only because of immersing in drawn water, and, in this case, we insist that the decision accorded to one set of food establishes the condition of the other. If, at C, the man is deemed clean, then in the other instance he must be deemed unclean. This is a second case and a happy conclusion to the whole. What follows is not really pertinent.

A.   Two women who engaged in preparing a bird which is suitable to produce [only one] sela' of blood,

B.   after a while, on this one a sela' of blood is found,

C.   and a sela' of blood is found on the other –

D.   both of them are in disarray (MQLQLWT; B. Nid. 58b: *unclean*).

T. 2:12, p. 267, lines 1-3

While only one stain derives from the bird, both are deemed unclean. Why? One stain cannot be attributed to the bird and therefore is certainly unclean. Both are deemed unclean, just as at M. 2:1G, doubt involving a major source of uncleanness.

6

The Facts of Mishnah-Tosefta Relationships [3]: The Tosefta as a Supplement to the Mishnah

In this chapter I present passages of the Tosefta that are essentially free-standing. I give only a brief selection, which is in proportion to the small proportion of the Tosefta comprised by passages of the present classification. But the two selections suffice to show how the Tosefta presents materials that stand entirely distinct from the Mishnah.

I include the Mishnah paragraphs to which the passages are appended, simply to show how the Tosefta's materials bear no necessary or even implicit relationship to the Mishnah passage before us. My comments of course are kept brief, since a free-standing passage, by definition, speaks quite eloquently in its own behalf. Free-standing materials are of two kinds. First, some autonomous materials work on topics important to a passage in the Mishnah and are placed by Tosefta's framers in a position corresponding to the thematic parallel in the Mishnah. What marks these materials as autonomous is that, while they intersect with the Mishnah's topic, their interest in that topic bears no point in common with the Mishnah's treatment of the same topic.

A second criterion, which is complementary, is that we can understand what follows without referring to the Mishnah for any purpose. The second type of autonomous materials addresses topics omitted in the Mishnah, and that type is included only because, in the Mishnah, there may be a tangential reference to the topic treated by Tosefta's composition. The criterion of classification, then, is even simpler than that governing the first type. The Tosefta's authorship has collected this kind of material we know not where. It certainly could have been composed in the same period as the writing of the Mishnah or the components that later were drawn together into the Mishnah. The proportion of this type of writing to the Tosefta as a whole for the Division of Purities is approximately one-sixth, and for the other divisions, somewhat smaller. Here, too, I give the Mishnah passage that is pertinent, so that readers may judge for themselves the accuracy of my description and the cogency of my classification of the Tosefta's writings.

Mishnah-tractate Miqvaot Chapter Ten

10:8 A. [If] one ate unclean food or drank unclean liquids [wine, honey, milk, etc.], immersed, then vomited them up –

B. they are unclean,

C. because they are not cleaned with the body.

D. [If] he drank unclean water, immersed, and vomited it up –

E. it is clean, because it is cleaned with the body.

F. [If] one swallowed a clean ring, entered the Tent of the corpse, was sprinkled and repeated the sprinkling [on the third and seventh day] and immersed and then vomited it up –

G. lo, it is as it was [clean].

H. If one swallowed an unclean ring, he [is made unclean and] immerses, eats heave-offering [since the unclean object which is swallowed up does not make the man unclean, M. Kel. 8:5], then he vomited it up –

I. it is unclean and [because he touches it when he vomits, it] renders him unclean.

J. An arrow which is stuck in a man – when it is apparent to the eye, [even if it is unclean, because it is embedded inside the body, as at H] he immerses and eats his heave-offering.

M. 10:8 (F-I: B. Hul. 71b)

The point of M. 10:5-6, that water is different from other liquid, is carried forward at A-E. The immersion does not avail the unclean food or liquid, so once they are vomited up, they remain unclean. But immersion does avail unclean water, D-E. Therefore when the man immerses and cleans the body, his immersion also cleans the water.

The distinction between F-G and H-I obviously is the condition of the ring. It is not made unclean when the man goes into the Tent of the corpse, because it is tightly sealed in his body (T. Kel. B.Q. 6:10). When he becomes clean and vomits it up, there is nothing to make it unclean. If he swallowed an unclean ring, it makes him unclean and he immerses. The immersion does not avail the ring. But while it is inside him, it does not make him unclean. Therefore when he vomits up the ring it is unclean as it was, and it again makes him unclean.

J is autonomous of the foregoing, but its relevant point is clear. When the arrow is stuck inside the man, it will not interpose when he immerses, like the ring of F-I.

A.   [If] one swallowed an olive's bulk of corpse matter and entered a house, it is clean, for whatever is swallowed by man or cattle or beast or fowl is clean [= does not impart uncleanness].

B.   [If] it decomposed or emerged from below [the rectum], they are clean.

C.   [If] one drank unclean water and vomited it up, it is unclean, because it was made unclean when it went out.

D.   [If] one immersed, or [if] it decomposed or it came out below, it is clean.

E.   [If] one drank other [unclean] liquids [besides water], even though he immersed and vomited them out, they are unclean, because they are not made clean in the body.

F.   If they decomposed or went forth, they are clean.

> T. 7:8, p. 283, lines 18-20, p. 284,
> lines 1-4

The rule of A accords with T. Oh. 12:3, part IV, p. 250. The main points are in harmony with M. 10:8A-E, with stress on the difference between water, C, and other liquids, E. At C there is no process of purification. D, by contrast to E, has effective immersion. Decomposition through the natural processes is deemed in all instances to remove the uncleanness, B, D, F.

A.   A cow which drank unclean water and vomited it up – it is unclean, because it is not made clean in the body.

B.   If it decomposed or went out below, it is clean.

> T. 7:9A, p. 284, lines 5-6

The rule is identical to the foregoing.

A.   He into whose knee an arrow penetrated –

B.   Rabbi [Judah] says, "It does not interpose."

C.   And sages say, "Lo, this interposes."

D.   Under what circumstances [B]?

E.   In the case of one made of metal.

F.   But in the case of one made of wood, lo, this interposes.

G.   And if the flesh formed a membrane over it, all agree that it does not interpose,

H.   for whatever is swallowed up in man, cattle, beast, and fowl is clean.

I.   [If] pieces of gravel or splinters went into the cracks beneath his feet –

J.   R. Jacob [Aqiva] says, "It does not interpose, because it is like the privy parts."

> T. 7:9B, p. 284, lines 6-13

T. corresponds to M. 10:8J, but its issue ignores M.'s distinction. On that basis I classify the matter as complementary. D-F apply to B. Metal does not interpose (B, E) because removing it may endanger life. Sages hold one takes note of metal as of wood (*TR* IV, p. 47). At G we have an arrow which does not rise above the surface, as in M., with T.'s own reason added, H. I-J are separate and add to the definition of privy parts. Now comes the autonomous unit. Once again we observe a uniform order of types of materials.

A.   A cow which drank purification water, and one slaughtered it within twenty-four hours –

B.   this was a case, and R. Yosé the Galilean did declare it clean, and R. Aqiva did declare it unclean.

C.   R. Tarfon supported R. Yosé the Galilean. R. Simeon ben Nanos supported R. Aqiva.

D.   R. Simeon b. Nanos dismissed [the arguments of] R. Tarfon. R. Yosé the Galilean dismissed [the arguments of] R. Simeon b. Nanos.

E.   R. Aqiva dismissed [the arguments of] R. Yosé the Galilean.

F.   After a time, he [Yosé] found an answer for him [Aqiva].

G.   He said to him, "Am I able to reverse myself?"

H.   He said to him, "Not anyone [may reverse himself], but you [may do so], for you are Yosé the Galilean."

I.   [He said to him,] "I shall say to you: 'Lo, Scripture states, *And they shall be kept for the congregation of the people of Israel for the water for impurity* (Num. 19:9).

J.   "'Just so long as they are kept, lo, they are water for impurity – and *not* when a cow has drunk them.'"

K.   This was a case, and thirty-two elders voted in Lud and declared it clean.

L.   At that time R. Tarfon recited this verse:

M.   *"I saw the ram goring westward and northward and southward, and all the animals were unable to stand against it, and none afforded protection from its power, and it did just as it liked and grew great* (Dan. 8:4) –

N.   "[this is] R. Aqiva.

O.   *"As I was considering, behold, a he-goat came from the west across the face of the whole earth, without touching the ground; and the goat had a conspicuous horn between his eyes.*

P.   "[Sens: This is R. Yosé the Galilean and his reply.] *He came to the ram with the two horns, which I had seen standing on the bank of the river, and he ran at him in his mighty wrath. I saw him come close to the ram, and he was enraged against him and struck the ram and broke his two horns* – this is R. Aqiva and R. Simeon b. Nanos.

Q.   *"And the ram had no power to stand before him* – this is Aqiva.

R.   *"But he cast him down to the ground and trampled upon him* – this is R. Yosé the Galilean.

S.   *"And there was no one who could rescue the ram from his power* – these are the thirty-two elders who voted in Lud and declared it clean."

T.   *[Then the he-goat magnified himself exceedingly; but when he was strong, the great horn was broken, and instead of it there came up four conspicuous horns toward the four winds of heaven]* (Dan. 8:5-8).

> T. 7:11, p. 285, lines 3-21, p. 286,
> lines 1-6 = Sif. Num. 124Q,
> Horovitz, p. 158, lines 12-20, p.
> 159, lines 1-4, part IX, pp. 244-245

The connection to the present problem is via M. Par. 9:5E-H (part IX, p. 159): "A cow which drank purification water – its flesh is unclean for twenty-four hours. R. Judah says, 'It is annulled in its intestines.'" Yosé the Galilean agrees with Judah. The point of G is that Yosé the Galilean was able to demonstrate that so long as the water is guarded, it is capable of rendering something unclean when purposelessly used, but once it is no longer kept under proper, Israelite oversight – as in the intestines of the cow – it is no longer unclean. The composition of T. 7:11 is of course free-standing.

Mishnah-tractate Hullin Chapter Two

2:9   A.   They do not perform an act of slaughter [in such a way that the blood falls] either into seas, or into rivers, or into utensils.

        B.   But one slaughters [so that the blood falls] into a dish (WGN) filled with water, or, [when on board] a boat, onto the backs of utensils [Danby: or over the outside of vessels on a ship (so that the blood flows into the sea)].

        C.   They do not slaughter [in such a way that the blood falls] into a hole [Pa, N, P, K, C omit: *of any kind*].

        D.   But one makes a hole in his house, so that the blood will flow down into it.

        E.   And in the market one may not do so,

        F.   so that one will not imitate the *minim* [in their ways].

M. 2:9

While F explains E, it also serves A, C. We have two matched rules, one negative, the other positive, A-B, C-D, and then the conclusion of E-F. The reason A and C are forbidden is that disposing of the blood in the specific ways is interpreted as slaughter for the service of the demons of the specified places or collecting the blood for that purpose.

    A.   *They do not perform an act of slaughter [in such a way that the blood falls] either into seas or into rivers* [M. Hul. 2:9A].

    B.   But into turbid water [one may do so].

    C.   *But one performs an act of slaughter [in such a way that the blood falls] into a dish of water, or, on a ship, on the backs of utensils* [M. Hul. 2:9B-C].

    D.   And if one has no place on a ship [in which to perform the act of slaughter in the way just now prescribed], one performs the act of slaughter [so that the blood flows over the side of the ship and thence (*TR* II, p. 227)] into the sea.

    E.   And if one does not want to make his house dirty, he performs an act of slaughter [so that the blood flows] into a utensil or into a hole [M. Hul. 2:9C, D].

    F.   *But in the market one may not do so,* because he [thereby] carries out [the act in accord with] *the rules of minim* [M. Hul. 2:9E].

    G.   And if he has done so, it requires examination.

T. 2:19 Z, p. 503, lines 5-9

A.   Meat which is found in the hand of a gentile is permitted for gain. [If it is found] in the hand of a *min*, it is prohibited for gain.

B.   That which goes forth from a pagan temple, lo, it is deemed to be meat from the sacrifices of corpses.

C.   For they have stated, "The act of slaughter of a *min* [is deemed to be for the purposes of] idolatry" [M. Hul. 2:7E].

D.   Their bread [is deemed] the bread of a Samaritan, and their wine is deemed wine used for idolatrous purposes, and their produce is deemed wholly untithed, and their books are deemed magical books, and their children are *mamzerin.*

T. 2:20 Z, p. 503, lines 9-11

A.   People are not to sell anything to them or buy anything from them.

B.   And they do not engage in any business whatsoever with them.

C.   And they do not teach their sons a craft.

D.   And they do not seek assistance from them, either financial assistance or medical assistance.,

T. 2:21 Z, p. 503, lines 12-13

A.   MᶜSH B: R. Eleazar b. Damah was bitten by a snake.

B.   And Jacob of Kefar Sama came to heal him in the name of Jesus, son of Pantera.

C.   And R. Ishmael did not allow him [to accept the healing].

D.   He said to him, "You are not permitted [to accept healing from him], Ben Dama."

E.   He said to him, "I shall bring you proof that he may heal me."

F.   But he did not have time to bring the promised proof before he dropped dead.

T. 2:22 Z, p. 503, lines 13-16

G.   Said R. Ishmael, "Happy are you, Ben Dama. For you have expired in peace, but you did not break down the hedge erected by sages. For whoever breaks down the hedge erected by sages eventually suffers punishment, as it is said, *He who breaks down a hedge is bitten by a snake* [Qoh. 10:8]."

T. 2:23 Z, p. 503, lines 16-18

A.   MᶜSH B: R. Eliezer was arrested on account of *minut*. They brought him to court for judgment.

B.   That *hegemon* said to him, "Should an elder of your standing get involved in such things?"

C.   He said to him, "The Judge is reliable in my view. [I rely upon the Judge.]"

D.   That *hegemon* supposed that he referred only to him, but he referred only to his Father in heaven.

E.   He [the *hegemon*] said to him, "Since you deemed me reliable for yourself, so thus I have ruled: Is it possible that these grey hairs should err in such matters? [Obviously not, therefore:] *Dimissus* [pardoned]. Lo, you are free of liability."

F.   And when he left court, he was distressed to have been arrested on account of matters of *minut*.

G.   His disciples came to comfort him, but he did not accept their words of comfort.

H.   R. Aqiba came and said to him, "Rabbi, may I say something to you so that you will not be distressed?"

I.   He said to him, "Go ahead."

J.   He said to him, "Perhaps someone of the *minim* told you something of *minut* [heresy] which pleased you."

K.   He said to him, "By heaven! You remind me, once I was strolling in the camp of Sepphoris. I bumped into Jacob of Kefar Sikhnin, and he told me a teaching of *minut* in the name of Jesus ben Pantiri, and it pleased me. So I was arrested on account of matters of *minut*, for I transgressed the teachings of Torah: *Keep your way far from her and do not go near the door of her house...* (Prov. 5:8)."

L.   For R. Eliezer did teach, "One should always flee from what is disreputable and from whatever appears to be disreputable."

                              T. 2:24 Z, p. 503, lines 18-30

T. 2:19 cites and glosses M. 2:9, explaining, at D, how, in duress, one may allow the blood to flow into the sea (M. 2:9B), and, also, why one may collect the blood in a hole or utensil (M. 2:9D), so harmonizing M. 2:9D and M. 2:9C. On T. 2:19B, see *TR* II, p. 226. Turbid water produces no reflection, so one may let blood drip into it. Then the language of M. 2:9E-F is slightly revised for clarity, with special attention to the meaning of HQH of M. 2:9F. Thereafter, the general principle that one does not slaughter for gentiles (M. 2:7C-E) is carried forward and expanded. On T. 2:24, see my *Eliezer ben Hyrcanus* (Leiden, 1973: E.J. Brill), I, pp. 400-403. T. 2:22, 23, and 24 show us how Tosefta presents completely free-standing materials, parachuting them down more or less ad lib.

7

Are There Really Tannaitic Parallels to the Gospels?

"The Gospels do not contain passages in which it is unmistakably clear that the understanding of one Gospel depends on a knowledge of the content, if not the text, of another, but the understanding of Tosefta often depends on a knowledge of the Mishnah...."

I. Did Morton Smith Understand the Relationship between the Mishnah and the Tosefta?

Since, as Chapter Two shows us, Smith claimed to compare the relationship between Matthew and Luke to the relationship between the Mishnah and the Tosefta, and since, as Chapters Three through Six have made clear, we really do know in rich detail how the latter two documents do relate, let us begin by asking the simple question, did Smith know what he was talking about? Despite the entirely sound observation cited above, the answer is, not at all. Bungling and bumbling, saying something and then contradicting it, making a boldface and then apologizing for his temerity, Morton Smith understood nothing at all about the relationship between the Mishnah and the Tosefta. Three points of relationship suffice to highlight the man's ignorance:

1. The Tosefta depends entirely for its sequence and topical program on the Mishnah. It is not an independent and free-standing document, which can be understood on its own, for example, read from beginning to end. Smith never refers to that fact, which would have proven the opposite of his thesis, since Matthew does not depend on Luke, or Luke on Matthew. We can read Matthew without Luke and understand every word in Matthew, and vice versa. But we

131

cannot read the Tosefta without line-by-line reference to the
Mishnah. Of that fact, Smith was ignorant.

2.   The Tosefta's compilation of materials is in three parts:
materials that cite and gloss Mishnah sentences, materials
that complement Mishnah sentences, and materials that
merely in topic or theme supplement the Mishnah's. Smith
did not recognize, even in his own sample, the diverse
relationships of the several passages he inspected. He
furthermore did not know that the Tosefta was made up of
three distinct types of materials, each with its own
relationship to the Mishnah. Therefore he also did not
classify the types of materials shared by Matthew and Luke
and ask how one type related to some other. We cannot
analyze the Tosefta without differentiating its materials by
the criterion of how they relate to the Mishnah, but we can
analyze Luke or Matthew without differentiating their
materials by the criterion of how they relate to the other
Gospel. Of that fact, Smith was ignorant.

3.   The Tosefta in general orders the three types of materials
that it contains in terms of the relationship of each set to its
counterparts in the Mishnah: citation and gloss, then
complement, then supplement. We can make no sense of the
order and structure of the Tosefta without examining the
classifications of materials in the Tosefta and assessing the
relationship of each classification to the Mishnah's
counterparts. But, it goes without saying, the order and
structure of Matthew unfold without any concern for the
relationships of Matthew's materials to their counterparts in
Luke, and vice versa. Of that fact, Smith was ignorant.

The upshot is that Smith did not understand the relationship
between the Mishnah and the Tosefta, and therefore his allegation that
the relationship between those two documents is "parallel" to the
relationship between Matthew and Luke rests on nothing more than his
declaration that that is the case. Smith made things up as he went along
and called the result "innovative." But the sole innovation is that for his
fabrications he got a Ph.D. from the Hebrew University, which at that
time did not give doctorates for fiction.

It is time for a null hypothesis (something of which Smith, in his
entire career, was ignorant). Let us now form the argument the way that
Smith should have and identify the propositions that, as to the facts, he
had to have proven to make his case. Specifically, if one wishes to allege
that the relationship between the Mishnah and the Tosefta is comparable

to the relationship between Matthew and Luke, then these are the facts that we have to be able to demonstrate. In the formulation, I use the Mishnah-Tosefta relationship as the known, the Matthew-Luke relationship as the unknown, though matters could have been stated in reverse.

1. Luke depends entirely for its sequence and topical program on Matthew. Smith does not imagine that he has to prove that fact, but, if he had tried, he would have failed.
2. Luke contains a mass of materials that cite verbatim and gloss those of Matthew, and that can be understood only by reference to their counterparts in Matthew. Smith never attempted to demonstrate that fact, which of course is false.
3. Luke contains further materials that can be fully understood only in the context of Matthew, even though these do not cite Matthew verbatim. Smith did not introduce such a possibility or imagine it.
4. Luke contains some small quota of materials not found in Matthew at all. Smith does show that each of the Gospels' accounts of the Sermon on the Mount has materials absent in the other.
5. Luke orders his materials in accord with their relationship to counterparts in Matthew, and not in accord with some plan of exposition governing his document and no other. Smith does not address this issue at all, nor did he see why it would enter into the argument.

Of course, the conditions just now defined for comparison are absurd; only No. 4 pertains, and that, of course, has no bearing on the relationships between the two documents. That is, the characterization of the relationship between Luke and Matthew is not advanced by the knowledge that the two documents at some points contain each its own, unique passages; that knowledge concerns the contents, not the relationships, of the documents.

So, it must follow, as to the data on documentary relationship, if we wanted to compare and contrast to the relationship between the Mishnah and Tosefta the relationship between Matthew and Luke, we should begin by defining how the one document relates to the other, and then asking whether the alleged counterparts relate in that way. Smith, we see in Chapter Two, has simply not done his homework. But it is not only Smith's sloth and ignorance that account for the vacuity of his "demonstration" in his Chapter Seven. The reason, I shall suggest in a moment, is that he did not define his problem with sufficient clarity to

identify the data he needed to examine. Even had he shown the wit and
energy to do the work, he bungled the conceptual problem so miserably
that hard work would have yielded a still less satisfactory result than his
penchant for a few "illustrations" and "examples" does.

In Smith's defense, I hasten to add, in his time people had not done
the work summarized in the preceding four chapters, so he cannot be
blamed for not knowing what he did not know. But then, by the late
1940s, New Testament scholarship had long since known about the
relationships between Matthew and Luke as whole documents. And
among these relationships, there was one that was fully exposed: the
relationship of Matthew, Mark, and Luke, to Q. I look in vain in Smith's
account of "parallels of parallelism" to the issue of Q: Does Smith think
that there is a "Q" from which the framers of both the Mishnah and the
Tosefta drew? If he does, then what shall we make of his pretentious
declaration, "I cannot recall even a word by any Jewish scholar
remarking – for example – that the problem of the relationship between
Tosefta and the Mishnah is similar to the synoptic problem, and this in
spite of the fact that they are so similar as to be practically inseparable,
and that any theory begun from a study of the one literature should have
immediate application in the study of the other"? In fact, the problem of
the relationship between Tosefta and the Mishnah bears no resemblance
whatever to the synoptic problem. And the rest of Smith's bombast is
just that: "so similar as to be practically inseparable" indeed! We owe
him only one fact. He is right that "any theory begun from a study of the
one literature should have immediate application in the study of the
other," but the consequences of that application – showing difference,
not "parallels of parallelism" – Smith could not have drawn. In fact,
Smith was merely babbling.

I do not think Smith was listening to what he was saying. But if
Smith had proved sentient to his own words, he would have raised the
first question anyone asks when dealing with the synoptic problem, and
that is, the matter of Q. But Q does not occur in this chapter of his or
elsewhere in the book, and Smith never proposes to raise the question of
a common source – or the lack of a common source. In other words,
Smith tells us everything but the main thing. He has missed the point of
his own dissertation. Clearly, it is time to rewrite Smith's dissertation for
him – the right way.

But first, let us turn from the fundamental flaw of incompetent work
to the details of the exercise. That is, if Smith has done the main thing
wrong, can we say he has done anything right? The answer,
unfortunately for the future use of his scholarship, is negative: not at all.
He not only has not done the work he should have done. The work that
he did do is hopelessly confused by his intellectual incompetence. My

survey in Chapter One of his other seven units shows ample evidence of gross bungling. Here, in the main chapter, we see how Smith's muddled thinking rendered worthless even the work he did do. Stated simply: Smith classified together in a single category diverse data of markedly different categories – the classic bungle of a confused mind.

II. Smith's Conceptual Bungling

By "complete parallels" Smith means parallels of relationships between whole documents in the one literature as compared with those of the other. When Smith refers to "complete parallels," it is, however, the source of a stunning mistake. He sometimes refers to one thing, sometimes to another, and the result is absolute chaos. Part of his statement is satisfactory, and part shows a profoundly muddled mind.

[1] Part of the time, he means, "parallels in the relationship of complete documents," that is, Luke is to Matthew as the Tosefta is to the Mishnah.

[2] But by "parallels of parallelism," what he also means is, "shared materials," or "passages common to two or more documents."

That a passage occurs in two documents yields a comparison of how two documents use the same passage. It does not justify a comparison of the two relationships of the two documents viewed in their entirety: "parallels in the relationship of complete documents." Here is where Smith shows his confusion: he seems to have forgotten his own definition when he got down to work. For the "relationship of complete documents" and "passages common to two or more documents" form completely different categories of comparison and contrast. Smith ends up sometimes comparing the relationship of apples of two species to the relationship of apples of two other species, which is what he says he is going to do. But most of the time, he compares elephants to Australians, finding out they both have ears, but Australians don't have tails. And when I claim that is a mark of stupidity, it is because an intelligent person notices in his own work what is silly or stupid – we all can say silly or stupid things – but the unintelligent person celebrates everything he has done. In the concluding unit of this chapter, I shall draw some general conclusions from the present case.

Let me expand on the confusion at hand, since readers will find as astonishing as I do the rather obvious errors that Smith makes. When he says, "large numbers of complete parallels," he clearly means, "passages that occur in common." This interpretation of what he says is clear when he adds, "But, apart from these pairs, there are to be found many passages common to all the midrashim." This second formulation introduces different types of relationships from the first – relationships of discrete and free-standing passages that occur in two or more documents simply are not the same thing as relationships of complete documents, and hence, comparison of the former will yield this, that, and the other thing, while comparisons of the latter will yield only one thing (or one thing and its opposite).

Now, as a matter of fact, the occurrence of the same passage in two or more documents is not the same thing as the parallel in patterns of relationship between two documents on the one side and two on the other. Indeed, these phenomena (whether or not we speak of parallels at all is no longer relevant) do not resemble one another. It is entirely possible that two or more documents will use the same composition or even composite without those documents running parallel at all. Some materials in them are shared; at those points, the documents intersect; but the documents are not parallel to one another and otherwise do not even relate to one another. They relate, rather, to a common source – where the original composition or composite is primary, as distinct from where it is inserted and added on; or they relate only through that common passage.

Is this what Smith means here? Well, yes and no. Sometimes he does, and sometimes he doesn't, and more often than not, he forgets what he is talking about anyhow. In the passage at which we began, Smith refers to "passages common to all the midrashim," so he must be speaking of parallel usages of a single passage. But he forthwith proceeds to state, "Scholars have paid little attention to this parallel which exists between the Gospels on the one hand and that of the books of TL on the other, viz.: that in both literatures the books are related to one another chiefly by 'complete' parallelism." The ambiguity is removed by his explicit statement: "I cannot recall even a word by any Jewish scholar [he means, of course, scholar of Judaism] remarking...that the problem of the relationship between Tosefta and the Mishnah is similar to the synoptic problem, and this in spite of the fact that they are so similar as to be practically inseparable, and that any theory begun from a study of the one literature should have immediate application in the study of the other." Here, Smith leaves no doubt, he refers not to shared passages but shared structures of relationship.

Here Smith's pathetic bungling – his confusion of two distinct phenomena – has exacted a heavy price. For the evidence relevant to the one hypothesis – shared materials – has no bearing upon the other hypothesis at all. And that brings us to Appendix C. Smith introduces it in these words: "As regards complete parallels, the relation between one book of the Gospels and another is similar in many details to the relation between one book and another of TL." And that once more focuses upon book-to-book relations. But forthwith he compares passages, not books. Indeed, he does not even allude to whole books and their relations, as I shall show in a later section of this chapter.

As was his way, Smith proceeds to the usual obsequious apologies and paralyzing qualifications. I refer the reader to Chapter Two's verbatim repetition, "I know of course.... I know also that.... Therefore I am sure that the comparison of the two relatively small pairs of parallels here chosen will not display all the sorts of parallels of parallelism to be found between the Gospels and TL...." As usual, he claims too much and then nothing whatsoever. He says he will show a number of important details, "and...this will suffice." But then there are (inconvenient) differences, "and only an examination of all the material, passage by passage – an examination which would require a synopsis for its undertaking and a work of several volumes for its completion – would make possible an exact review of these similarities and differences and an adequate estimate of the evidence for and against any historical theory as to the nature of the traditions behind the works studied. Any pretensions of historical significance thus specifically excluded, I can proceed to the comparison of the two pairs...." This of course is Smith's standard dissertation obfuscation: saying something, then denying it, then retracting it, then going ahead and saying it again.

Smith's account of his "parallels" in Appendix C, beginning in his paragraph, "The striking parallel...," proceeds to the – now-expected – series of banalities and stupidities. He has now parallels "emphasized by similarity in content," which is parallel to his great insight into form-analysis, that sermons have beginnings, middles, and endings. Here he has "passages contain lists of good or bad characteristics...," and the rest is incomprehensible blather. Then he has a contrast, blessings as against curses. That would be another piece of space filler, were it not that he has Matthew and the Mishnah on one side, Luke and Tosefta on the other. So this gives us the appearance of the comparison of whole documents. But he makes nothing of it, and he does not propose that Luke relates to the Tosefta as does Matthew to the Mishnah (complete parallels?). In fact, he says nothing. The next paragraph, beginning with "13 contains rules...," begins a long paraphrase of his evidence, and if he has any conclusion in the paragraph, readers will have to pick it out for themselves; I see nothing but this, that, and the other thing.

Smith's capacity to blather, saying everything and its opposite, in total oblivion to his starting point and alleged thesis, is brilliantly exemplified in his next paragraph, "The relationship between...." Here he tells us that the "relationship between a passage in Matthew and one in Mark has no counterpart in TL." What that shows is Smith has wandered over into the comparison of passages of documents, not whole documents, and what he is telling us is that there is no parallel of parallelism here, meaning, the relationship of a passage shared by the two Gospels and that of "TL" is not parallel. But he draws back: the Gospels' passages contradict, and "contradictions between Tosefta and the Mishnah are very frequent." Here Smith invokes heaven and earth to tell us what everybody knows anyhow. He then goes on to examples of what everyone should be willing to stipulate; but why stipulate facts when you can give whatever you want to fill space.

The next "discovery" is that the Mishnah has material absent in the Tosefta, just as Matthew has sections lacking in Luke. Here Smith reverts to the comparison of whole documents. But the comparison is – once more – simply trivial. All we find out is that, while Matthew and Luke compare in some ways, they differ in others, and the same is so for the Mishnah and Tosefta. The next paragraphs, "The last of these laws...," and, "Yet one more detail...," show once more how doctorands will fill up their pages with incoherent and irrelevant facts, if they are confident that their *Doktorväter* will not notice or will not care. After a mass of irrelevancies, Smith concludes, "To sum up, briefly: It has been found that the relations between the complete parallels found between Peah 1-3 and Peah T 1 are very similar to the relations between the complete parallels found between the sermon on the mount in Mat and its equivalent in Lk. This parallelism extends even to many details." That is how Smith packages a mass of petty aperçus and a mess of confused, often irrelevant observations about this, that, and the other thing.

Smith's final statement forms a confession that he has entirely missed the point of his data, and it pays to contemplate *ipsissima verba:*

> However, there are very important differences. The differences in the order of the elements between one Gospel and another are more frequent than those between the Mishnah and Tosefta. The Gospels do not contain passages in which it is unmistakably clear that the understanding of one Gospel depends on a knowledge of the content, if not the text, of another, but the understanding of Tosefta often depends on a knowledge of the Mishnah. From such facts it would be easy to develop a historical theory to the effect that the relationship of Tosefta to the Mishnah was closer than that of one Gospel to another because of the different ways in which written sources had been used. But either the demonstration or the refutation of such a theory would require a complete examination of the material.

Here Smith has stumbled into a corner of the field that, in Chapters Three through Six, I have surveyed in amplitude. If he had done a thorough job, instead of confusedly throwing together this and that and the other thing and declaring himself the first to see anything at all, he would have said the following:

1. the Gospels do not contain passages in which it is unmistakably clear that the understanding of one Gospel depends on a knowledge of the content, if not the text, of another;
2. the Gospels do not contain passages in which it is unmistakably clear that on Gospel has cited verbatim a passage spelled out in full in the other;
3. one Gospel does not organize its materials in total dependence upon the order and structure of another.

That is to say, Smith ought to have proved that there are no parallels of parallelism yielded by the examination of complete documents and their relationships – the point with which he began. And he ought to have recognized that the issue of how free-standing compositions shared by two or more documents compare and contrast has no bearing at all on how the documents as a whole relate.

Smith's collection of facts, some relevant, many not, his capacity to say, deny, say again, contradict, and finally claim whatever he wants to anyhow, his implacable refusal to do the work required but insistence that a few dubious examples suffice – all of these traits mark the work as amateurish and jejune, the author as uncertain of himself and confused, the results as pretentious and misleading. But these are traits of the man: flawed character, conscience, and intellectual capacity. That the chapter at hand presents a fraudulent, not only a flawed, thesis is shown by intellectual, not personal, failings. And that brings me at the end to the main point.

To summarize: Smith's conceptual bungling consists of three extraordinary errors.

1. Smith has simply confused his categories, not realizing that he collected data in a single classification that belong in two or more distinct classifications, so, in his confusion, Smith has compared as the same thing two different things.
2. Smith thinks that compositions ("passages") that are similar indicate a relationship between two documents, though they show only an intersection at the shared composition.
3. Smith has missed the main point of his comparison.

That is the mark of intellectual mediocrity, and it is the point on which I rest my case. It is to that third point, the point that Smith never raised at all, that we now turn. It was important to me in my time, because I was taken in by his assertion of his own uniqueness. I really did believe that the special boy was special.

III. The Relationship between the Tosefta and the Mishnah and the Synoptic Problem

"I cannot recall even a word by any Jewish scholar remarking – for example – that the problem of the relationship between Tosefta and the Mishnah is similar to the synoptic problem, and this in spite of the fact that they are so similar as to be practically inseparable, and that any theory begun from a study of the one literature should have immediate application in the study of the other."

When I first read those words, some three decades ago, the scales fell from my eyes. Such a thought had never entered my mind, and, as I have already explained, I had never heard such a thing. I determined to learn from Gospel research all of those theories begun in that literature that would have immediate bearing upon the study of rabbinic literature. Now we shall see how good results can flow from a proposition not proved, and not even fully understood, by the person who announced it.

Nothing in Smith's evidence substantiated this declaration of his, and most of his evidence proves monumentally irrelevant to it. Not only so, but having made that statement, as we have seen, Smith himself walked away, not identifying the main traits of Luke-Matthew relationships. Indeed, there is an element of sheer irresponsibility here: he spoke of "synoptic problem," without a word about Q, and with practically no attention to Mark. He declares at the outset he will compare Matthew's and Luke's Sermon on the Mount. But the key to the synoptic problem surely is Q. So, as I said, even on the Gospels' side of things, which Smith presumably knew, Smith simply misses the main point of his comparison. So both components of his comparison – Mishnah-Tosefta relationships, Matthew-Luke relationships – prove ignorant and fraudulent.

Now, Smith's greatest contribution to my education was in providing me with a model of how work should be done. So let me conclude this examination of his only book on Judaism by showing how that book should have been written. Specifically, since Smith omitted the main point of comparison and contrast, the relationship of Mark, Matthew, and Luke, to Q, and a second point of equal interest, the relationship of the principles of organization – the protocol that governed the selection of data and its arrangement – governing in Matthew, Luke, and Mark, on the one side, to the governing principles of selection and arrangement in the Mishnah and the Tosefta, let me ask two questions.

1. Do any documents in rabbinic literature draw on the equivalent of a Q? If so, then there is a basis for asking whether any two documents of rabbinic literature, drawing

on a common Q, relate in the same way as do Matthew,
Luke, and Mark, in relationship to their Q.

2.   Do any documents in rabbinic literature give evidence of a
shared protocol of selection and arrangement of data? If so,
then there is a basis for asking whether any two documents
of rabbinic literature share a common protocol governing the
selection and arrangement of data, the way Matthew, Mark,
Luke, and John accept a common protocol in presenting
Jesus Christ, differing in common from the protocol that
governs other New Testament re-presentations of the same
figure: biography, for instance, having its rules, which differ
from the rules that told Paul or the author of Hebrews how
to set forth their picture of the same Jesus Christ.

Smith's "parallels of parallelism" so poorly formulates matters that
he simply missed the point at hand; he never in fact discussed the issue
he (so confusedly) raised. So we are hardly bound by his choice of
documents – the Mishnah and the Tosefta – and may look elsewhere for
a more promising arena for comparison. Smith for his part knew only a
bit of rabbinic literature and nothing about the Talmuds, which he
consulted but never studied. He could not have done what we are about
to do, because he was ignorant and not only because he was not very
smart.

I turn forthwith from the Mishnah-Tosefta problem to the problem of
the two Talmuds. That is for two reasons. First of all, we now realize,
there is no "parallel of parallelism" between Matthew and Luke on the
one side and the Mishnah and the Tosefta on the other. The Tosefta
quotes the Mishnah and formulates much of its materials in dependence
upon the Mishnah – no Q there. Not only so, but, for much the same
reason, since the Tosefta depends for order, structure, and topic upon the
Mishnah, we cannot characterize the relationship of the two documents
as one of dependence upon a common, prior, shared protocol.

But what if Smith had exerted himself a bit – the dominant quality of
the dissertation being a resort to labor-saving devices throughout – and
had actually turned to documents read as such, not just to passages that
float hither and yon. That is, if he had taken seriously his own thesis
concerning a "parallel of parallelism," he would have identified as his
best candidate for the identification of a rabbinic parallel not the
Mishnah and the Tosefta but the two Talmuds. Here, the Yerushalmi
and the Bavli come to center stage. They share the Mishnah and the
Tosefta. They also undertake the same task, which is Mishnah-Tosefta
relationships. And, finally and most important, even by Smith's time it
was well known that the two Talmuds draw upon a shared corpus of

sayings that occur in no prior, completed document but that do occur in both Talmuds – surely an open invitation to a comparison with Q. If Smith had done the work with commitment and energy, rather than giving excuses why it is too much trouble to examine all the data, would he have found his parallel of parallelism? I shall now answer that question for him, since it is the one his dissertation promised to answer but failed even to consider. He would have come up with nothing, but, at least, it would have been a noteworthy and important negative result. The failed experiment teaches more than the successful one – for people in honest search of learning.

IV. Do Any Documents in Rabbinic Literature Draw on the Equivalent of a Q?

Do we find in the two Talmuds an appeal to common prior source or collection of earlier authorities' sayings, in the context of Gospel research, a "source" or *Quelle* (Q). Stories in the Talmuds about communications sent from one community of sages to another, citations of one locale's principal authorities in the Talmud of the other, allegations that the Babylonian sages humbly accepted the priority of those of the Land of Israel, the appearance of sages of the one country in the Talmud of the other – these well-attested facts form ample grounds for the hypothesis of a "Q." So we rightly ask, Do the Bavli and Yerushalmi draw on (a) "Q"? That is to say, is there a corpus of sayings available to the authors of compositions and framers of composites used in both Talmuds and prior to and independent of each? If such a source of sayings circulated, then the Bavli cannot be said to stand independent of the Yerushalmi, since it would then be joined to the Yerushalmi not only by common sources upon which both draw or comment, but something far more definitive of the character of the Bavli in the tradition of the Yerushalmi.

Now, it is a demonstrable fact that, here and there, the Bavli cites the same saying in the same wording that the Yerushalmi presents in its composition on a given Mishnah pericope. That is in three aspects. First, it is the simple fact that, occasionally, sayings not found in any prior document are shared in the same or nearly the same wording by the Yerushalmi and the Bavli. That is not surprising. Stories in both Talmuds speak of constant communications among the authorities of each country's Jewish polity. That the Bavli had access to sayings assigned to the Yerushalmi's authorities is shown on virtually every other page of the document, where Simeon b. Laqish or Yohanan or their colleagues are cited. What I take that to mean is, the stories about circulating sayings are matched by the data themselves, which show the Babylonians' utilizing sayings in the names of the other country's sages.

But whether or not collections of such sayings existed, as a counterpart to "Q," and, if they did, what such collections looked like, is a separate question.

For a saying to occur in the rabbinic "Q," I should want it to be cited in both Talmuds, in the same context or for the same purpose. If a saying imputed to a Yerushalmi figure occurs only in the Bavli, for example, in a dispute involving Rab and Samuel, Simeon b. Laqish and Yohanan, that may show that the Babylonians had access to sayings from the Land of Israel (if we take the names at face value), but it does not show that a common corpus of sayings circulated in both countries and influenced the formation of both Talmuds along the same lines (yielding a Bavli dependent on Q dependent on the Yerushalmi or closely tied to it); it shows the exact opposite. If a saying assigned to a Yerushalmi sage occurs in both the Yerushalmi and the Bavli but not in the same context, for example, "R. Simeon b. Laqish says, 'It is unfit,'" that is inconsequential, because it is simply indeterminate.

But if, in the same setting, for example, of Mishnah exegesis or analysis of legal principle or premise, the same saying occurs in the same way in both documents (but in no other prior or contemporary document, for example, the Mishnah, Tosefta, or Sifra), and if that saying is so worded as to be particular to the issue (not just "R. Yohanan declares unclean"), or distinctive to the context, then we may propose that that saying derives from a circulating collection of sayings of Yerushalmi sages (or Babylonian ones, for that matter); and then there was a "Q." And if there was a "Q," then, while not directly connected, the Bavli stands in an established relationship to the Yerushalmi – as against my interpretation of the facts I have established, which is, the Bavli is independent of the earlier Talmud (within the amply specified qualifications about prior common sources of the Torah, Scripture, and the Mishnah, for example).

Here I shall have to follow Smith's dubious example of declining to reproduce all the evidence. It will have to suffice if I state very simply that, in the sample I examined, there are too few such sayings, to suggest that the framers of the Bavli drew to any extent on a corpus of set sayings in the formation of their compositions. But the issue is not quantity but effect. If there was such a "Q," the part of it the existence of which we can demonstrate through hard evidence was both trivial and lacking in all influence. I have simply never found a case in which that shared saying, from a hypothetical "Q," influenced the authors of the two Talmuds' compositions to say the same thing in the same way. To the contrary, shared sayings were used in different ways, with the consequence that, if there was a "Q," it made no difference to the authors of the Bavli's compositions as they contemplated their exegetical or hermeneutical program.

A specific case is now called for. If there was a "Q," what would it have looked like? Here is a candidate for consideration: At M. Niddah 1:1 neither set of authors does more than give a reprise of received materials. But if I had to specify the character of the received materials, I should have to say that, as to wording, they do not appear the same in both Talmuds; it is the gist that can be shown to play a role in both Talmuds' compositions, not the wording – so surely no "Q" by any definition that pertains. I underline what I take to be the candidate for "Q."

[I.A] Samuel said, "This teaching [of A] applies only to a virgin and an old lady. But as to a pregnant woman and a nursing mother, they assign to her the entire period of her pregnancy or the entire period of her nursing [respectively, for the blood ceases, and what does flow is inconsequential, so there is no retroactive contamination at all]."

[B] Rab and R. Yohanan – both of them say, "All the same are the virgin, the old lady, the pregnant woman, and the nursing mother [= B]."

[C] Said R. Zeira, "The opinion of Rab and R. Yohanan accords with the position of R. Haninah, and all of them differ from the position of Samuel."

VIII.1 A. And of what case did they speak when they said, "Sufficient for her is her time"? In the case of the first appearance of a drop of blood. But in the case of the second appearance of such a drop of blood, she conveys uncleanness to whatever she touched during the preceding twenty-four hours.

B. Said Rab, "The statement [But in the case of the second appearance of such a drop of blood, she conveys uncleanness to whatever she touched during the preceding twenty-four hours] applies to all the listed cases."

C. And Samuel said, "It refers only to the virgin and the old lady, but as to the pregnant woman and the nursing mother, throughout all the days of pregnancy or through all the days of nursing, it is sufficient for them to reckon uncleanness not retroactively but only from the time of observing a flow."

D. And so said R. Simeon b. Laqish, "The statement **[But in the case of the second appearance of such a drop of blood, she conveys uncleanness to whatever she touched during the preceding twenty-four hours]** applies to all the listed cases."

E. And R. Yohanan said, "It refers only to the virgin and the old lady, but as to the pregnant woman and the nursing mother, throughout all the days of pregnancy or through all the days of nursing, it is sufficient for them to reckon uncleanness not retroactively but only from the time of observing a flow."

F. *The dispute follows the lines of a dispute among Tannaite versions:*

[D] For R. Eleazar said in the name of R. Haninah, "On one occasion Rabbi gave instruction in accord with the lenient rulings of R. Meir and in accord with the lenient rulings of R. Yosé."

[E] What was the nature of the case?

[F] [If] the feotus was noticeable, and then [the woman] produced a drop of blood –

[G] R. Meir says, "She is subject to the rule of the sufficiency of her time [of actually discovering the blood]."

G. "A pregnant woman or a nursing mother who were **[11A]** bleeding profusely – throughout all the days of pregnancy or through all the days of nursing, it is sufficient for them to reckon uncleanness not retroactively but only from the time of observing a

flow," the words of R.
Meir.

[H] R. Yosé says, "She imparts uncleanness retroactively for twenty-four hours."

H. R. Yosé and R. Judah and R. Simeon say, "The ruling that sufficient for them is the time of their actually seeing a drop of blood applies only to the first appearance of a drop of blood, but the second imparts uncleanness for the preceding twenty-four hours or from one examination to the prior examination."

[I] [If] she produced many drops of blood, then missed three periods, and afterward produced a drop of blood,

[J] R. Meir says, "She imparts uncleanness retroactively for twenty-four hours."

[K] R. Yosé says, "She is subject to the rule of the sufficiency of her time [of actually discovering blood]."

[L] Now if you say that they assign to her the entire period of her pregnancy or the entire period of her nursing, what need do I have for the lenient ruling of R. Yosé? The teaching of R. Meir [in such a case] produces a still more lenient ruling than does that of R. Yosé. [For so far as Meir is concerned, if we read his view in the light of Samuel's opinion (A), the nursing mother and the pregnant woman enjoy the stated leniency throughout the period of nursing or pregnancy. The issue, then, is that Meir deems this drop of blood (I) as a second one. Yosé regards the cessation of the period as consequential.]

[M] Said R. Mana before R. Yosé, "Or perhaps we should assign [Rabbi's ruling] to the case of the milk [dealt with above,

in which Meir and Yosé
dispute about whether
the woman who hands
over her son to a wet
nurse retains the stated
leniency. At issue then is
whether the matter
depends upon the status
of the woman's milk or
on the status of the
child]."

[N] He said to him, "The
matter was explicitly
stated in regard to the
present issue."

I see no material differences as to the gist of the law, between the two
Talmuds' representation of the matter. But this kind of intersection has
proven very, very rare in our sample. So all we can conclude is that we
have a fine example of what the two Talmuds would have looked like,
had the Bavli's authors satisfied themselves with a reprise of the
Yerushalmi, a reprise constructed by reference not to the Yerushalmi
itself but to some sort of handbook of sayings. "Q" here would then
have consisted of something that yielded the underlined wording in the
respective documents, that is to say, that would have permitted the
Bavli's composition's author to word matters as he did. If this were our
sole evidence, then we should have to posit a "Q" consisting of
paraphrases and allusions, the gist of what was said, not the wording;
but then the analogy collapses, that is not what "Q" consists of or how it
contributes to the received Gospels.

Second, some items that appear to attest to a "Q" of sayings, not the
gist, show the opposite, for what appears to be a shared saying may turn
out, on closer examination, to be two distinct sayings, one for each
Talmud. Hence, even where a saying appears to originate in the rabbinic
counterpart to "Q," in fact it shows the opposite: not a well-crafted
sourcebook of sayings, but a rather slovenly process of tradition,
operating so that handing on whatever was shared was botched. Let me
give a single example of such a phenomenon, one in which (as a matter
of fact) the Yerushalmi's version in fact is superior to the Bavli's.

M. M.Q. 3:4: We have a somewhat odd situation at Y. 3:4III and B. 3:4
I.2. As it stands, the latter is incomprehensible, and it clearly presupposes
the former. Then there is no discussion, at B.'s version, of Rab's views:

[III.A]	Someone lost his *tefillin* on the intermediate days of a festival. He came to	I.2 A.	*Rab instructed R. Hananel, and some say, Rabbah bar bar Hanna instructed R.*

R. Hananel [who was a scribe and who would prepare a new set for him]. He sent him to R. Abba bar Nathan. He said to him, "Give him your *tefillin [phylacteries]* and go, write a new set for yourself."

[B] Said to him Rab, "[It is permitted to] go and write them for him [without practicing deception]."

[C] The Mishnah stands at variance with the view of Rab: A *man may write out tefillin and mezuzahs for his own use [M. 3:4G].*

[D] Lo, for someone else he may not do so.

[E] Interpret the passage to speak of not doing so merely by writing them out and leaving them [for future sale].

Hananel, "The decided law is this: He may write them out and sell them in the ordinary way if it is to make his living."

As we have it, B.'s version is strange and out of context; read as a continuation of B. 3:4 I.1, the statement does not intersect with Y.'s case at all; but then how explain the reference to Hananel?! So, in all, here is a case in which a fragment of a formulation has been inserted, and without the Yerushalmi, the fragment is not to be interpreted.

Yet a second look calls that judgment into question. In fact, Rab's instructions to Hananel in B. have to do with writing tefillin and selling them on the intermediate days of the festival if it is to make a living; Y.'s formulation does not introduce that consideration at all. And the reason that the consideration of making a living is introduced at B. 3:4 I.2 is Yosé's reference to it at I.1D! So, in fact, while somewhere in the dim past of both Talmuds' compositions may lie a statement of Rab to Hananel (or: Rabbah bar bar Hanna!), the use of the same by each depends entirely on considerations particular to each Talmud respectively. Here is no instance in which making sense of the Bavli requires that we resort to the Yerushalmi or to "Q"; to the contrary, all we have to do is back up one line to make sense of the Bavli's formulation entirely in the Bavli's own terms.

Do the Bavli and Yerushalmi draw on (a) "Q"? At some points, they do draw on finished, and available materials, ordinarily, sayings floating hither and yon. It is very common that these finished materials occur also in the Tosefta, which is hardly surprising, but, occasionally, the finished materials are not located in any other document. So there could have been a "Q," but not like a "Q" of the size and importance of the one that is attested by Matthew and Mark and used by Luke. But if there was a shared corpus of sayings besides those in available documents, what difference does that fact make for the description of the Bavli? None. The Bavli emerges, all the more so, as a free-standing document, written by its compositions' writers and its composites' compilers, for whatever purpose suited them. They used traditions, whether deriving from Scripture or the Mishnah or the Tosefta or other compilations bearing the sign of Tannaite status; this they did for their own purposes, in their own way, for the presentation of their own statement. They used traditions, they were not traditional. More to the point, the relationship between the two Talmuds in no way exhibits a parallel to the relationship of Matthew, Luke, Mark, and Q.

V. Do Any Documents in Rabbinic Literature Give Evidence of a Shared Protocol of Exegesis or Common Convention Governing the Selection and Arrangement of Data?

Since the Gospels share a protocol that governs in them all – the teachings of Jesus being set forth in the context of a biography, with numerous points in common, on the one side, and a shared protocol of arrangement (all end with Passion narratives, for instance, and these are situated in the same place in each of the Gospels), we may ask whether a parallel of parallelism may be found here. That is, do the two Talmuds follow a single convention of exegesis of the same Mishnah passage? Do they follow a common protocol in the selection and arrangement of their Mishnah commentaries? If they do, then Smith could have identified here a very compelling case for his "parallel of parallelism."

Let me spell out this null hypothesis. An established, conventional protocol, governing the problematic identified in a given Mishnah paragraph by both Talmuds, can link the Talmuds and compromise the independence of the second one. So we now ask: If there is no shared corpus of sayings, then does a topical protocol define both Talmuds' Mishnah exegesis, that is, a protocol of topics or problems associated with a given Mishnah pericope but not articulated therein? Such a protocol would have told the exegetes of that pericope, or the compilers of compositions deemed pertinent to that pericope, what subject they should treat (over and above the subject of the pericope); or what problem they should investigate (over and above the problem explicit in the pericope). Obviously, every Mishnah pericope treated differently in the two Talmuds gives evidence that there was no such protocol of topics or problems. But more specific evidence can be adduced, where the Mishnah pericope does not demand attention to a topic, but both Talmuds address said topic. It is at Mishnah Moed Qatan 3:5-6, where the absence of a protocol of problems, over and above those of Scripture, emerges:

[XXXIX.A] For they have said, "The Sabbath counts in the days of mourning, but does not interrupt the period of mourning, while the festivals interrupt the period of mourning, and do not count in the days of mourning" [M. 3:5C].

[B] "[The festivals do not count,]" R. Simon in the name of R. Yohanan [explained], "Because one is permitted on them to have sexual relations."

[C] R. Jeremiah dealt with R. Judah b. R. Simon, saying to him, "Do all the disciples of R. Yohanan report this tradition? Not one person has ever heard this tradition from him, except for your father!"

[D] Said to him R. Jacob, "If it was said, it was said only by those who say, 'Thus and so is the matter' [without knowing what they are talking about]!

[E] "For R. Joshua b. Levi said, 'Lo, [on the festival] it is forbidden [for a mourner] to have sexual relations.'"

[F] For R. Simon said in the name of R. Joshua b. Levi, "Have they not

II.1 A. For they have said, "The Sabbath counts [in the days of mourning] but does not interrupt [the period of mourning], [while] the festivals interrupt [the period of mourning] and do not count [in the days of mourning]":

B. *Judeans and Galilaeans* —

C. *These say,* [2 3 B] "Mourning pertains to the Sabbath."

D. *And those say,* "Mourning does not pertain to the Sabbath."

E. *The one who says,* "Mourning pertains to the Sabbath," *cites the Mishnah's statement,* The Sabbath counts [in the days of mourning].

F. *The one who says,* "Mourning does not pertain to the Sabbath," *cites the Mishnah's statement,* but does not interrupt [the period of mourning]. *Now if you take the view that mourning applies to the Sabbath, if mourning were observed, would there be any question of its interrupting the counting of the days of mourning?*

G. *Well, as a matter of fact, the same passage does say* The Sabbath counts [in the said, 'A mourning does not apply on a festival, but people observe mourning discretely'?"

[G] What is the context for this discretion? It has to do with sexual relations [which are not to be performed on the festival by a mourner].

[H] [Reverting to the discussion broken off at B:] They objected, "Lo, in the case of the festival, lo, the mourner is prohibited from having sexual relations, and yet it does not count [toward the days of mourning]. Also in regard to the Sabbath, since a mourner is forbidden to have sexual relations, the Sabbath should not count [among the days of mourning, and yet it does, so the reason proposed at B is not likely]."

[I] Said R. Ba, "It is possible that seven days can pass without a festival, but it is not possible that seven days can pass without a Sabbath[, and if the Sabbath does not suspend the rites of mourning, there will be eight days of mourning, and not seven]."

days of mourning]*!*

H. *The inclusion of that phrase is on account of what is coming, namely,* [while] the festivals interrupt [the period of mourning] and do not count [in the days of mourning], *so the Tannaite formulation to balance matters also stated,* The Sabbath counts [in the days of mourning].

I. *And as to the position of him who says,* "Mourning pertains to the Sabbath," *does the passage not say,* but does not interrupt [the period of mourning]?

J. *That is because the framer of the passage wishes to include,* the festivals interrupt [the period of mourning], *so for the sake of balance he stated as well,* The Sabbath...does not interrupt [the period of mourning].

II.2 A. *May we say that at issue is what is under debate among the Tannaite authorities in the following:*

B. As to one whose deceased [actually] lies before him, he eats in a different room. If he does not have another room, he eats in the room of his fellow. If he has no access to the room of his fellow, he makes a partition and eats [separate from the corpse]. If he has nothing with which to make a partition, he turns his face away and eats.

C. He does not recline and eat, he does not eat meat, he does not drink wine,

he does not say a bless-
ing before the meal, he
does not serve to form a
quorum, and people do
not say a blessing for
him or include him in a
quorum.

D.   He is exempt from the
requirement to recite the
Shema and from the
Prayer and from the
requirement of wearing
phylacteries and from all
of the religious duties
that are listed in the
Torah.

E.   But on the Sabbath he
does recline and eat, he
does eat meat, he does
drink wine, he does say a
blessing before the meal,
he does serve to form a
quorum and people do
say a blessing for him
and include him in a
quorum. And he is liable
to carry out all of the
religious duties that are
listed in the Torah.

F.   Rabban Simeon b.
Gamaliel says, "Since he
is liable for these
[religious duties], he is
liable to carry out all of
them."

G.   And [in connection with
the dispute just now
recorded], R. Yohanan
said, *"What is at issue
between [Simeon and the
anonymous authority]? At
issue is the matter of
having sexual relations.*
[Simeon maintains that
the mourner on the
Sabbath has the religious
obligation to have sexual
relations with his wife,
and the anonymous
authority does not
include that require-

ment, since during the mourning period it does not apply.]"

H.   Is now this what is at stake between them, namely, one authority [Simeon b. Gamaliel] maintains, "Mourning pertains to the Sabbath," and the other takes the view, "Mourning does not pertain to the Sabbath"?

I.   *What compels that conclusion? Perhaps the initial Tannaite authority takes the view that he does there only because of the simple consideration that the deceased is lying there awaiting burial, but in the present case, in which the deceased is not lying there awaiting burial, he would not take the position that he does. And, further, perhaps Rabban Simeon b. Gamaliel takes the position that he does in that case because, at that point [prior to burial] the restrictions of mourning do not pertain, but, here, where the restrictions of mourning do pertain, he would concur [that the mourning does pertain to the Sabbath].*

II.3   A.   [24A] *R. Yohanan asked Samuel*, "Does mourning pertain to the Sabbath or does mourning not pertain to the Sabbath?"

B.   He said to him, "Mourning does not pertain to the Sabbath."

Now what is interesting here is not that the passages do not intersect. It is that there is no protocol or convention that links the two Talmuds' reading of the same Mishnah passage.

To the contrary, the case suggests there was none. We see that the Bavli introduces the case of one's deceased's actually lying there in the room, and links that case with the present dispute. But the Yerushalmi treats that situation in a completely different context, namely, at Y. 3:5 VI. What makes that evidence probative is simple. The passage where the Yerushalmi treats the cited question serves *not* our Mishnah pericope at all, but rather M. Ber. 3:1. Since it has nothing to do with the Mishnah passage to which, in the Bavli, the topic is tied, here is no argument from silence. It is, rather, decisive evidence that no topical protocol told sages in both the Land of Israel and Babylonia where and how to address a given theme that was not in the Mishnah but somehow deemed connected to it. Where the framers of the Yerushalmi thought a given subject, not introduced by the Mishnah but held relevant to it, should be addressed, the authors of the compositions and composites of the Bavli had no such notion, and, it goes without saying, vice versa.

Reverting to the comparison of Gospels' relationships to Talmuds' relationships, let me spell out the hypothetical parallel of parallelism. Here again, an analogy may clarify for New Testament scholars what is at stake here. It is clear that for the authors of the four canonical Gospels as well as all of the extracanonical ones, a shared protocol, not spelled out, dictated the subjects that should be treated and the order in which they should occur. That is to say, if we propose to talk about Jesus Christ, his life and teachings, we follow an established program. We are going to discuss, for example, the Passion, and, moreover, the Passion is going to appear at the end of the narrative. A biographical narrative will intrude throughout. That protocol governs in all four Gospels, without regard to the character of the Passion narrative, on the one side, or the program of sayings and stories to be utilized in the articulation of the various Gospels, respectively, on the other: a fine example of a blatant topical (narrative) protocol.

If such a protocol were in play, then when discussing a given Mishnah paragraph, compilers of both Talmuds would have introduced the same themes, not mentioned in the Mishnah (whether in the paragraph at hand or in some other paragraph) but held in common to belong to the clarification of that Mishnah paragraph. But where a topic not introduced in a given Mishnah paragraph is treated by both Talmuds, the framers of one Talmud will deal with that topic in one place, those of the other, in a different place; nothing tells them both to treat the same topic in the same context. That is so when it comes to matters of lore; where we have the same story, it will not always serve the same purpose; and it is true when it comes to matters of law.

We have seen in the sample of evidence just now reviewed that there is no substantial, shared tradition, either in fully spelled-out statements in so many words, or in the gist of ideas, or in topical conventions, or in intellectual characteristics. The Bavli presents an utterly autonomous statement, speaking in its own behalf and in its own way about its own interests. The shared traits are imposed and extrinsic, formal: documents cited by one set of writers and by another. The differentiating characteristics are intrinsic and substantive: what is to be done with the shared formed statements taken from prior writings. The framers of the Bavli in no way found guidance in the processes by which the Yerushalmi's compositions and composites took shape, either in the dim past of the document, or, it goes without saying, in the results of those processes as well. The Talmuds differ not in general only, but in detail; not in how they make their statements or in what they say but, at a more profound level, in their very generative layers, in the intellectual morphology characteristic of each. What Smith could have demonstrated is that there is no parallel of parallelism. Such a negative result would have reinforced his teachers' insistence that nothing was to be learned for rabbinic literature from Gospels' research; but that they knew anyhow, and for that they would have given Morton Smith no Ph.D. It suffices to conclude very simply that, assessed by the results spelled out here, they would have been right, though they would not have known why.

VI. What, Today, Is to Be Learned from the Career of Morton Smith?

This doctoral dissertation of course bears a misleading title and makes promises it never keeps. For Smith's *Tannaitic Parallels to the Gospel* yields these facts:

[1]   The Tannaitic parallels to the Gospels prove trivial and obvious.
[2]   The Tannaitic differences from the Gospels prove weighty and formidable.
[3]   The real point of comparison – the matter of Q – is neglected, but, had it been pursued, would have yielded a book called *Tannaitic Differences from the Gospels.*

But for that book, Smith would have gotten no Ph.D., because, after all, everybody knew then, as we all know now, that the Tannaite writings and the Gospels are different from one another. Others may evaluate the further principal books that Smith wrote. I am inclined to think that, in the next generation, Smith will be forgotten or, when read, provide lessons on how not to pursue a career of learning. Even from the document at hand, we may draw conclusions for the coming ages to consider in evaluating Smith's work.

The sorry record of Smith's scholarship serves as a warning to scholars now and in the future. It yields the twin lessons:

[1]   learn from other people, and
[2]   criticize your own ideas.

From others Smith got facts, but no insight. And as to his own ideas, Smith more adeptly criticized other people's conceptions than his own. I learned from Smith not only what he had to teach about writing a book, but, over the years afterward, also how not to conduct a scholarly career. To me, Smith's failures of wit and character served as a warning. The work of other people I find stimulating and suggestive; when it is poor, as, in my field, I ordinarily find it to be, I learn what not to do and look in my own work for the flaws I find in that of others. As to my own ideas, the restlessness and dissatisfaction that characterize my oeuvre show the simple fact that I revise and rework, ever changing what I have done, always reshaping – but then, moving on, too, to new problems.

The most published scholar of my generation, I may state very simply: Each major project of mine forms a scathing review of the one before it. I have worked in a series of large-scale enterprises, taking up major problems of text, history, history of ideas, history of religion, and working through those problems of description, analysis, and interpretation, presented by a set of sources; and each such enterprise differs from the foregoing in not only topic but problematic; and every one of them improves upon its predecessor; and all of them, each in sequence, repudiates not the results but the urgency and consequence of its predecessor.

Never satisfied with what I have done (and, admittedly, rarely impressed with what others in my field have done either), I move on to new things, but always in a straight line, so forming a coherent, incremental work. Rejecting dilettantism, I have followed a single, straight path, accumulating not only learning and experience, but also a rich store of dissatisfaction with earlier achievements. Each project has formed the logical successor's problem, and each new project addressed flaws in its predecessor. Overall, I never repeat work I have finished (though I try to provide a reprise of the main results for diverse audiences), but I always build upon prior projects and improve them. Just as one who wants money never gets enough money, so one who wants learning never gets enough either – if curiosity is the motive and quest for understanding the goal.

Specifically, it is important in the context of his later career to reread Smith's most important writing, since here we see the cost of failure to continue to learn and work. Smith was not a very productive scholar, he was not a very painstaking or patient scholar, he was hasty in drawing conclusions and sloppy in presenting them, because he did not pursue the main lines of any investigation beyond the beginnings. That explains why he was so superficial. And the flaws, we now know, were present in the beginning: he absolutely refused to cover all the necessary data, he persisted in insisting that a little "sample" would have to suffice, since it was too much trouble to do the whole required labor. Well, I did the entire work, and that is why I have shown he was simply wrong. The superficiality of his research then is one characteristic trait, accounting for the opinionated mode of discourse he selected: he had to talk everybody down, because he feared to argue in a civil way.

But that does not define the sole lesson to be learned from him. There is another, as I have already implied. Smith was not only opinionated, he also was a dilettante. He had opinions on many more subjects than he ever closely investigated, as the utterly disparate topics on which he wrote books shows. That fact has been frequently seen in the pages of this book. We have time and again observed how his superficial and impressionistic grasp of Mishnah-Tosefta relationships led him to misrepresent those relationships. This was, alas, so that he could make a point no one else had ever made (or, knowing the facts, would make). So the second lesson is this: Work always, if not on the same thing, then along some one line, continuously; and argue against yourself.

Smith thought he knew more about more things than he actually did, and intoxicated by his exaggerated sense of his learning, he stumbled more than a few times. With his usual self-assurance, Smith announced results treated here but never returned to them. He did not pursue the paths he claimed he had discovered. He never therefore found out whether he was right or wrong in his original pronouncements. Smith, adept as passing his opinion, therefore never built upon the foundations he laid down. Consequently, he also never found out that, in fact, most of his results would prove trivial and obvious, and the really important proposals would not stand the test of further work on the same documents. Smith learned from others only information, rarely insight, and never well-crafted proposals contrary to his own preconceptions. He was a true believer – in himself.

Smith's tragic, fruitless career reminds coming generations that scholarship, an art form in the end, not only expresses the scholar's learning, imagination, and wit, but also forms a monument to the scholar's character and conscience. Flaws of the one turn out, upon examination, to replicate failings of the other. Power and politics gain a certain ephemeral prominence for the one who values the former and relies upon the latter. And many do, because it is what they have. For

Smith, power meant, the power to destroy persons and careers by a mere expression of his opinion, a conception Smith shared with other powers of his day, Gershom Scholem, Salo W. Baron, Louis Finkelstein, Solomon Zeitlin, Saul Lieberman, and Ephraim E. Urbach, in "Jewish Studies," for example. And for them all, politics meant gossip and character assassination, carried on behind the curtain or within the closed committee.

In his day, many feared Smith and his clones, and only a very, very few in the world he dominated defied him. I am proud that, when the occasion demanded, I was one of the few. By publicly condemning his *Secret Gospel's* outcome, *Jesus the Magician,* I opposed anti-Christianism just as so many Christian scholars, from Moore through Sanders, have opposed anti-Judaism. I take pride that, when it was time to stand up and be counted, I said in print that Smith's portrait of Jesus was not history but contemptible, hateful ideology. There were no costs of consequence. True, Smith never forgave me, and he spent his best energies for years and years to come to try to destroy me. But he never came close. He merely ruined his own career – if, after his *Clement of Alexandria and a Secret Gospel of Mark* and *The Secret Gospel: The Discovery and Interpretation of the Secret Gospel According to Mark* and *Jesus the Magician,* he can be said to have had a career at all.

Morton Smith was a victim of his own vice. Smith believed too much in his own infallibility. We who, for longer or shorter periods of his life, were his disciples and brought him our goodwill and our admiration, in the end did not serve him well. We gave too much, too devotedly, so he mistook our gifts for a tribute none imagined, or could pay. He heard what we never said. I look back with satisfaction that I did make an honorable statement, and I take his abuse to attest to the fact that I succeeded in making my message heard.

There is one more lesson to be drawn. Intelligence and patient, everyday work at learning for the early years prove commonplace in the academy, defining the requirement for admission. But, once tenured, professors tend to an excess of certitude and to sloth; hard work on some one problem over a long period of time is therefore episodic. Even with the security of tenure, in the academy genuine independence of judgment and patient autonomy prove still rarer. But self-criticism, restless dissatisfaction with one's own results – among scholars that inner provocation is only seldom found or felt. People prefer to celebrate what they have done than to contemplate what they have left to do. In the end, bombast and intimidation fail. For enduring learning builds upon intelligence, sustained, hard work, which many have, but, above all, that independence of judgment and a bottomless store of self-criticism that mark only the few who, from one generation, will speak to the future.

Appendix One

Smith's Legacy of Conceptual Bungling: The Case of Lee I. Levine

The Rabbinic Class of Roman Palestine in Late Antiquity (Jerusalem: Yad Ishak Ben-Zvi; New York, 1989: Jewish Theological Seminary of America). Pp. 223. N.P.

Smith had no patience for problems of category formation, with the result that he found himself trapped by unexamined categories and paralyzed by methods long since abandoned in the generality of learning. The result, as we saw in Chapter Seven, was total confusion; his entire dissertation turns out to collapse in ruins around Smith's confusion on matters of definition.

His disciple, Lee Levine, in the book examined here, exhibits Smith's incapacity to define with care and wit the categories that he uses, to examine the methods he employs, and to defend the formulations he sets forth. To the contrary, like Smith, Levine here shows himself a conceptual bungler. That bungling affects not only his category formations but his arguments, and, in this regard, he proves himself inferior to his master, who had a rich capacity for vigorous (if not very rigorous) argument.

Dean of the Jewish Theological Seminary's Jerusalem center, Levine treats these subjects: first, "the challenges of the third century," with attention to the sages during the first centuries C.E., urbanization, institutionalization, and a new attitude toward the people, the role of Judah I in shaping the rabbinic class, the sages in a new historic context: the Galilee, the urban aristocracy, and the patriarch; second, "the status of the rabbinic class," with attention to the ideal of Torah study, the uniqueness of the sages, special privileges of the sages, the social support system of the rabbis, the size of the rabbinic class, the economic support system, stratification within the rabbinic class, was there a Sanhedrin in Palestine during the Talmudic era, and pluralism and tension among the sages. He treats, third, "the sages within Jewish society," the sages and Galilean Jewry, the image of the sages, the responsiveness of the sages to the needs of the community, the sages and *ammei haaretz*, friction between the sages and the people, the place of the sages in Jewish society; and fourth, "the sages, the patriarch, and community life," the dominant position of the patriarch in late antiquity, sages at the time of various patriarchs, the sages as *parnasim*, the sages and the urban aristocracy, the patriarchate and the urban aristocracy, rabbinic attitudes toward communal involvement, the sages and the patriarch: tension and cooperation. The book ends with "the status of the sages in late antiquity: an assessment."

This account of the contents shows us that Levine surveys evidence in a thematic way, rather than arguing a coherent proposition. His difficulty in sustaining a coherent argument affects not only the book as a whole, but even the chapters, subdivisions, and paragraphs, which tend to shade over from one thing to something else. Indeed, the book looks like an anthology, with lots of sources and some free-associative remarks tacked on. But three problems render the volume a mere curiosity, of no scholarly value whatsoever.

First, we turn to Levine's conceptual bungling, worthy of his teacher. Levine's theoretical framework, involving the Marxist term, "class," proves jerrybuilt and sustains no solid structure of inquiry. That is not surprising, since, in his ignorance, Levine seems unaware, in invoking the metaphor of "class," that his use of so Marxist a category will puzzle an entire generation of scholarship in Greco-Roman antiquity, which finds many problems in a category Levine invokes so innocently. In his defense, it must be said that he uses the word "class" in a very private way. By "class" he means merely "a group for whom social and religious issues are of prime importance, yet it differs from a 'party' primarily with respect to its political involvements or, more precisely, the lack thereof. This does not mean that a 'class' is devoid of all political aspirations.... Rather it sees itself first and foremost as a religious elite and functions primarily as such. By this definition...the rabbis...resembled a 'class.'" I suspect that so idiosyncratic a definition of so common and problem-laden a term will startle people with a firmer grasp of problems of social metaphors than Levine evidently has. I should have thought he would want to have learned from scholars of class status and class structure in antiquity, beginning, after all, with M.I. Finley, *The Ancient Economy* (1985), *Studies in Ancient Society* (1974), and the like. They would have taught him that invoking the category "class" for antiquity presents difficult problems of socio-economic theory, starting with the difficulty of identifying pertinent data to justify the economic analysis of society to begin with. But, alas, Levine seems oblivious to the fact that his generative category, "class," derives from a very specific theory of political economy; not a single line of his book suggests he grasps the implications of his choice of "class." By his own definition, he could have used any number of other analogies, with equal lack of discernment. "Class" means more or less what he wants it to mean, which is everything and its opposite, depending on the context.

Second, Levine's use of archaeological evidence, in the judgment of qualified scholars, is simply incompetent. Here I defer to Fergus Millar (*Journal of Theological Studies* 1991, 42:275-276), who points out that "the most important single piece of recent archaeological evidence bearing on this topic...is treated in very cursory fashion. Indeed it is not even translated precisely." In a few sharp words, Millar has dismissed Levine's use of evidence that, as "professor of Jewish History and Archeology at the Hebrew University since 1971," he should be assumed to have mastered decades ago.

Third, Levine's use of the literary evidence, bearing the veneer of a critical method, proves gullible and everywhere uncritical. In this regard he is a true heir of Morton Smith's fundamentalism. There is scarcely a line of analysis of the documents he quotes on every page; he never characterizes his literary sources or explains their traits or tendencies; they are just a mass of reliable information, so far as he is concerned. To be sure, as is the custom, he acknowledges that there are critical problems in using ancient literary sources (pp. 16ff.). But, without a trace of demonstration or analysis, he simply alleges, "Our sources are most abundant for Palestine of the third and fourth centuries, and the increase in quantity is paralleled by a greater degree of historical credibility." This is because the writings were redacted near the time of events they describe or masters they cite. But why that fact (if it is a fact) makes the documents more credible he does not explain.

More to the point, even though general considerations may point toward greater plausibility, we still have to analyze, point by point, each piece of literary evidence and assess in its own terms whether it tells us about something that really happened or something someone thought happened, and, if the latter, who thought so and why. Levine evades this question, which is critical to the enterprise, by a series of mere assertions: "Undoubtedly, reports of particular incidents are often a reliable type of evidence. Contrastingly, when a sage expresses his opinion about a matter or his hope for a certain situation, it is unclear whether his words accord with reality, whether they had any effect on it, or whether these were merely pious hopes." Why the former is the case Levine does not tell us. Like Smith in his glory days, Levine seems to think that if he merely says something, that makes it so. Rather, he hastens to assure us that "the problem of historical reality is somewhat less acute," because, in this book, his concern is "with the rabbis themselves, their position in the community, attitudes toward others, involvement in the life of the community.... Their opinions and desires are no less significant than incidents and events; it is our task to understand them and place them in some sort of historical perspective."

The result, upon examination, proves as empty as most of Smith's intellectual legacy. What these pieties add up to is simply nothing. For when it comes to actual use of sources, we have the same old rabbinic fundamentalism, for example, "On one occasion R. Abbahu was even approached by a gentile woman for the same purpose." Footnote: "J. Nazir 9, 1, 57c. On the release from vows in the second century, see T Pesahim 2, 16, ed. Lieberman, p. 147; M Nedarim 5, 6; 9, 5; M Gittin 4, 7." Now what this adds up to (and I choose at random among thousands of candidates) is simply [1] X (really) did so and so, because [2] the source says so; and then, as further evidence, come [3] references to (also uncriticized) sources pertaining to a period two centuries earlier: temporal categories do not apply to Levine's "torah," any more than in the theology of Judaism they do to the Torah of Moses. Millar's judgment on Levine's misuse or uncritical use of literary sources is simply, "Although the normal expressions of caution appear, no such serious analysis is carried out." Levine is a fine example of the "pseudorthodoxy" – a critical veneer covering a core of pure credulity – Morton Smith ridiculed two decades ago, but accurately embodied in his work on Judaism.

Invoking a Marxist category he simply has not taken the trouble to master and explain, claiming to use archaeological evidence he does not competently use, alleging to consult in a critical manner literary sources he cites with perfect faith but absolutely no critical judgment, Levine exhibits contempt for scholarship as it is practiced in the academy. No wonder the publisher, Jewish Theological Seminary, by way of up-front prophylaxis, has given the book its own review, in a foreword by Ismar Schorsch, Chancellor of the Jewish Theological Seminary, who is also the publisher of the book. Schorsch praises the book: "Never has the rabbinic elite of the third and fourth centuries been so fully drawn as to yield a portrait graced by the majestic blend of all available sources – primary and secondary, literary and archaeological, Jewish and non-Jewish. The simplicity and incisiveness of the text conceal the endless process of distillation. This blend will undoubtedly become the reference point for the generation of scholars to come." Many having read the book will find that judgment bizarre.

Discounting the usual hyperbole of a blurb, coming from one's own college president no less, one can account for the disparity between the hopelessly uncritical, indeed incompetent character of the book and its publisher's accompanying blurb only by the theory that, the chancellor either has not read the book and is saying what he thinks politic, or has read the book but has not actually understood its disgraceful ignorance. But quite plausibly, Schorsch calls Levine "vintage Seminary," pointing to his studies with Saul Lieberman there; with that judgment no one can disagree. This is precisely the quality of scholarship to be anticipated from a "vintage Seminary" product, now professor at the same institution.

Appendix Two

Smith's Legacy of Selective Fundamentalism in the Writing of S.J.D. Cohen: Believing Whatever You Like

Smith thought that, on the basis of philology – correctly interpreting the meaning of the words of a text – we can recover history, meaning, things that actually happened. He was a philological fundamentalist. But of course, unlike Bible-believing Christians, Smith picked and chose out of Scripture what he would believe, and he declared the rest "pious fraud." But we have seen to whom appropriately belongs the epithet, "fraud." The premise of his *Jesus the Magician* is, the fragment that completes the narrative tells us about Jesus something that we did not know before. So the text yields history – once a process of selectivity and arrangement has told us what we have to accept as fact, and what we may dismiss as fiction. But Smith never defined that process, he only appealed to its consequence. That is because he did not find patience to reflect on questions of method, on the one side, and because he knew in advance pretty much whatever he was going to find out (or "prove"), on the other. The failure to identify premises as to the character of historical knowledge Smith condemned in his indictment of "pseudorthodoxy." But he did not recognize that, in believing in the text whatever he wished, he was a pseudo-scholar: an ideologue claiming to prove his case through what were facts selected or even fabricated, not objectively established through processes others can replicate.

Among Smith's disciples (and my critics), Professor Shaye J.D. Cohen, who succeeded to my chair at Brown University, believes what he wants and disbelieves the rest, and so practices that selective fundamentalism that Smith formulated. In the blatant instance before us, what I shall show is that the thesis takes up a question that Cohen could only have asked in the assumption that answers of a historical order exist in the rabbinic literature he cites. While eager to distinguish himself from the other gullibles, Cohen emerges as nothing other than a true believer – in what he wants to believe.[1] That is what I mean by believing whatever you like: assuming the facticity and historicity of sources when it suits your purpose, and ostentatiously dismissing the same sources when it does not. The same modes of thought that for Smith yielded Jesus as a magician for Cohen produced an article we shall now examine.

In "The Significance of Yavneh: Pharisees, Rabbis, and the End of Jewish Sectarianism," *Hebrew Union College Annual* 55, 1984, pp. 27-53, Cohen presents an important thesis. If the sources presented the facts he imagines that they do, it might even be a thesis worth investigating; but we cannot investigate a thesis that rests on believing everything in the sources we find plausible and disbelieving the rest; that is not scholarship, it is mere self-indulgence: making things up as we go along, passing our opinion on this and that, and, in general, talking as though saying something proved it. But an allegation is neither evidence nor argument, nor is paraphrasing a source or free-associating about it the equivalent to either evidence or argument; it is just empty blather.

In order to make certain he is represented accurately, I cite his own précis of his article, which is as follows:

> After the destruction of the second temple in 70 C.E. the rabbis gathered in Yavneh and launched the process which yielded the Mishnah approximately one hundred years later. Most modern scholars see these rabbis as Pharisees triumphant, who define "orthodoxy," expel Christians and other heretics, and purge the canon of "dangerous" books. The evidence for this reconstruction is inadequate. In all likelihood most of the rabbis were Pharisees, but there is no indication that the rabbis of the Yavnean period were motivated by a Pharisaic self-consciousness (contrast the Babylonian Talmud and the medieval polemics against the Karaites) or were dominated by an exclusivistic ethic. In contrast the major goal of the Yavnean rabbis seems to have been not the expulsion of those with whom they disagreed but the cessation of sectarianism and the creation of a society which tolerated, even encouraged, vigorous debate among members of the fold. The Mishnah is the first work of Jewish antiquity which ascribes conflicting legal opinions to named individuals who, in spite of their disagreements, belong to the same fraternity. This mutual tolerance is the enduring legacy of Yavneh.

---

[1] I go over my critique of Cohen originally published in *Reading and Believing: Ancient Judaism and Contemporary Gullibility* (Atlanta, 1986: Scholars Press for Brown Judaic Studies).

Now what is important is not Cohen's theory, with which I do not undertake an argument, but whether or not to formulate and prove his theory, he has exhibited that gullibility that seems to characterize pretty much everyone else.

Let us now proceed to ask how Cohen uses the evidence, investigating the theory of the character of the sources that leads him to frame his questions in one way and not in some other. What we shall see, first of all, is that Cohen takes at face value the historical allegation of a source that a given rabbi made the statement attributed to him. At pp. 32-33 Cohen states:

> The text narrates a story about a Sadducee and a high priest, and concludes with the words of the wife of the Sadducee:
>
> A.   "Although they [= we] are wives of Sadducees, they [= we] fear the Pharisees and show their [= our] menstrual blood to the sages."
> B.   R. Yosé says, "We are more expert in them [Sadducean women] than anyone else. They show (menstrual) blood to the sages, except for one woman who was in our neighborhood, who did not show her (menstrual) blood to the sages, and she died [immediately]" (Bab. Niddah 33b).

Cohen forthwith states, "In this text there is chronological tension between parts A and B. A clearly refers to a woman who lived during second temple times, while B has R. Yosé derive his expertise about Sadducean women from personal acquaintance." Why Cohen regards that "tension" as probative or even pertinent I cannot say. Now we may wonder whether Cohen believes Yosé really made the statement attributed to him. We note that Cohen does not specify the point at which "the text" was redacted. The fact that the Babylonian Talmud reached closure in the sixth or seventh century makes no difference. If the text refers to Yosé, then it testifies to the second century, not to the seventh.

We shall now hear Cohen treat the text as an accurate report of views held in the time of which it speaks. How does he know? Because the text says so: it refers to this, it refers to that. What we have is a newspaper reporter, writing down things really said and giving them over to the National Archives for preservation until some later reporter chooses to add to the file: gullibility of a vulgar order indeed. Here is Cohen again, in the same passage, starting with the pretense of a critical exercise of analysis:

> In this text there is chronological tension between parts A and B. A clearly refers to a woman who lived during second temple times, while B has R. Yosé derive his expertise about Sadducean women from personal acquaintance. He recalls a Sadducean woman who lived in his

neighborhood and died prematurely because (R. Yosé said) she did not
accept the authority of the sages to determine her menstrual status.

To this point Cohen simply paraphrases the text, and now he will verify
the story. It seems to me that Cohen takes for granted Yosé really made
the saying attributed to him, and, moreover, that saying is not only
Yosé's view of matters, but how matters really were. He says so in so
many words: "This baraita clearly implies that R. Yosé is referring to
contemporary Sadducean women. If this is correct, R. Yosé's statement
shows that some Sadducees still existed in the mid-second century but
that their power had declined to the extent that the rabbis could assume
that most Sadducees follow rabbinic norms." It seems to me beyond
doubt that Cohen takes for granted that what is attributed to Yosé really
was said by him, and, more interestingly, Yosé testifies to how things
were not in one place but everywhere in the country. "If this is correct"
Cohen concludes not that Yosé thought there were still a few Sadducees
around, but that there were still a few Sadducees around. There is a
difference. Cohen does not tell us what conclusions he draws *if this is not
correct*, because, in point of fact, that possibility he declines to explore.

Nonetheless, he wants to verify the story. How? By finding another
text that tells the same story.

The version of the Tosefta is similar:

A.   "Although we are Sadducean women, we all consult a sage."
B.   R. Yosé says, "We are more expert in Sadducean women that
      anyone else: they all consult a sage except for one who was among
      them, and she died" (Tosefta Niddah 5:3).

The Tosefta does not identify Pharisees with sages, a point to which we
shall return below, and omits the phrase "who was in our
neighborhood." Otherwise, it is basically, the same as the Babylonian
version.

Now the reader may rightly wonder, perhaps Cohen intends something
other than historical narrative about views Yosé held or opinions he
taught. Maybe Cohen proposes to write a history of the tradition about a
given matter. In that case simply citing this and that serves a valid
purpose. I concur.

But Cohen leaves no doubt as to his intention. Let us listen as he tells
us what *really* happened: Since Yosé made his statement, Yosé's
statement tells us about the second century. Then Yosé's statement
proves that there were Sadducees in the mid-second century but they
had no power. I find no evidence whatsoever that Cohen grasps the
critical problem of evaluating the allegations of sources. He looks into a
source and comes up with a fact. If he finds two versions of the same
story, the fact is still more factual. Gullibility, pure and simple! And, if

that were not enough, he gives us the "proof" of "according to rabbinic tradition." That tradition suffices: "They always failed, of course, but they resisted; by the second century they stopped resisting." Let us review those clear statements of his:

> This baraita clearly implies that R. Yosé is referring to contemporary Sadducean women. If this is correct, R. Yosé's statement shows that some Sadducees still existed in the mid-second century but that their power had declined to the extent that the rabbis could assume that most Sadducees follow rabbinic norms. Contrast the Sadducees of the second temple period who, according to rabbinic tradition, tried to resist rabbinic hegemony (see below). They always failed, of course, but they resisted: by the second century they stopped resisting. This is the perspective of R. Yosé.

The "if this is correct" changes nothing. As soon as the "if" has been said, it is treated as a "then." "Then" it is correct, so Cohen here tells us the story of the Sadducees in the first and second centuries. In the first century they resisted "rabbinic norms," whatever they were, but in the second century, they gave up. This is Cohen's conclusion, based on his failure to ask how the Bavli and the Tosefta's compilers or the author of the story at hand knew the facts of the matter. The sole undisputed fact is that they represent the facts one way, rather than some other. But that does not suffice. Thus far we have seen a use of evidence entirely as gullible as that of Koester and Sanders.

Now, again, let us give Cohen his due. Any fair-minded reader may claim that what we have is a mere lapse. Cohen may have made a minor lapse that we should forgive. So let us see how he analyzes sources. At p. 42 he says:

> Rabbinic tradition is aware of opposition faced by Yohanan ben Zakkai at Yavneh but knows nothing of any expulsion of these opponents (Bab. Rosh Hashanah 2b). Yohanan ben Zakkai was even careful to avoid a confrontation with the priests (Mishnah Eduyyot 8:3).

Now what have we here? "Rabbinic tradition" indeed. What can that possibly mean? All rabbis at all times? A particular rabbi at a given time? Church historians these days rarely base their historical facts on "the tradition of the Church." Would that we could write a life of Jesus based on the tradition of the Church, how many problems we could solve. Cohen does not favor us with an exercise in differentiation among the sources. His is an undifferentiated harmony of the Jewish Gospels. Indeed, to the opposite, he looks into "rabbinic tradition," undifferentiated, unanalyzed, and gives us a fact: *Bab. Rosh Hashanah 2b*. What can that be? It is a story about someone. What does the story tell us? Is it true? Why should we think so? Cohen does not ask these questions. He alludes to a page in the Talmud, and that constitutes his fact, on which, it goes without saying, he proposes to build quite an edifice. So the Talmud is a kind of telephone book, giving us numbers through which we make our connections. In no way does he establish a critical method, which tells us why he believes what he believes and disbelieves what he rejects.

But he does have a clear theory of matters. Where sources concur with Cohen's thesis, he accepts them, and where not, not. Cohen wants to prove that earlier there were disputes, later on disputes ended. Now some sources say that earlier there were no disputes, later on there were disputes. So Cohen rejects the historicity of the sources that say there were no disputes earlier and accepts that of the ones that say there were no disputes later. This slight of hand I find on p. 48. Here he cites T. Hagigah 2:9, "At first there was no dispute in Israel." He proceeds to point to an "irenic trend," Mishnah Yebamot 1:4 and Eduyyot 4:8, which alleges that while the Houses disputed various matters, they still intermarried and respected each other's conformity to the purity rules. Then Cohen: "But this wishful thinking cannot disguise the truth. The two Talmudim find it almost impossible to understand this statement. The Houses could not marry or sup with each other. They were virtually sects – *kitot* the Palestinian Talmud calls them (Yer. Hagigah 2:2). At Yavneh sectarian exclusiveness was replaced by rabbinic pluralism, collective authority was replaced by individual authority." What Cohen has done is to reject the statements in earlier sources – Mishnah, Tosefta – and adopt those in later ones (the Palestinian Talmud). He has done so simply by fiat. He cites what they say, and then he calls it wishful thinking. The truth, he discovers, is in the judgment of the Palestinian Talmud. I find this strange, for two reasons. First, it is odd to reject the testimony of the earlier source, closer to the situation under discussion, in favor of the later. Second, it is not entirely clear why and how Cohen knows that the Mishnah's and Tosefta's statements represent wishful thinking at all. Had he cited the Talmudic discussions of the passage, readers would have found that the problem confronting the later exegetes is not quite what Cohen says it was. The Talmuds do not say that the parties were "virtually sects." That statement, it is true, occurs where Cohen says it does – but that is not on the passage of M. Yebamot 1:4 etc. that Cohen is discussing. It is on another passage entirely. The Talmudic discussion on the Mishnah passage and its Tosefta parallel is a legal one; the sages are troubled by the statement that people who disagree on laws of marriage and of purity can ignore those laws. The Talmudic discussion in no way sustains Cohen's statement. If now we reread the sequence of sentences, we find an interesting juxtaposition:

1. The two Talmudim find it almost impossible to understand this statement.

2. The Houses could not marry or sup with each other. They were virtually sects – *kitot* the Palestinian Talmud calls them.

3. At Yavneh sectarian exclusiveness was replaced by rabbinic pluralism, collective authority was replaced by individual authority.

Now sentence three does not follow from sentence two, unless sentence two has had something to do with "sectarian exclusiveness" replaced by "rabbinic pluralism." But the passage cited by Cohen does not say that, it has no bearing on that proposition. Cohen writes as though the evidence supports his thesis, when, in fact, the evidence has no bearing on that thesis. The sentences in fact do not follow from one another. No. 1 is factually inaccurate. No. 2 makes the valid point that the Yerushalmi calls the sects *kitot*. That is an undisputed fact. It however bears no consequences for the statements fore or aft. And no. 3 is parachuted down, Cohen's own judgment. So, to repeat, he believes what he wishes to believe, the later sources' allegations, disbelieves what he does not wish to believe, the earlier sources' statements, finds in a source not related to anything a statement he wishes to believe, cites that, then repeats – as though it had been proved – the fundamental thesis of his paper. I find this extraordinarily confusing.

It follows that Cohen's reading of the source begins with a generous view of the a priori accuracy of his own convictions about what the source is saying. Yohanan's "care" in avoiding a confrontation is Cohen's allegation, for the source does not quite say that. It says, in point of fact, not that he avoided confrontation, but that he did not think he could force the priests to do what they refused to do. That is the exact language of the source, though, as we see, Cohen is notoriously indifferent to detail in his headlong rush to prove his point; all the rest is Cohen's indulgence of his own convictions. Now the statement imputed to Yohanan ben Zakkai may mean he was careful about avoiding confrontation. It may also mean he did not feel like wasting his time on lost causes. It may mean a great many other things. Cohen does not know. He simply cites the tractate and its chapter and paragraph number, and lo, another fact, another proof. Once more, a properly incredulous reader must wonder whether I misrepresent the facts about Cohen's gullibility.

I shall now show that Cohen can tell us "the truth," because *he* knows which source is giving us facts and which source is giving us fancies. That explains why what gets a question mark "(at Yavneh?)" half a dozen lines later loses the question mark and becomes a fact: "At

Yavneh sectarian exclusiveness was replaced by rabbinic pluralism." On
what basis? Let us hear. For this purpose we review the materials just
now set forth. At pp. 48-49 he says:

> Some of the rabbis were aware that their ideology of pluralism did
> not exist before 70. "At first there was no dispute (mahloqet) in Israel"
> (Tos. Hagigah 2:9 and Sanhedrin 7:1). How did disputes begin?
> According to one view in the Tosefta, disputes were avoided by the
> adjudication of the great court which sat in the temple precincts and
> determined either by vote or by tradition the status of all doubtful
> matters. In this view, when the great court was destroyed in 70,
> disputes could no longer be resolved in an orderly way and mahloqot
> proliferated. According to another view, "once the disciples of Hillel
> and Shammai became numerous who did not serve [their masters]
> adequately, they multiplied disputes in Israel and became as two
> Torahs." In this view Jewish (i.e., rabbinic) unanimity was upset by the
> malfeasance of the disciples of Hillel and Shammai, a confession which
> would later be exploited by the Karaites. What happened to the
> disputes between the Houses? They ceased at Yavneh, how we do not
> know. Amoraic tradition (Yer. Yebamot 1:6 [3b] and parallels) tells of a
> heavenly voice which declared at Yavneh, "Both these [House of Hillel]
> and these [House of Shammai] are the words of the living God, but the
> halakha always follows the House of Hillel." As part of this ironic trend
> someone (at Yavneh?) even asserted that the disputes between the
> Houses did not prevent them from intermarrying or from respecting
> each other's purities (Mishnah Yebamot 1:4 and Eduyyot 4:8; Tos.
> Yebamot 1:10-12) but this wishful thinking cannot disguise the truth.
> The two Talmudim find it almost impossible to understand this
> statement. The Houses could not marry or sup with each other. They
> were virtually sects – *kitot* the Palestinian Talmud calls them (Yer.
> Hagigah 2:2 [77d]). At Yavneh sectarian exclusiveness was replaced by
> rabbinic pluralism, collective authority was replaced by individual
> authority. The new ideal was the sage who was ready not to insist upon
> the rectitude of ("stand upon") his opinions. The creation of the
> Mishnah could now begin.

This repeated reading of Cohen's statements allows us to avoid the
charge of quoting him out of context or only in part. I believe I have
quoted him accurately, verbatim, and in context. So let us review the
substance of the case.

When Cohen says, "...were aware," he treats the thesis of his article
as the fact of the matter. Who were these rabbis? And how do we know
of what they were, or were not, aware? Did they live at Yavneh, in 70?
Or did they live in the early third century, when the Mishnah had
reached closure, or did they live a hundred years later, when the Tosefta
was coming to conclusion? Cohen does not tell us. But he clearly thinks
that their awareness is evidence of historical fact. Now these in the
aggregate constitute historical statements, for example, "The Houses
were virtually sects." Why Cohen valorizes Y. Hag. 2:2 – a late source –

and dismisses the evidence of the Mishnah and Tosefta is something that causes a measure of surprise. In fact he has set out to prove at the end of his paragraph the very point he takes for granted at the outset of his paragraph. Philosophers call that begging the question.

Cohen's review of the stories makes a feint toward criticism. He cites diverse views, balancing one view against another. But from Cohen we do not have a history of people's opinions, we have facts. "What happened to the disputes between the Houses? They ceased at Yavneh, how we do not know." Here Cohen tells us that Neusner has shown that some of "the House disputes were later scholarly constructs, but these are not our concern." I do not know why it is not our concern. The Mishnah contains substantial evidence that the names of the Houses served to identify positions held by later disputants, of the mid-second-century it would appear. Materials deriving from the period after the Bar Kokhba War are particularly rich in allusions to Houses' disputes that take up moot principles otherwise debated entirely in the age beyond Bar Kokhba's war. We clearly have mid-second century literary conventions. I do not mean to suggest that the names of the Houses served as more than literary conventions; I demonstrated that they served at least as literary conventions. Why? Were there "Houses of Shammai and Houses of Hillel" in the time of Yosé, in the mid-second century? Is that why so many sayings about the relationships among the Houses are assigned, in fact, to mid-second-century authorities? But the assignments of those sayings occur in documents edited only in the third century, at which point (some stories have it) the patriarch, Judah, discovered that he descended from Hillel. So perhaps the disputes of the Houses served a polemical purpose of the patriarchate, since the ancestor of the patriarchate – everyone knew – kept winning the disputes. These are only possibilities. In answering the question as Cohen phrases it, all we have are possibilities, few of them subject to tests of falsification or validation.

Cohen knows facts, the unbelieving among the rest of us, only possibilities: "They ceased at Yavneh, how we do not know." Well, just what ceased at Yavneh, if the names of the Houses persisted as literary conventions and points of polemic for a hundred years and more. It must follow that Cohen's claim of knowledge of an "irenic trend" rests on nothing more than two things, first, the source's claim of such a trend, second, Cohen's opinion as to the facts. This is proved by the stories cited from M. Yeb. 1:4 and M. Ed. 4:8 and so on. Let us review in sequence Cohen's statements:

1.   But this wishful thinking cannot disguise the truth.

2. At Yavneh sectarian exclusiveness was replaced by rabbinic pluralism, collective authority was replaced by individual authority.

3. The new ideal was the sage who was ready not to insist upon the rectitude of his opinions.

4. The creation of the Mishnah could now begin.

All of these statements may well be true. But in the paragraph I have cited, in which these statements occur, not a single source, not a single piece of evidence, proves any such thing. I cite No. 1 to prove that Cohen claims to make a historical statement. No. 2 then tells us he sees a movement from sect to church (though he does not appear to have read Max Weber, who saw much the same movement). Cohen has not proved that the "new ideal" of the sage antedates the Mishnah, in which it is said that that is the ideal. But he has ignored the fact that the Mishnah imputes that irenic position to none other than the House of Hillel – who lived long before "Yavneh." And what all this has to do with "the creation of the Mishnah" only Cohen knows. So, in a climax of total confusion, if a passage in the *Mishnah* refers to the time of the Houses, but Cohen thinks that the fact does *not* apply to the time of the Houses, he ignores the allegation of the Mishnah's passage. If a passage in the Yerushalmi, two hundred years later, refers to the earlier period and says what Cohen thinks was the fact, then that later passage is true while the earlier one is not. It looks to me as though he is more or less making things up as he goes along.

What does he do in the case at hand? He assigns that allegation neither to the context of the age of the Mishnah itself, as, to begin with, I would find plausible, nor to the age of which the passage itself speaks, namely, the time of the Houses (before 70, so Cohen), as other fundamentalists, consistent in their gullibility, would insist. In Cohen's mind, the passage testifies to an age of which it does not speak, and also in which the document that contains the passage was not redacted. This is pure confusion, and I can find, in the rest of Cohen's article, still more utter chaos. But Cohen is consistent: if he does not think something happened, then he also will not believe sources that say it happened, even though they are early sources. We already have noticed that if a passage in a later rabbinic document refers to an earlier time and Cohen does think the fact applies to that early time, then he of course produces the source to prove the point that, to begin with, he wishes to make. So he prefers the later source that conforms to his thesis over the earlier one that does not. He has the best of all worlds, living, as he seems to wish, in a private garden of his own. To put matters differently, Cohen seems to make things up as he goes along and call the result history. But how would he know? In the age of which he writes, he was not around, and in the age in which he writes, he is not doing critical history the way historians do it, except in the ghetto.

Let us not forget where we started. Does Cohen believe that if the source says someone said something, then he really said it? Well, yes, on the one side Cohen does believe it, when the source says something Cohen thinks the source should have said the man said, as in the case of Yosé. But no, on the other side Cohen does not believe it, when the source says something Cohen thinks the source should not have said the man (or group) said, as in the case of the Houses when they are represented in an irenic mode. So Cohen's scholarship emerges as rather credulous except when he is confused. And let us at the end not miss the simple point that his thesis to begin with rests on the conviction that the sources as we have them present us with the facts we require to test – and prove – a thesis of that order and not some other. That framing of the question attests to a profound gullibility indeed. Because Cohen assumes the rabbinic literature answers the questions he has in mind, he asks those questions. He learned that from Smith.

Index

Abba bar Nathan, 148

Abba Saul, 101

Abbahu, 164

abomination, 101

adultery, 59

Akiba, 49, 56-57

Albeck, C., 42, 44

Alexandria, 28, 158

Allen, W., 43

altar, 1, 108

Amen, 76, 81

Amora, 70-71, 174

analogy, 109, 121, 147, 154

anonymity, 152

Apocrypha, 15

appendix, 11, 25, 36, 45-46, 50, 66, 136-137, 161, 167

Aqiva, 89-93, 108-110, 125-126, 129

Aramaic, 32, 43

ark, 83

attributions of sayings, 21

authorship, 67, 73-74, 81, 86, 123

autonomy, 158

B. Ket., 101

B. Qid., 104, 109

Ba, 83-85, 151

Babylonia, 8, 19-20, 65-66, 71, 83, 88, 154

Babylonian, 65, 68, 142-143, 170

Babylonian Talmud, 44, 69, 86, 168-169

Baptist, 49

Bar Kokhba War, 175

baraitot, 69, 170-171

Baron, Salo W., 6, 19, 158

Barzilai, Isaac, 6, 19

Bavli, 67, 74, 76, 86, 88, 141-144, 147-149, 154-155, 171

Ben Nannos, 126

Benoit, Fr. P., 47

Berakhot, 74-76, 78, 82, 88

betrothal, 100

Biban, 84

Bible, 9, 15-16, 20, 22, 28, 167

blemish, 108

blood, 94-100, 122, 127, 129, 144-146, 169

Braude, William G., 24

Bultmann, Rudolph, 16, 30, 37

Burney, C., 43

canon, 18, 42, 66, 154, 168

catalogue, 32, 34

category formation, 4, 26-27, 161

Christ, 31, 141, 154

Christianity, 2-3, 5, 9-10, 17, 20-22, 26-27, 42-43, 158, 167-168

Church, 171, 176

cleanness, 69, 75-77, 79, 84-85, 89-94, 101, 104-108, 110-122, 124-126, 145

Clement, 5, 10, 28, 30, 158

cogency, 65, 86, 111, 124

Cohen, Shaye J.D., 12, 167-177

comparison, 41-42, 45, 78, 109, 133, 135-142, 154-155

compilation, 103, 132, 149

composite, 88, 102, 136

Conservative Judaism, 8

continuity, 73

contrast, 4, 18, 66, 68, 106-107, 113, 119, 125, 133, 135, 137, 139-140, 163, 168, 171

corpse, 124-125, 151

Dan., 126

Danby, Herbert, 69, 89, 94, 104, 111, 127

Davies, W.D., 6, 19, 23-24

Dead Sea Scrolls, 29

death, 23, 25, 30, 49, 95, 97, 100, 169-170

debt, 24

Deut., 41

Dibelius, 16, 30

disciple, 11, 17, 27, 49, 77, 79, 85-86, 129, 150, 158, 161, 167, 174

Divine Name, 76, 81

divorce, 22, 59

divorcée, 108-110

documentary study, 18

domain, private, 104-105, 108, 110, 121

domain, public, 104-105, 108-110, 121

dough-offering, 84

East, 32

Eduyyot, 171-172, 174

Eleazar, 95-96, 98, 107, 145

Eleazar b. Damah, 128

Eliezer, 9, 17, 27, 57, 94-99, 101, 129

Eliezer ben Hyrcanus, 9, 17, 19, 27, 129

Elijah, 70

English, 23, 42, 66, 73

exegesis, 15-16, 34, 68, 70-73, 87, 103, 143-144, 149, 172

Father of Uncleanness, 90, 106

festival, 76, 84, 101, 147-148, 150-151

Fiebig, P. 42

Finkelstein, Louis, 158

Finley, M. I., 162

fire, 75, 79, 85-86

flame, 77-78, 81

flood, 63

foetus, 95, 97, 101

footnote, 10, 23, 36, 38, 164

forbidden, 48, 127, 150-151

form-analysis, 34, 137

fraud, 21, 24, 29-30, 38, 167

fundamentalism, 12, 26-27, 163-164, 167

Galilee, 161

Gardner-Smith, 47

Gen., 97

gentile, 39, 60, 75-76, 78, 81, 101, 128-129, 164

German, 42

Gittin, 164

gloss, 67, 78, 87-90, 94, 96, 102, 108, 129, 132-133

God, 1-2, 33, 36, 51, 58, 61, 174

Goodenough, Erwin R., 4, 47

Gospels, 1-4, 6, 15-17, 20, 26-28, 30-39, 41-50, 87, 102, 131-133, 136-140, 142, 147, 149, 154-155, 158, 171

GRA, 70, 119-120

Grace, 75

Greco-Roman, 5, 22, 162

Greece, 3, 16, 32, 35, 42-43

Hagigah, 172, 174

halakhah, 174

halisah, 108

Hallah, 84

Hananel, 147-148

Hanin bar Ba, 84

Havdalah, 75, 77, 79-80, 82-85

Hawkins, J., 48

heave-offering, 124

Heaven, 58-59, 62-63, 126, 128-129, 138

Hebrew, 5, 23-24, 32, 35, 38-39, 42, 66, 69, 168

Hebrew Union College, 24, 168

Hebrew University, 17, 34, 38, 132, 163

Hebrews, 141

hermeneutics, 2, 144

Herod, 49

Herr, M.D., 69

high priest, 169

Hillel, 174-175

Hillelites, 102

history, 2-6, 8-10, 15-22, 26-27, 37, 70, 156, 158, 163, 167, 170, 175-177

history of religion, 10, 26, 156

Hiyya, 84

Hoffmann, D., 44

Holy Things, 45, 93-94

House of Hillel, 55, 75-86, 100, 174, 176

House of Shammai, 55, 75-86, 100, 174

Houses (of Shammai and Hillel), 17, 102, 172-177

Howard, W., 43, 47

Hullin, 127

husband, 100

hypocrite, 62

hypothesis, 33, 132, 136, 142, 149

idiom, 32-34, 41

idol, 75, 81

idolatry, 51, 128

interpretation, 22, 27-28, 36, 69, 73, 135, 143, 156, 158

Isa., 97

Ishmael, 128

Islam, 3, 27

Israel, 23, 65-66, 69-71, 74, 82-83, 88, 126, 142-143, 154, 172, 174

Israelites, 47-48, 76, 78, 81, 127

Jacob, 19, 125, 150

Jacob of Kefar Sama, 128

Jacob of Kefar Sikhnin, 129

Jeremiah, 150

Jerusalem, 1, 7, 10, 12, 36-38, 44, 69-70, 161

Jesus, 1-3, 9-10, 16, 20-21, 23-31, 36-37, 49, 128-129, 141, 149, 154, 158, 167-168, 171

Jesus ben Pantiri, 129

Jew, 5, 7-8, 10, 12, 15-16, 18-20, 22, 24, 43-44, 134, 136, 140, 142, 158, 161-164, 168, 171, 174

Jewish Theological Seminary of America (JTSA), 7, 15-16, 161

John the Baptist, 49

Jonathan, 102

Jose, 47-49, 57-58

Joshua, 57, 90, 95-97, 101

Joshua b. Levi, 84, 150

Judah, 52, 54, 56-57, 71, 85, 91, 94, 100, 127, 146

Judah b. R. Simon, 150

Judah ben Beterah, 57

Judaism, 1, 3, 5, 8, 10-11, 17-24, 26, 38, 65-69, 136, 140, 158, 164, 168

judgment, 5, 11, 28, 31, 61, 69, 88, 124, 128, 148, 158, 163-165, 172-173

Katsh, 104

Kelim, 70, 89

Kittel, G., 42

Kuhn, Thomas, 7

Laban, 19

lamp, 50, 77, 81

Land of Israel, 23, 65-66, 70-71, 74, 82, 88, 142-143, 154

Latin, 32, 42

law, 1-2, 4, 17, 28, 33, 36, 45, 49-52, 59-60, 62, 70, 73, 76, 78, 84-85, 87, 92-93, 95-98, 109, 138, 147-148, 154, 172

Levi, 84

Levine, Lee I., 12, 161-165

Levite, 53

Leviticus, 76

liability, 55, 128

Lieberman, Saul, 10, 23-24, 44, 46, 69-70, 76-78, 80-81, 92-93, 97, 118, 158, 164-165

Lisowsky, 108, 116-117

literature, 2, 5, 8, 15-18, 20-23, 26, 32, 34-40, 41-43, 47, 68, 74, 134-136, 140-142, 149, 155, 168, 177

logic, 35

Lord, 2-3, 63, 102

Luke, 3, 66-67, 102, 103, 131-135, 137-138, 140-141, 149

M. Ber., 154

M. Ed., 175

M. Git., 95, 164

M. Hul., 127-128

M. Kel., 84, 89, 93, 124

M. M.Q., 147

M. Miq., 117
M. Nedarim, 164
M. Par., 95, 114, 127
M. Toh., 107, 111-112, 117
M. Yad., 90
M. Yeb., 172, 175
Maaser Sheni, 47
Maimonides, 69, 94, 104, 111
mamzer, 128
Mana, 82, 146
Mann, J., 46
Mark, 27, 32, 134, 137, 140-141, 149, 158
marriage, 95, 97, 102, 108, 172-174
Marxism, 162, 164
Matthew, 3, 66-67, 102, 103, 131-135, 137-138, 140-141, 149
meat, 128, 151-152
Meir, 54, 84, 89-91, 93, 95, 97, 100-102, 107-108, 121, 145-147
Melamed, E., 44
menstruation, 98
metaphor, 162
method, 4, 10, 25-27, 31, 163, 167, 172
midrashim, 42, 44, 70, 136
Millar, Fergus, 163-164
Miqvaot, 103, 110, 124
Mishnah, 3-4, 11, 17-18, 32, 40, 41, 43-50, 65-76, 78, 81-86, 87-89, 92, 94, 103, 110, 123-124, 127, 131-138, 140-143, 148-150, 153-154, 157, 168, 171-172, 174-176
Mishneh LaMelekh, 120

Moed, 69
Moed Qatan, 150
Moore, 158
Moses, 164
Muilenberg, James, 15
murder, 27, 59
Nashim, 69
Nazir, 164
Neusner, Jacob, 23-24, 175
New Moon, 96
New Testament, 2, 15-18, 22-23, 26, 28, 30, 38-39, 134, 141, 154
Neziqin, 69
Niddah, 70, 94, 144, 169-170
Nock, Arthur Darby, 4-5, 30
Num., 126
Numbers, 42
Old Testament, 2, 7, 15-16, 34, 39, 45
Omnipresent, 102
orthodoxy, 168
paganism, 128
Palestine, 161-163
Palestinian, 7, 16, 68-69, 172-174
parables, 34, 61
parallelism, 4, 11, 31, 33, 35-36, 41-43, 45, 50, 134-139, 141-142, 149, 154-155
Pardo, Isaac, 70
patriarchs, 161-162, 175
Paul, 141
peace-offering, 47-48
Peah, 44, 46, 48-58, 138
Pentateuch, 70

pericope, 70-71, 90, 105, 109-110, 112, 115, 142, 149-150, 154

Pharisees, 8-9, 17, 19, 27, 45, 168-170

philology, 3, 16-17, 20, 31, 36-37, 42, 167

philosophy, 9, 12, 26, 31, 33-34, 175

phylactery, 148, 152

politics, 7, 11, 16, 157-158, 162-163, 165

prayer, 34, 83-84, 152

prejudice, 10

priest, 47-48, 53, 109, 169, 171, 173

prohibition, 47, 101, 128, 151

prophet, 59, 62

proposition, 37, 66, 73, 88, 132, 140, 162, 173

Prov., 102, 129

Ps., 102

pseudepigrapha, 15, 70

purification, 117-118, 125

purification water, 126-127

Q (Quelle), 38, 110, 134, 140-144, 147-149, 155

Quesnell, Quentin, 28-30

Qoh., 128

Rab, 71, 143-144, 147-148

Rabbah bar bar Hanna, 147-148

Rabbi, 24, 70, 129, 145-146, 169, 171

rabbinic, 5, 8, 15-23, 26-27, 35, 38-40, 42, 46, 68, 74, 76, 88, 140-143, 147, 149, 155, 161-162, 164, 168, 170-174, 176-177

rabbis, 24, 92, 161-162, 164, 168, 170-171, 174

Rashi, 100

redaction, 67-69, 71-73, 96, 114

rejoicing, 59

religion, 3, 6, 10, 15, 19, 21-22, 24-27, 30, 33, 37, 60, 152, 156, 162

remarriage, 102

Rengstorf, Karl Heinrich, 69

rhetoric, 34

Rome, 3, 5, 22, 32, 161-162

Rushdie, Salman, 27

Sabbath, 76-78, 80, 83-84, 101, 150-153

sacrifice, 108, 128

Sadducees, 169-171

sage, 8, 30, 54, 56-57, 70, 76-77, 79, 86, 90, 95-96, 98, 102, 106-107, 110-111, 117, 125, 128, 142-143, 154, 161-163, 169-170, 172, 174, 176

salvation, 16

Samaritan, 55, 76, 81, 128

Samson of Sens, 69, 91, 108, 114-117, 119, 126

Samuel, 24, 71, 84, 144, 146, 153

sanctification, 76, 78, 82-84, 107

sanctuary, 94

Sanders, E.P., 158, 171

Sanhedrin, 162, 174

Saul, 24

Schlatter, A., 43

Scholem, Gershom, 10, 158

Schorsch, Ismar, 164-165

Schweitzer, Albert, 16, 30, 43

scribe, 45, 47, 105, 148

Scripture, 26, 70, 86, 97, 126, 143, 149-150, 167

sea, 29, 127, 129

Sermon on the Mount, 34, 44, 50, 102, 133, 138, 140

sexual relations, 150-152

Shabbat, 32

Shabbetai, 84

Shammai, 95, 174

Shammaites, 86, 102

Shema, 152

Sifra, 41, 143

Sigge, T., 47

Simeon, 99-100, 106, 108-110, 146, 152

Simeon b. Gamaliel, 101-102, 152-153

Simeon b. Laqish, 40, 84, 142-143, 145

Simeon b. Nanos, 126

Simon, 41, 47-48, 52, 55, 58, 150

sin, 1

Sinai, 28

slaughter, 127-129

slave, 58

Slotki, 100

Smith, Morton, 1-13, 15-40, 41, 66-67, 87, 102, 103, 131-143, 149, 155-158, 161, 163-164, 167-168, 177

Stewart, Zeph, 4

Strack-Billerbeck, 46

Sukkah, 84

Sumkhos, 97

Synoptics, 8, 16, 35, 38, 41, 43, 46-47, 134, 136, 140

T. Kel., 90-91, 94, 124

T. Oh., 125

T. Par., 114

T. Pesahim, 164

T. Toh., 117-118

Talmud, 7, 40, 44, 65-66, 69-70, 72-75, 81-82, 86, 88, 141-144, 147-150, 154-155, 168-169, 171-174

Talmud of Babylonia, 66, 71, 88

Talmud of the Land of Israel, 23, 65-66, 70-71, 74, 82, 88

Tanna, 69

Tannaite, 1-3, 6, 15-18, 21, 31-32, 34-38, 41, 50, 70, 131, 145, 149, 151, 153, 155

Tarefon, 57

Tarfon, 89, 91, 93, 108-110, 126

Taubes, Jakob, 6, 19

tax collector, 60

taxonomy, 73

tefillin, 147-148

Temple, 50, 94, 128, 168-169, 171, 174

Temurah, 45

Testaments, 3

theology, 2-3, 6-8, 12, 15, 19, 28, 34, 37, 73, 161, 163-164

tithe, 47-48, 53, 57

tithe, second, 47

TL (Tannaitic literature), 1-2, 32-36, 38, 41-45, 49, 136-138

Tohorot, 70

topic, 11-12, 71-73, 123, 131-133, 141, 149-150, 154-157, 163

Torah, 2, 19, 69, 76, 129, 143, 152, 164

Torah study, 161

Tosefta, 3-4, 11, 18, 40, 41, 43-47, 49-50, 65-76, 78, 81-82, 86, 87-88, 94, 103, 113-114, 123-124, 129, 131-138, 140-141, 143, 149, 157, 170-172, 174-175

tradition, 8, 13, 16-17, 19, 21, 27, 45, 137, 149

transgression, 51, 129

translation, 18, 21, 23, 66-67, 69-71, 73, 93

uncleanness, 47, 76-77, 79, 84-85, 89-101, 103-122, 124-127, 143-146

unconsecration, 77, 79, 85

Union Theological Seminary, 6, 15, 19

unit of thought, 66, 89

Urbach, E. Ephraim, 10, 158

Usha, 110

Ushan, 96

violation, 3, 9

virgin, 95-98, 144

virginity, 97

vow, 164

Weber, Max, 176

Wernle, P., 43

wife, 49, 57, 152, 169

Windisch, H., 47

witness, 8, 39

woman, 94-102, 122, 144-147, 164, 169-171

wrath, 23, 126

writ of divorce, 22

Y. Ket., 101

Yavnean, 90, 168

Yavneh, 108, 168, 171-176

Yebamot, 172, 174

Yerushalmi, 66, 74, 76, 82, 86, 88-89, 141-143, 147-148, 154-155, 173, 176

Yohanan, 40, 71, 84, 142-145, 150, 152-153, 173

Yohanan ben Zakkai, 6, 8, 10, 17, 20-21, 171, 173

Yosé, 84, 89-91, 93-96, 99-100, 104, 106-108, 110, 112, 114, 126, 145-148, 169-171, 175, 177

Yosé b. R. Hanina, 84

Yosé b. Rabbi, 83

Yosé the Galilean, 126-127

Zabim, 46

Zadok, 53

Zalman, Elijah ben Solomon, 70

Zeira, 83, 144

Zeitlin, Solomon, 29, 158

Zeraim, 69

Zuckermandel, 44, 46, 69, 93, 97

South Florida Studies in the History of Judaism

240001	Lectures on Judaism in the Academy and in the Humanities	Neusner
240002	Lectures on Judaism in the History of Religion	Neusner
240003	Self-Fulfilling Prophecy: Exile and Return in the History of Judaism	Neusner
240004	The Canonical History of Ideas: The Place of the So-called Tannaite Midrashim, Mekhilta Attributed to R. Ishmael, Sifra, Sifré to Numbers, and Sifré to Deuteronomy	Neusner
240005	Ancient Judaism: Debates and Disputes	Neusner
240006	The Hasmoneans and Their Supporters: From Mattathias to the Death of John Hyrcanus I	Sievers
240007	Approaches to Ancient Judaism: New Series, Volume One	Neusner
240008	Judaism in the Matrix of Christianity	Neusner
240009	Tradition as Selectivity: Scripture, Mishnah, Tosefta, and Midrash in the Talmud of Babylonia	Neusner
240010	The Tosefta: Translated from the Hebrew: Sixth Division Tohorot	Neusner
240011	In the Margins of the Midrash: Sifre Ha'azinu Texts, Commentaries and Reflections	Basser
240012	Language as Taxonomy: The Rules for Using Hebrew and Aramaic in the Babylonia Talmud	Neusner
240013	The Rules of Composition of the Talmud of Babylonia: The Cogency of the Bavli's Composite	Neusner
240014	Understanding the Rabbinic Mind: Essays on the Hermeneutic of Max Kadushin	Ochs
240015	Essays in Jewish Historiography	Rapoport-Albert
240016	The Golden Calf and the Origins of the Jewish Controversy	Bori/Ward
240017	Approaches to Ancient Judaism: New Series, Volume Two	Neusner
240018	The Bavli That Might Have Been: The Tosefta's Theory of Mishnah Commentary Compared With the Bavli's	Neusner
240019	The Formation of Judaism: In Retrospect and Prospect	Neusner
240020	Judaism in Society: The Evidence of the Yerushalmi,Toward the Natural History of a Religion	Neusner
240021	The Enchantments of Judaism: Rites of Transformation from Birth Through Death	Neusner
240022	The Rules of Composition of the Talmud of Babylonia	Neusner
240023	The City of God in Judaism and Other Comparative and Methodological Studies	Neusner
240024	The Bavli's One Voice: Types and Forms of Analytical Discourse and their Fixed Order of Appearance	Neusner
240025	The Dura-Europos Synagogue: A Re-evaluation (1932-1992)	Gutmann
240026	Precedent and Judicial Discretion: The Case of Joseph ibn Lev	Morell
240027	Max Weinreich *Geschichte der jiddischen Sprachforschung*	Frakes
240028	Israel: Its Life and Culture, Volume I	Pedersen
240029	Israel: Its Life and Culture, Volume II	Pedersen
240030	The Bavli's One Statement: The Metapropositional Program of Babylonian Talmud Tractate Zebahim Chapters One and Five	Neusner

240031	The Oral Torah: The Sacred Books of Judaism: An Introduction: Second Printing	Neusner
240032	The Twentieth Century Construction of "Judaism:" Essays on the Religion of Torah in the History of Religion	Neusner
240033	How the Talmud Shaped Rabbinic Discourse	Neusner
240034	The Discourse of the Bavli: Language, Literature, and Symbolism: Five Recent Findings	Neusner
240035	The Law Behind the Laws: The Bavli's Essential Discourse	Neusner
240036	Sources and Traditions: Types of Compositions in the Talmud of Babylonia	Neusner
240037	How to Study the Bavli: The Languages, Literatures, and Lessons of the Talmud of Babylonia	Neusner
240038	The Bavli's Primary Discourse: Mishnah Commentary: Its Rhetorical Paradigms and their Theological Implications	Neusner
240039	Midrash Aleph Beth	Sawyer
240040	Jewish Thought in the 20th Century: An Introduction in the Talmud of Babylonia Tractate Moed Qatan	Schweid Neusner
240041	Diaspora Jews and Judaism: Essays in Honor of, and in Dialogue with, A. Thomas Kraabel	Overman/MacLennan
240042	The Bavli: An Introduction	Neusner
240043	The Bavli's Massive Miscellanies: The Problem of Agglutinative Discourse in the Talmud of Babylonia	Neusner
240044	The Foundations of the Theology of Judaism: An Anthology Part II: Torah	Neusner
240045	Form-Analytical Comparison in Rabbinic Judaism: Structure and Form in *The Fathers* and *The Fathers According to Rabbi Nathan*	Neusner
240046	Essays on Hebrew	Weinberg
240047	The Tosefta: An Introduction	Neusner
240048	The Foundations of the Theology of Judaism: An Anthology Part III: Israel	Neusner
240049	The Study of Ancient Judaism, Volume I: Mishnah, Midrash, Siddur	Neusner
240050	The Study of Ancient Judaism, Volume II: The Palestinian and Babylonian Talmuds	Neusner
240051	Take Judaism, for Example: Studies toward the Comparison of Religions	Neusner
240052	From Eden to Golgotha: Essays in Biblical Theology	Moberly
240053	The Principal Parts of the Bavli's Discourse: A Preliminary Taxonomy: Mishnah Commentary, Sources, Traditions and Agglutinative Miscellanies	Neusner
240054	Barabbas and Esther and Other Studies in the Judaic Illumination of Earliest Christianity	Aus
240055	Targum Studies, Volume I: Textual and Contextual Studies in the Pentateuchal Targums	Flesher
240056	Approaches to Ancient Judaism: New Series, Volume Three, Historical and Literary Studies	Neusner
240057	The Motherhood of God and Other Studies	Gruber
240058	The Analytic Movement in Rabbinic Jurisprudence	Solomon
240059	Recovering the Role of Women: Power and Authority in Rabbinic Jewish Society	Haas

240060	The Relation between Herodotus' *History* and Primary History	Mandell/Freedman
240061	The First Seven Days: A Philosophical Commentary on the Creation of Genesis	Samuelson
240062	The Bavli's Intellectual Character: The Generative Problematic: In Bavli Baba Qamma Chapter One And Bavli Shabbat Chapter One	Neusner
240063	The Incarnation of God: The Character of Divinity in Formative Judaism: Second Printing	Neusner
240064	Moses Kimhi: Commentary on the Book of Job	Basser/Walfish
240065	Judaism and Civil Religion	Breslauer
240066	Death and Birth of Judaism: Second Printing	Neusner
240067	Decoding the Talmud's Exegetical Program	Neusner
240068	Sources of the Transformation of Judaism	Neusner
240069	The Torah in the Talmud: A Taxonomy of the Uses of Scripture in the Talmud, Volume I	Neusner
240070	The Torah in the Talmud: A Taxonomy of the Uses of Scripture in the Talmud, Volume II	Neusner
240071	The Bavli's Unique Voice: A Systematic Comparison of the Talmud of Babylonia and the Talmud of the Land of Israel, Volume One	Neusner
240072	The Bavli's Unique Voice: A Systematic Comparison of the Talmud of Babylonia and the Talmud of the Land of Israel, Volume Two	Neusner
240073	The Bavli's Unique Voice: A Systematic Comparison of the Talmud of Babylonia and the Talmud of the Land of Israel, Volume Three	Neusner
240074	Bits of Honey: Essays for Samson H. Levey	Chyet/Ellenson
240075	The Mystical Study of Ruth: *Midrash HaNe'elam* of the Zohar to the Book of Ruth	Englander
240076	The Bavli's Unique Voice: A Systematic Comparison of the Talmud of Babylonia and the Talmud of the Land of Israel, Volume Four	Neusner
240077	The Bavli's Unique Voice: A Systematic Comparison of the Talmud of Babylonia and the Talmud of the Land of Israel, Volume Five	Neusner
240078	The Bavli's Unique Voice: A Systematic Comparison of the Talmud of Babylonia and the Talmud of the Land of Israel, Volume Six	Neusner
240079	The Bavli's Unique Voice: A Systematic Comparison of the Talmud of Babylonia and the Talmud of the Land of Israel, Volume Seven	Neusner
240080	Are There Really Tannaitic Parallels to the Gospels?	Neusner
240081	Approaches to Ancient Judaism: New Series, Volume Four, Religious and Theological Studies	Neusner
240082	Approaches to Ancient Judaism: New Series, Volume Five, Historical, Literary, and Religious Studies	Basser/Fishbane